Unreasonable Force

Unreasonable Force

New Zealand's journey towards banning the physical punishment of children

Beth Wood, **Ian Hassall** and **George Hook**

with **Robert Ludbrook**

Save the Children
New Zealand

Save the Children
New Zealand

Save the Children fights for children's rights. We deliver immediate and lasting improvements to children's lives worldwide.

Save the Children works for:

- a world which respects and values each child
- a world which listens to children and learns
- a world where all children have hope and opportunity.

ISBN:	978-0-473-13095-4
Authors:	Beth Wood, Ian Hassall and George Hook with Robert Ludbrook
Editor:	George Hook
Proof-reader:	Eva Chan
Publisher:	Save the Children New Zealand
First published:	February 2008
Printer:	Astra Print, Wellington

To order copies of this publication, please write to:

Save the Children New Zealand
PO Box 6584
Marion Square
Wellington 6141
New Zealand
Telephone +64 4 385 6847
Fax +64 4 385 6793
Email: info@savethechildren.org.nz
Website: http://www. savethechildren.org.nz

DEDICATION

Our tamariki mokopuna (children) carry the divine imprint of our tupuna (ancestors), drawing from the sacred wellspring of life. As iwi (indigenous nations) we share responsibility for the well-being of our whānau (families) and tamariki mokopuna. Hitting and physical force within whānau is a violation of the mana (prestige, power) and tāpu (sacredness) of those who are hit and those who hit. We will continue to work to dispel the illusion that violence is normal, acceptable or culturally valid. We will continue to advocate for whānau education based on cultural models that provide alternatives to violence. Our capacity for resilience as indigenous people is fed and nourished by our language, traditional practices and oral traditions.

We dedicate this important piece of work to the children of Aotearoa New Zealand – may they grow in peace.

> *Maha rawa wā tatou mahi te kore mahi tonu, tawhiti rawa to tatou haerenga te kore haere tonu.*
>
> *We have done too much to not do more, we have come too far to not go further.*
>
> *Sir James Henare*

Naida Glavish JP
Chairperson
Te Runanga o Ngāti Whātua (Tribal Authority)

CONTENTS

ACKNOWLEDGEMENTS

Over the years that preceded the passing of the legislation that banned the use of force for correcting children in New Zealand, a great many people contributed their time, energy and knowledge towards achieving changes in our law, attitudes and habits as they relate to physical punishment. Their contributions have all been valuable and the authors thank them sincerely and acknowledge their individual roles in bringing about change. Some of these people are mentioned in the book but many are not. The efforts of all those who contributed to change are deeply valued.

In relation to this book, we would like to acknowledge the help received from the following Members of Parliament: Sue Bradford, Hon. Brian Donnelly, Lynne Pillay and Dianne Yates. We would like also to thank our reviewers who looked critically at one or more chapters: Prof. Bill Atkin, Janet Bagshaw, Archdeacon Glynn Cardy, Alison Cleland, Mike Coleman, Dr Marie Connolly, Revd Dr Anthony Dancer, Associate Prof. Joan Durrant, Dr Kirsten Hanna, Rae Julian, Cathy Kern, Mercy Jumo, Revd Dr Margaret Mayman, Gordon McFadyen, Peter Newell, Hon. Deborah Morris-Travers, Dominique Pierre Plateau, Rt Revd Richard Randerson, Christine Richardson, Marie Russell and Peter Shuttleworth. Of course, the opinions expressed in this book are the responsibility of the authors as are any errors of fact.

We would like to thank those who supplied photos: Green Party (page 48), Barnardos New Zealand (pages 16, 18, 89, 119, 120, 139, 155 and cover photo), Office for the Children's Commissioner (pages 113 and 118), Anglican Church Media Office (page 99), *Dominion Post* (pages 17, 167, 178, 183 and 186) and *New Zealand Herald* (page 181). We also thank those who supplied cartoons: Tom Scott (pages 24 and 192) and Mike Moreu (page 184).

Finally we need to thank Save the Children New Zealand for making this book possible and in particular John Bowis, Debbie Jack, Sonya Hogan, Ariana Paretutanganui-Tamati and Mercy Jumo for their support and encouragement.

Beth Wood, Ian Hassall and George Hook

FOREWORD

In May 2007, the rights of New Zealand children were significantly enhanced with the passing of the Crimes (Substituted Section 59) Amendment Act, which repealed the old section 59 defence used by parents charged with assaulting their children. The new law specifically bans the use of force for the purpose of correcting children. Essentially, it made physical punishment of children in New Zealand illegal.

Children's human rights are not, as is sometimes assumed, about giving children everything they want, nor are they about parents losing authority. Human rights, particularly the human rights of children, set standards about the way human beings ought to treat each other justly, respectfully and equally. Basically, they aim to ensure that people do not exploit their positions of power over children and young people and cause them to suffer.

The United Nations Convention on the Rights of the Child (UNCROC), the international treaty that identifies a set of rights for all children, was adopted by the United Nations General Assembly in 1989 and ratified by New Zealand in 1993. Fundamental to the Convention is the understanding that parents and the extended family are central to children's lives, and that adults are expected to exercise their legitimate authority in their relationship with their children.

This Convention is monitored by a UN Committee called the Committee on the Rights of the Child (CRC). This Committee has consistently found that physical punishment of children breaches three of their fundamental human rights: the right to physical integrity, the right to protection from harm, and the right to equal protection under the law.

It is appropriate that we celebrate our new law and the leadership shown in changing this law. It is an opportunity for New Zealand to do things that will decrease our reliance on physical punishment of children, and encourage a public and family environment where positive parenting is the norm. This has implications for New Zealand and other countries that may take heart from this change.

This book traces the journey to law reform in New Zealand and looks at the many factors that contributed to this. As with other advances in human rights, people do not give up old habits and beliefs easily. There has been conflict, soul searching and heated debate in our country – and this will no doubt continue. In time, we will look back and wonder how we ever considered not changing the law. We should remember that this legislative change received more public submissions than any other piece of legislation in our history. Many of these were opposed to change, but there were significant numbers of individuals and groups of organisations who supported the proposed change.

We can be justly proud of what we did for our children. They will benefit from family relationships in which physical punishment plays no legitimate part. We can then say that we are closer to our goals of realising the inherent dignity of children and respecting their right to safety, which have always been the goals of this legislative change. However, we must also be mindful that the price of this is eternal vigilance. Old habits die hard. There are still moves to have the new legislation overturned. Like all significant social change, it takes time, leadership and consistency to bed down these changes. In time, fewer children will be hit, punished physically and killed. That must surely be the most worthy goal of all.

Dr Cindy Kiro, Children's Commissioner of New Zealand

PREFACE

In June 2007, Beth Wood informally approached Save the Children New Zealand with an idea about writing a book on the events surrounding the recent law change in New Zealand that might prove useful to overseas child advocates. After receiving an encouraging response, the authors developed a proposal for the book which Save the Children then agreed to fund and publish. Their steadfast support has been apparent throughout the intense writing and editing phases. This support reflects the leadership role that Save the Children has undertaken both nationally and internationally in advocating for the right of children to be protected from all forms of violence including physical punishment.

This book is primarily an account of how New Zealand came to prohibit parents from physically punishing their children. It describes the events leading up to the enactment in May 2007 of the Crimes (Substituted Section 59) Amendment Act, which put that prohibition in place. Reference is made to the history, going back at least forty years in New Zealand, of opposition to physical punishment of children and its sanctioning by the law, but the focus of the book is primarily on the two years preceding the final passage of the Bill. It was during this period, beginning in June 2005 with the introduction into Parliament of a short bill to repeal section 59 of the Crimes Act 1961, that New Zealand became gripped by an intense debate on the subject of physical punishment and the role of the law in sanctioning or prohibiting it.

Three of the authors are well-known as proponents of law reform and although we have not attempted to provide a neutral account of the journey, we have aimed to accurately describe the history, intent and effect of the new law. We have written this book in the hope that it will play a part in changing adult behaviour and further protecting children. We also hope that it will set the record straight by correcting any misinformation that might undermine positive social change.

Legal provisions for parents to use 'reasonable force' for the purpose of 'correction' are found in the statutes of many countries but increasingly this has come into question. New Zealand was the eighteenth nation to either revoke such a provision or ban physical punishment outright, but advocates for children in many countries continue to struggle with overturning similar legal provisions.

The purpose of this book is two-fold. Firstly, we aim to inform, assist and encourage people worldwide who wish to end physical punishment of children, particularly those who live in countries with English-derived political and legal systems where New Zealand's experience will be most relevant. To this end, we have highlighted comments throughout the text that encapsulate what has been learnt from the New Zealand experience.

Secondly, we aim to provide New Zealanders with a readable account of the 'story so far' in the struggle to advance children's well-being and rights, and then to identify what remains to be done with respect to ensuring that all children live lives free of violence.

The first part of the book focuses on the context and history of New Zealand's journey towards banning physical punishment.

The opening chapter begins with a sketch of the extraordinary events of the 2nd of May 2007, which included an unprecedented agreement between the Government and the Opposition, a street demonstration, a cathedral service, and finally a session in Parliament when the passage of the Bill into law became assured. We then go on to explore the background to these events.

Chapter two provides a sequence of the milestones reached along the journey, which the reader can use to locate significant events and follow relevant developments in research, governance, child welfare, law enforcement, advocacy and law reform.

In the second part of the book, we look in some detail at different facets of the journey, in particular, the impact of rights, law, religion, advocacy, public attitudes, media and politics on the debate and its final resolution.

The third chapter explores the origins of children's rights in international law, the reluctance of many New Zealanders to accept the notion that children possess rights, and how different rights-based instruments and organisations contributed towards ensuring that particular fundamental human rights of children are now better reflected in New Zealand law.

Chapter four is concerned with the legal issues. The origins of the law that allowed New Zealand parents to hit their children are traced together with the limitations on its application that evolved over time. Contemporary applications of the law are considered including its use and misuse, and the growing conflict between it and the evolving canon of civil law offering children greater protection and the benefits of full citizenship. Divided opinion within the legal profession is surveyed before the implications of the new law are finally examined.

The contributions that opposing religious perspectives made to the debate is discussed in chapter five. We survey briefly the religious affiliations of contemporary New Zealanders, then look at the impact of the Christian faith on the child-rearing practices of indigenous peoples before discussing the biblical roots of physical punishment. The critical emergence of Christian support for repeal is reviewed, as well as the nature of Christian opposition to law reform. We also describe the rise of vocal anti-repeal Christian lobby groups and their use of overseas experts. Finally we provide a brief account of how the claims made by these experts were rebutted by advocates.

In chapter six we give an account of the advocacy done on behalf of children by a wide variety of agencies and individuals. This advocacy aimed at securing children's rights and better meeting their needs. Over time these initiatives developed into an effective, well-coordinated network that promoted the repeal bill at every opportunity offered in the media, in political discourse, and in public debate.

In chapter seven we look at the range of attitudes that New Zealanders expressed about the place of physical punishment in raising children and the role of the law in mediating this. We then discuss the difficulties in shifting public opinion, particularly when a ban on physical punishment became a very real possibility. The chapter concludes with a survey of the human factors that lay behind people's unwillingness to change, and how these factors might be responded to.

The media was the public's main source of information and as such it played a critical role in the national debate. In chapter eight, the attitudes of the media towards child discipline and its link with child abuse are explored first. We then look at how the media responded during the passage of the Bill and key themes that emerged while the media hosted the public debate. Next we consider briefly the impact of the media on public opinion and politicians, and finally reflect upon the challenges and opportunities that interacting with the media presents for advocates.

The contributions and responses of politicians and political parties are the subject of chapter nine. Political reformers had to contend with strongly expressed, divergent public and media opinion, lobbying pressure from proponents and opponents of the Bill, a United Nations recommendation to repeal the existing law, as well as pressure from their political party and/or parliamentary caucus. The critical role of strongly principled and determined political leaders is made clear, particularly that of the Bill's sponsor, Sue Bradford.

In the final part of the book on completing the journey, we examine in chapter ten the meaning and implications of the law change for New Zealand children and their families. We then look at the responses occurring even at this early stage in the life of the new law. Finally we discuss what remains to be done to ensure that the new law brings benefits to all New Zealand children.

Writing this book has proved to be a journey in itself. As we have reflected upon the events that led up to repeal, we are left with an immense sense of admiration for all those who contributed towards achieving the goal of banning physical punishment of children in New Zealand. We hope that the account we have provided throughout the pages of this book will prove both informative and engaging for readers.

AUTHORS

Beth Wood has a background in social work, child policy and child advocacy. She was a co-founder in 1997 of EPOCH New Zealand, a voluntary organisation dedicated to ending physical punishment of children. She sought the repeal of section 59 from 1993 onwards, and became a leader in networking, lobbying and advocating for repeal. Beth has recently retired from the position of Advocacy Manager at UNICEF New Zealand.

Ian Hassall is a New Zealand paediatrician and children's advocate. He was New Zealand's first Commissioner for Children from 1989 to 1994. His career has entailed working for children and their families as clinician, strategist, researcher and advocate. At present he is a Senior Lecturer in the Children and Families Programme of the Institute of Public Policy at AUT University. Ian advocated publicly for the repeal of section 59 from 1993 onward through the planning and execution of campaigns, engagement in public debate, submission to the parliamentary select committee, seminar presentations, newspaper articles, blog contributions and radio interviews.

George Hook has a background in teaching and educational publishing, particularly in authoring and editing textbooks. Currently he is working as a freelance author and book editor. George became involved as a private citizen in lobbying government ministers and leaders of political parties shortly before the issue of repeal surfaced on Parliament's agenda. He continued his behind-the-scenes lobbying during the period in which the Bill progressed into law.

Robert Ludbrook is a children's lawyer with a long-standing interest in children's rights. In 1986, he founded the Youth Law Project in Auckland, which evolved into YouthLaw Tino Rangatiratanga Taitamariki in the mid-nineties. For many years, Robert has been involved in promoting children's rights in New Zealand, including their right to legal protection from physical punishment. Robert's contributions to this book can be found in the legal issues and children's rights chapters.

Part One

Background to the Journey

Chapter 1

SETTING THE SCENE

The 2nd of May 2007 will remain a significant day in the memories of many New Zealanders, particularly those who over a long period of time had sought to change the law relating to physical punishment of children. It was the day on which it became certain that the use of force for the purpose of correcting children would soon no longer be legally defensible. It was a day of strong emotions and high drama.

In a surprise mid-morning media conference, the Prime Minister Helen Clark, the Leader of the Opposition John Key, the leader of United Future Party Peter Dunne, and Green Party Member of Parliament Sue Bradford, sponsor of a Member's Bill to repeal the statutory defence used by parents accused of assaulting their children, announced that they had struck a deal to allow the passage of the Bill into law. It had been the subject of highly visible public and media contention during the preceding three weeks of the parliamentary recess.

John Key, Helen Clark, Sue Bradford and Peter Dunne at the media conference

After the rare spectacle of the leaders of the two main political parties, Labour and National, in public agreement, the Prime Minister joined other Members of Parliament in St Paul's Anglican Cathedral across the road from Parliament. Here, senior clerics from a wide range of Christian denominations were attending an ecumenical prayer vigil for children in support of the Bill. They called for peace in New Zealand families. Supporters gradually filled the cathedral and during the service the great bell tolled ten times – one ring for each child killed through family violence during a typical year in New Zealand.

At the same time, a thousand-strong demonstration against the Bill, organised by the Destiny Church,[1] took place in the grounds in front of the Parliament buildings. Leaders of the demonstration presented their views to parliamentary representatives on the steps of Parliament.

Destiny Church-led rally against repeal with a dissenting placard in the midst of the protestors (courtesy of the Dominion Post*)*

A short time later, the cathedral congregation processed across the street and assembled around the steps of the Parliamentary Library and in silence presented a message in support of repeal, signed by many church leaders, to Helen Clark and Sue Bradford.

Presentation of the message in support of repeal

The session of Parliament that was the target of the two gatherings recommenced consideration of the proposed legislation at 4 pm. Later that evening, a very large majority of Members of Parliament had voted to support the Bill, which now included the agreed amendment announced at the earlier press conference. The speeches during this session were a startling mix of graciousness and point-scoring, of small-minded party politicking and visionary unity.[2] The final passage of the Bill into law became a formality at that point (see chapter 9).

Accordingly, on the 16th of May, Parliament voted overwhelmingly to pass the Crimes (Substituted Section 59) Amendment Bill into law, and on the 21st of June 2007 the new law finally came into force (see appendices 3 and 4).

The Change in the Law

Any visitor to New Zealand observing these extraordinary events must have wondered what it was about the old law that attracted so much attention and contention. It was a brief passage, section 59, in the omnibus Crimes Act 1961, which read:

> ***59 Domestic discipline***
>
> *(1) Every parent of a child … is justified in using force by way of correction towards the child, if the force used is reasonable in the circumstances.*

Similar clauses are found in the laws of many countries, especially those which have English-derived legal systems. Such provisions enable parents to successfully defend themselves in prosecutions for assaulting their children on the grounds that the assault was for the purpose of correcting their children's behaviour and that the force used was reasonable in the circumstances. Of course, whether the force used was reasonable or not would have to be assessed by a judge or, in New Zealand at least, by a jury if the accused so elected.

Those who supported the repeal of section 59 in New Zealand were inclined to see it as an unjust and damaging legal relic from a past in which men were able to beat their wives, servants, children or animals with impunity. Some of those opposed to the repeal of section 59 saw the legal provision as a reflection of a God-given parental right to bring up their children in the way that they saw fit, using physical punishment where necessary as a disciplinary tool.

Although the old section 59 was eventually replaced with a new section 59, entitled *Parental control*, rather than being simply deleted from the Crimes Act, the purpose of the new law is clear:

> *… to make better provision for children to live in a safe and secure environment free from violence by abolishing the use of parental force for the purpose of correction.*[3] (emphasis added)

Implicit in the new law (see the full text in appendix 3) is an elevation in the status of children. As a consequence of the change in the law, children must now be treated as citizens of no less consequence than adult New Zealanders, entitled to the same range of human rights, and afforded equal if not greater protection under the law, given their vulnerabilities. This does not imply they are to be treated as adults in all respects, or mean that their parents should be fearful of inappropriate state interference with their legitimate authority and parental responsibilities.

In summary, the new law:

- fully repealed the old section 59 'Domestic discipline' defence
- introduced a specific ban on the use of force for the purpose of correcting children
- overturned any rule of common law having the same effect
- ensured equal legal protection from assault for children as for adults
- prohibited parents from administering physical punishment to their own children within a school context
- achieved congruence with other recently passed child-related legislation in New Zealand
- complied with New Zealand's international and domestic human rights obligations
- provided legal protection for parents who restrain their children for purposes of care or safety
- provided for a review of the effectiveness and additional impacts of the new law after two years
- affirmed that the Police have the discretion not to prosecute when instances of minor parental assaults on children come to their notice.

In this book we will explore aspects of the long journey towards banning the use of physical punishment[4] by New Zealand parents when disciplining their children. Along the way we will share insights about factors and actions that were critical in influencing the final outcome here in New Zealand. Some of these may be relevant in other countries where advocates for children's rights are seeking to reform their laws. The context in which our journey occurred is important. What then is the setting in which New Zealand became the first English-speaking country in the world to ban physical punishment of children?[5]

The New Zealand Context

In this section we will consider the demographics and child-rearing practices of New Zealand as well as the legal and political systems.

The population

New Zealand is a small country in the South Pacific Ocean, over a thousand kilometres away from its nearest neighbour, Australia. In 2006 it had a population of about 4.2 million people, one million of whom were children and young people under 18 years of age.[6] It is a country populated by migrants. Māori, its first human settlers, journeyed to Aotearoa (New Zealand) from other Pacific Islands over 700 years ago and became the land's indigenous people – the tāngata whenua. The first European settlers, who eventually came to be called Pākehā, arrived much later in the early 1800s.

Currently, Māori make up 14% of New Zealand's population, more recent Pacific Island migrants 6%, migrants of Asian descent 8%, and the remaining inhabitants, who are mainly of European descent, form 72% of the population.[7] In the early years of the twenty-first century, before the new law came into force, physical punishment of children was common, although not universal, in all ethnic groups but this was not always so.

Traditional child-rearing practices

The earliest written records suggest that Māori children led relatively tranquil domestic lives compared with children growing up in the families that began arriving from Britain in increasing numbers as the nineteenth century progressed.

> *According to de Montaison, the people 'appear to live harmoniously in their villages. The young people greatly respect the old people.' These comments indicate both the esteem in which the kaumātua (elders) were held and the relative tranquillity of domestic life. European accounts from the early contact period suggested that, compared with Europe, Māori domestic life was relatively free of casual violence, for children were rarely hit ...* [8]

The early nineteenth century missionary the Revd Samuel Marsden of the Church Missionary Society wrote thus of Maori domestic life:

> *I saw no quarrelling while I was there. They are kind to their women*

> *and children. I never observed either with a mark of violence upon them, nor did I ever see a woman struck.*[8]

Early Māori writers, recalling life in the days before the European influence became so pervasive, also described a peaceful domestic scene that contrasted strongly with the violence of customary intertribal conflict. They suggest that Māori never beat their children but were always kind to them, and that this seemed to strengthen the bond of affection which remained among Māori throughout life.[9]

Some contemporary Māori commentators believe that in the society of the old days adults were respectful of children or at least had laissez-faire attitudes towards children's behaviour and were not given to striking them.[10]

> *Our people did not hit their tamariki (children). That only came about through colonisation and through Christianity actually.*
>
> *Tariana Turia, Member of Parliament* [11]

But as the European presence in Aotearoa became more pervasive, Māori began to adopt the child-rearing advice of Christian missionaries or imitate the disciplinary practices of Pākehā settlers. Physical punishment of Māori children became more common.[12] New Zealand had become a British colony in 1840 under the provisions of the Treaty of Waitangi. As a result, many thousands of English, Irish, Scottish and Welsh migrants arrived, including missionaries, who brought with them a belief in the necessity and efficacy of physical punishment of children.

This belief was partly based on traditional practice and its apparent effectiveness in getting children to conform to adult expectations, but it was also founded on a religious justification derived from certain passages in the Old Testament. (This belief system is discussed in greater depth in chapter 5.)

The legal system

As well as bringing their convictions about child-rearing practices, the new settlers from Britain also brought with them their legal traditions. New Zealand's laws were largely derived from the English laws that were in existence at the time at which our statutes were drafted. The legal system that developed in New Zealand was based on both statutory and common law provisions, as it was in England. 'Common law' involved laws that had evolved as a result of rulings by judges in specific cases, as distinct from the statutory laws passed by Parliament. In England, during the nineteenth century at least, matters to do with the maltreatment of children by parents were dealt with under common law rather than statutory provisions, and this tradition carried over into the functioning of New Zealand's legal system.

In 1961, the new Crimes Act continued to confirm the common law principle that parents, caregivers and teachers could use force to correct children, and it also stated that the force used must be reasonable in the circumstances. This meant that legal reforms to ban physical punishment of children would have to address both statutory and common law provisions. (The complex legal issues involved are explored further in chapter 4.)

The political system

New Zealand's system of government was largely based on the Westminster model of representative parliamentary democracy, but important differences emerged during the twentieth century. In 1951, with the abolition of the Upper House, New Zealand's Parliament was reduced to a single House of Representatives. Then in 1996, the first-past-the-post electoral system was replaced with a mixed-member-proportional representation system (MMP), which meant that in practice major political parties must rely on the support, either formal or informal, of minor political parties in order to govern effectively as well as to pass new laws. Support for law reform that came from minor parties, or from individual members of minor parties, turned out to be a critical factor in the repeal of section 59 of the Crimes Act, the law that provided a statutory defence for parents charged with assaulting their children.

New Zealand's Parliament is located in Wellington and the Members of Parliament are either electorate representatives or party list members without electorates. The latter are provided with seats in order to achieve proportional representation within Parliament. (See appendix 5 for further information on New Zealand's system of government.) Fortunately, members of the public and lobby groups have relatively easy access to politicians either in their electorate offices or in their parliamentary offices. This was another critical factor along the pathway to repeal.

Violence in society

As the new millennium got under way, New Zealanders continued to be troubled by the significant levels of violence occurring within families – both violence towards partners and towards children.[13] A 2003 report from UNICEF stated that New Zealand had a high rate of child deaths from parental maltreatment.[14] The small number of children involved, the variability in the numbers of deaths each year, and the different ways in which child homicide deaths are counted in each country make accurate comparisons problematic.[15] Nevertheless, the report was well publicised and, combined with public disquiet over reported acts of lethal violence towards children, led to pressure being put on the Government to take action over what was perceived to be an unacceptable tolerance of violence within New Zealand communities.

Cartoonist Tom Scott delivers a sobering message (courtesy of Tom Scott)

Such was the level of concern that the New Zealand Government introduced two major policy initiatives in recent years aimed at reducing family violence. In 2002, the Ministry of Social Development released *Te Rito: New Zealand*

Family Violence Prevention Strategy,[16] and in 2006 the same ministry led the *Taskforce for Action on Violence Within the Family: The First Report*.[17]

Some of the appalling stories of the deaths of young children resulting from parental violence generated intense media interest and impassioned public outcries.[18] There was, of course, disagreement over whether a connection existed between a law sanctioning the use of 'reasonable force' to correct children and the deaths of children resulting from violent acts committed by their parents. Many opponents of repeal believed there was no connection and argued that the individuals responsible for the deaths of their children were unlikely to have even heard of section 59 let alone be influenced by it. The media-exposed cases that had informed New Zealanders about the circumstance of child homicide since the first well-publicised case in 1992 seemed to support this view. The perpetrators presented a common picture of being trapped in a world of violent family relationships, as well as drug and alcohol abuse, often continuing on from one generation to the next.

The alternative view was that the removal of section 59, as well as correcting a serious breach of the rights of children to live free from violence and the threat of violence, would have a longer term effect in reducing the amount of physical force used on children, and with that the risk of serious physical injury or death. Repeal of section 59 was a necessary precondition for developing a domestic culture of non-violence nation-wide. So long as section 59 remained in place, it stood as a statement asserting that physical force was still the norm for child-rearing practice, undermining any effort to limit the use of physical punishment. Some actions towards children that most would agree involved maltreatment occurred as a consequence of parents exercising their supposed right to hit their children for disciplinary purposes. International research into fatal and non-fatal child abuse has found that the parents involved often set out with the intention of dealing with obnoxious behaviour.[19]

Although it was not the main argument put forward by repeal campaigners in New Zealand, some connection between section 59 and child homicide was acknowledged by many people. Similarly, reformers argued that children learn about violence in their own home when they witness violence between their parents and when they experience parental violence personally or see it being used on their siblings, and sometimes model it. Well-publicised deaths of women at the hands of their partner or ex-partner added to an increasing public horror about family violence.

The Influence of Research

In New Zealand, as in some other parts of the world, academic research identified many negative effects associated with the physical disciplining of children. It also clearly identified the benefits of positive, non-violent parenting strategies. This knowledge played a significant part in convincing many members of a wide variety of professional groups (such as early childhood teachers, psychologists and social workers) that the use of physical discipline had undesirable consequences for children and was ineffective in changing their behaviour.

Two key research documents on the discipline and guidance of children were published by the Office of the Children's Commissioner in conjunction with the Children's Issues Centre at the University of Otago in Dunedin.[20] One of the comprehensive reviews of the literature that underpinned both publications demonstrated convincingly that the use of physical punishment increased the likelihood of disruptive or bad behaviour and was associated with a wide range of negative outcomes.[21]

The release of the first publication was timed to coincide with a seminal conference that occurred during June 2004 in Wellington. Entitled *Stop it – it hurts: Research and Perspectives on the Physical Punishment of Children,* the ground-breaking conference focused entirely on physical punishment of children and it included presentations from Māori and Pacific leaders opposed to the use of physical punishment, as well as a religious perspective and a review of the case law involved.[22] The research findings from the publication were utilised extensively to support the case for law reform in many of the submissions made to the Justice and Electoral Select Committee that eventually considered Sue Bradford's Bill during 2005–06.

A highlight of the conference was a keynote presentation by Professor Joan Durrant from the University of Manitoba in Canada.[23] She brought with her a wealth of information about the benefits of positive parenting and also an in-depth knowledge of the research into the Swedish experience following the banning of corporal punishment in 1979.

The Swedish situation subsequently turned out to be a double-edged sword with opponents of law reform consistently and publicly challenging the statistics about the positive effects of reform in that country.[24] Countering this publicity was difficult because the misinformation was attractive to members of the public who were apprehensive about, or antagonistic towards, law reform.

The Arguments For and Against Repeal

In New Zealand, a wide range of arguments was advanced both for and against repeal, many of which will have relevance to, or be encountered by, advocates for children's rights and law reform in other countries.

Supporters of law reform argued that repeal would, in practical terms:

- remove the special defence used by parents when they were prosecuted for significant assaults on their children;
- subject such assaults to the same standard for prosecution and determination of guilt as assaults on adults;

and therefore better protect children from physical abuse.

Underlying these practical reasons for not allowing section 59 to remain on the statute books were other, mostly values-based, reasons such as:

- it implicitly sanctions the use of force against children
- it implies that physical punishment is a socially acceptable part of child-rearing
- it is an infringement of children's rights to physical integrity and to live a life free of the threat of pain, humiliation or injury
- it is a denial of equal citizenship for children in fact and in law
- it denies children equal protection before the law
- it is painful and can be dangerous for children
- it normalises a form of interpersonal violence

- it teaches children that interpersonal violence is an expression of 'love' in a context where one person dominates another
- it is not an effective way of teaching children how to behave well
- it forces children to become either servile or rebellious
- it is contrary to Christian principles and practice.

The contrary arguments that were raised by opponents of reform were that the practical effect of repeal would be to:

- deny parents their presumed right to discipline their children as they saw fit according to their belief systems
- create an unwarranted intrusion by the state into family life
- leave parents vulnerable to prosecution for mildly smacking or restraining their children and therefore criminalise good parents
- deny parents the use of an effective tool for raising children
- lead to children being raised poorly, lacking in boundaries and self-discipline.

Backing up these practical arguments were other values-based arguments that justified the use of physical punishment, such as:

- it is a necessary part of controlling children's behaviour
- it helps children develop into well-behaved, good citizens
- it conforms with biblical injunctions
- when applied in a mild and moderate manner it does children no physical or emotional harm.

The Long-term Goal

The ultimate aim of most advocates for reform was that over time New Zealand would become a country in which everyone knew that it was unacceptable to hit a child. It was always understood that the public would need information that explained what was wrong with using physical punishment and described the benefits of positive, non-violent child-rearing, as well as clarifying what the proposed law change would mean. The repeal of section 59 was seen as an important part of this long-term goal of changing attitudes and behaviour, but there were other, more immediate reasons to urge its repeal – to provide children with better legal protection against assault and to respect their human rights.

Not all members of the public, nor all politicians, accepted the long-term vision promoted by advocates of reform as being legitimate. Some believed that mild physical discipline was harmless, beneficial even in terms of improving the behaviour of children, although they were opposed to beating children. Many understood the need to change the existing law which disadvantaged children in the courts. But the lack of a common understanding of the overall aim of law reform and nervousness about the possible political consequences of repeal sometimes caused politicians who favoured reform to give different messages to different groups or make apparently contradictory statements about the aims of law reform (see chapter 9 for further commentary on the responses of politicians and the Government).[25]

Responding to Public Concerns

The biggest challenge faced by those promoting a change in the law was dealing with public opposition to the proposed change based on a genuine concern that good parents would be prosecuted needlessly. In New Zealand, some opponents of law reform sought to transform this concern into fear. 'Changing the law will lead to the criminalisation of good parents' was a refrain continually heard or read in the media throughout the years of the public debate and later on in the parliamentary debate. (The contribution of the media in defining and influencing the debate is more fully explored in chapter 8.)

Clearly, prosecuting parents who occasionally smacked their children would not be in the children's best interests because prosecution inevitably leads to family distress and disruption. However, it can appear confusing and contradictory to promote a legal ban on physical discipline and at the same time say 'But you won't get in trouble if you just do it mildly' in order to reassure anxious parents. This dilemma also contributed to the public being given some very mixed messages,[26] in particular by politicians who on the one hand supported repeal but on the other hand struggled to find ways of reassuring the public that they did not want to see parents who occasionally smacked their children being prosecuted for minor assaults.

One approach to changing the law suggested by some politicians and others seeking a compromise was to establish legal limits on physical punishment such as how a child may be hit, on what parts of the body, with what instruments, and what sort of impact on the child's body is permissible. Such approaches had already been adopted by England, Scotland, Canada, and New South Wales in Australia, for example. But advocates for law change in New Zealand were adamant that any move to describe in law acceptable forms of physical discipline would be unacceptable as it would continue to legitimise a form of interpersonal violence and not help in achieving the long-term goal of becoming a non-violent society.

Most reformers believed that just as adults are generally not prosecuted for minor assaults against other adults, parents would not be prosecuted for minor assaults against their children, although they might be investigated and warned. Sensible general prosecution guidelines for the Police were already in existence. Nevertheless, fear of prosecution was probably the most powerful negative factor influencing the public and politicians.

At the time the Bill was being debated in Parliament, there was some clearly visible support for change coming from a wide variety of organisations and individuals (see chapter 6 for further information), but organised opposition was persuasive and persistent, and the general public seemed to be leaning towards retaining the 'parental right' to use physical discipline. Despite the public disquiet, in the end the law was changed.

Conclusion

There are some anxieties about how the amendments introduced during the various stages of the parliamentary process will work. However, Sue Bradford's determination not to accept any amendment that would compromise her ultimate aim of ending the legal sanction of parental force resulted in legislation that not only repealed the statutory defence of the use of force for the purpose of correction, but also specifically bans the use of any force for the purpose of correction.

The public campaign to change the law in New Zealand was sustained over many years, but it intensified greatly after Sue Bradford's Bill to repeal section 59 was drawn from the ballot in June 2005.

Growing public concern over family violence and the existence of strong international research evidence discrediting the use of physical punishment were two of the critical factors underpinning pressure for change in New Zealand. Many other factors contributed to law reform becoming a reality in New Zealand, as did the contributions of numerous individuals and organisations. Most of these are highlighted in the following chapter on milestones along the journey, while the major issues surrounding reform are explored in greater depth in subsequent chapters.

Chapter 2

MILESTONES ALONG THE JOURNEY

Observations made during early contact between Europeans and Māori suggest that the indigenous people of New Zealand rarely hit their children but as Māori came to adopt the child-rearing advice of missionaries and the practices of the increasingly numerous settlers, physical punishment of children became more common over time.[27]

During the nineteenth and twentieth centuries immigrants to New Zealand from around the world, and in particular from the British Isles, brought with them long-held discipline and punishment customs, including physical punishment of children. For example, flogging was an accepted punishment for young male offenders in New Zealand until 1941.[28]

The colonists also imported the English and Scottish common law principle of *reasonable chastisement* – that parents, caregivers and teachers could use reasonable force to correct the behaviour of children. In 1893, this common law principle was first given statutory force in New Zealand when the Criminal Code was enacted by Parliament.

The Crimes Act passed by Parliament in 1961 re-enacted that earlier statutory provision by including a section that would be recognisable in many English-derived legal systems throughout the world. That section was the now notorious section 59.

It took 114 years to get the *reasonable chastisement* statutory defence repealed from New Zealand's law. On the 16th of May 2007, members of New Zealand's Parliament voted overwhelmingly to pass the Crimes (Substituted Section 59) Amendment Bill, which overturned the statutory defence contained in section 59 and also specifically banned the use of any force for the purpose of correcting children.

There have been numerous events, momentous and less so, national and international, that were milestones along this journey to reform. Many of these influenced the final outcome in some significant way. We have sought to record those events and to acknowledge some of those involved below. The events, and the associated publicity, helped to raise public awareness of the deficiencies and wrongness of physical discipline and the basic inequity of the law, and thus contributed to the final outcome. We may not have captured all of the significant milestones, nor does space allow us to acknowledge every valuable personal contribution, but we hope that those recorded illustrate the growing support and demand for reform over time. The milestones also illustrate the rich combination of influences that helped to bring about the eventual change.

The Milestones

1960s The Playcentre and Parents Centres movement are established and some parents question the punitive disciplinary practices in vogue.

1963 Marie Bell, a parent and educator, and others establish the parent co-operative school, Matauranga, in Wellington. No physical punishment is used in this school.[29]

1968 In a report entitled *Crime in New Zealand*, the Justice Department concludes that corporal punishment is objectionable because it is ineffective as a deterrent, and is degrading and unsuitable as a means of punishing juvenile offenders.[30]

1976 March 23: The United Nations adopts the International Covenant on Civil and Political Rights (later ratified by New Zealand in 1978), which states that 'no person shall be subjected to cruel, inhuman or degrading treatment or punishment'.[31]

1978 Jane and James Ritchie, psychologists from the University of Waikato in Hamilton, make a submission to the Parliamentary Select Committee on Violent Offending and advocate ending the use corporal punishment in the home.[32] The recommendation was not adopted.

1979 Sweden becomes the first country in the world to pass legislation specifically banning the use of corporal punishment. (Sweden had repealed its statutory defence in 1957.)

1979 November: At a major conference on *The Rights of the Child and the Law,* held during the International Year of the Child, the Ritchies argue strongly for the repeal of section 59 of the Crimes Act.[33]

1980 The New Zealand Committee for Children is established to carry on the work begun by the International Year of the Child Committee during the previous year. The new committee opposes the use of corporal punishment. The Committee's funding was withdrawn by Government in 1987 and the committee used its remaining funds to pay for a half-page advertisement in a popular magazine, the *New Zealand Listener*. The advertisement asked 'Do we really care about children?' and gave as one example of a negative attitude towards children the fact that children can be beaten without it being an assault.

1981 In their book *Spare the Rod,* the Ritchies make the first comprehensive New Zealand critique of corporal punishment of children and argue a strong case for legal reform.[34]

1981 The organisation Campaign Against Violence in Education (CAVE) holds its first seminar. Its aim is to end corporal punishment in schools.[35]

1982 The report of the Human Rights Commission on children and young persons homes administered by the Department of Social Welfare includes physical discipline amongst a range of practices it considers raise questions about New Zealand's compliance with Article 7 of the International Covenant on Civil and Political Rights.[36]

1985 The *Child Care Regulations* remove the right of workers to use physical discipline in child care centres.[37]

1986 The *Children and Young People (Residential Care) Regulations* ban the use of corporal punishment in all residential institutions run by the Department of Social Welfare.[38]

1989 July: The New Zealand Government appoints the first Commissioner for Children, Dr Ian Hassall, who advocates for the repeal of section 59.[39] (As do the successive Commissioners, Laurie O'Reilly, Roger

McClay, and Dr Cindy Kiro. See chapters 3 and 6 for further information on the critical role of the Children's Commissioner.)

1989 The *New Zealand Universities Law Review* publishes an article by John Caldwell, University of Canterbury Law School, which critically examines the law relating to corporal punishment of children.[40]

1989 November 20: The *United Nations Convention on the Rights of the Child* is adopted by the United Nations General Assembly (see chapter 3 for further discussion on the influence of the Convention).[41]

1990 An Education Amendment Act is passed which includes the prohibition of corporal punishment in all New Zealand state and private schools (see chapter 6).

1990 Lesley Max, an Auckland-based child advocate, publishes the book *Children: Endangered Species*. It includes the case against the use of physical punishment.[42]

1990 October 1: New Zealand signs the United Nations Convention on the Rights of the Child, signalling its intention to proceed to ratification.

1991 The Department of Social Welfare adopts a policy that states the use of corporal punishment in foster homes is unacceptable.

1992 The first real public outcry over the death of a child from maltreatment occurs when a two-year-old is seriously injured and left to die in pain and squalor. An influential article on the tragedy by Lesley Max is published in *Metro* magazine.[43]

1992 The Commissioner for Children, Dr Ian Hassall, publishes articles in the journal *CHILDREN* advocating the repeal of section 59 and criticising the use of corporal punishment.[44]

1993 March 13: New Zealand ratifies the *United Nations Convention on the Rights of the Child*. (The UN Committee on the Rights of the Child has consistently regarded the legitimisation of corporal punishment as being in contravention of the Convention.)

1993 Dr Gabrielle Maxwell, a researcher at the Office of the Commissioner for Children, publishes a report entitled *Physical Punishment in the Home in New Zealand,* which shows that some attitudes towards the use of physical punishment in the home are changing. Tolerance of severe forms of physical punishment has decreased and a wider range of non-physical forms of discipline is being used than 30 years earlier.[45]

1993 September: A major forum held in Wellington, organised by the Office of the Commissioner for Children, publicises the case for the repeal of section 59 and launches pamphlets advocating repeal and discouraging the use of physical punishment.

1994 September: The Office of the Commissioner for Children publishes new pamphlets aimed at encouraging parents not to use physical punishment. These include a pamphlet expressing children's views on how adults could help them behave. This is a rare consultation with New Zealand children on the topic of discipline.

Ian Hassall with pupils of Cannons Creek School at the launch of the pamphlet

1995 November: The Office of the Commissioner for Children launches *Hey? We don't hit anybody here,* a children's story book in three languages, written by Beth Wood, a Wellington-based children's rights advocate.[46]

1996 August: Several New Zealanders attend the conference of the International Society for the Prevention of Child Abuse and Neglect (ISPCAN), held in Dublin, Ireland. It is preceded by a one-day meeting on ending corporal punishment organised by Peter Newell from EPOCH (End Physical Punishment of Children) Worldwide. (See chapter 6 for more information on international influences.)

1997 EPOCH (End Physical Punishment of Children) New Zealand is established as a charitable trust, with one of its aims being the repeal of section 59 of the Crimes Act (see chapter 6).

1997 Jane and James Ritchie publish the book *The Next Generation: Child Rearing in New Zealand* and again advocate ending physical punishment and the repeal of section 59.[47]

1997 January: The UN Committee on the Rights of the Child recommends that the New Zealand Government should review section 59 of the Crimes Act and effectively ban all forms of physical violence to children (see chapter 3).[48]

1997 June: New Zealand's largest-circulation newspaper, the *New Zealand Herald*, publishes a major feature series entitled *Our Children*, which draws attention to the plight of many New Zealand children, including those who are ill-treated.[49]

1997 November: A private citizen, Philip Holdway-Davis, promotes a video on 'safe smacking', which advocates the use of an instrument to punish a child. This provokes extensive discussion in the media and some protest.[50]

1998 July: EPOCH New Zealand develops *Children are Unbeatable* – a resource kit that provides commonsense advice about parenting without hitting.

1998 August: A public education campaign conducted by the Children,

Young Persons and their Families Agency aims to reduce child abuse. *Breaking the Cycle* includes a component called *Let's beat smacking, hands down*, which seeks to discourage physical punishment.

1998 September: This year, the IPSCAN conference is held in Auckland, New Zealand. One presenter outlines the case against physical punishment of children. In a plenary session on modern, traditional and religious views of child-rearing in the Pacific, one invited speaker supports physical discipline and provokes opposition.

1998 November: EPOCH New Zealand begins engaging support for repeal through the establishment of a network of organisations publicly committed to the repeal of section 59 and non-violent parenting.

1999 May: The savage beating and death of a child who soiled his pants arouses a public outcry.[51]

1999 July: Robert Ludbrook, a prominent children's legal advocate, and Beth Wood present a paper on physical punishment at the well-attended Children's Issues Centre Conference in Dunedin.[52] (Over the years, a number of advocates for change regularly make presentations at conferences and other forums.)

1999 November: Peter Newell, Co-ordinator of EPOCH Worldwide, visits New Zealand and argues strongly for the repeal of section 59 in a number of presentations at different forums.

2000 February: An article in *North & South* magazine, entitled 'Disciplined to Death', tells the horrific story of a four-year-old who died as a result of physical discipline.[53] The author, Auckland journalist Deborah Coddington, advocates repeal of section 59.

2000 July: EPOCH New Zealand publishes a series of simple pamphlets on the repeal of section 59, called *Five Good Reasons*. Copies are distributed widely, particularly in the early childhood sector and through community organisations.

2000 October: As a result of recommendations from the UN Committee on the Rights of the Child, the New Zealand Cabinet directs officials to report on how other countries address the issue of compliance with the UN Convention on the Rights of the Child with regard to physical punishment (see chapter 9).[54]

2001 An American student, Jenny Brobst, who is completing a Masters of Law degree at Victoria University, Wellington, reviews the options for repealing section 59. She presents her findings at two well-attended forums.

2001 The Labour Government consults with the community, including children and young people, about the development of new public policy for children (later published as *New Zealand's Agenda for Children*). Children consulted speak out against 'getting the bash'.

2001 The International Save the Children Alliance takes a formal position opposed to corporal punishment of children.

2001 February: A parent brought to court in a provincial town is accused of hitting a child with a stick, causing significant bruising. He is acquitted under section 59, which leads to an outcry from some professional groups.[55]

2001 May: The Cabinet Social Equity Committee directs officials in the Ministries of Justice, Social Policy and Youth Affairs to report on the likely implications if section 59 is repealed and on educational measures that should be undertaken.[56]

2001 August: A National Party Member of Parliament, Bob Simcock, places a Member's Bill in the ballot, which calls for an amendment to section 59 to limit how children could be hit. (The bill was never drawn from the ballot.)

2001 October: Barnardos New Zealand, a child-focused non-governmental organisation, holds a forum on section 59 in Wellington. MPs from most political parties speak – some for and others against repeal. Barnardos makes the repeal of section 59 an advocacy priority, and thereafter takes a leading role in advocating for repeal (see chapter 6).

2001 October: The EPOCH New Zealand resource kit *Children are Unbeatable* is rewritten and published as *Choose to hug, not to smack: Awhitia, Kaua e Papakitia (parenting advice)* by EPOCH and the Office of the Commissioner for Children.[57] The kit is launched by the Minister of Social Services, Steve Maharey, at Mt Cook School in Wellington.

2001 November: The Ministry of Justice publishes research into public attitudes toward reforming the law as it relates to physical punishment.[58] The findings indicate that most adults surveyed want to retain the right to hit their children within the law, even, in a significant number of responses, with implements.

2001 November: Cabinet directs officials to prepare another report on the likely implications if section 59 is repealed or amended, and how these could be addressed.[59]

2001 November: Cabinet directs officials to prepare a proposal for a national public education campaign to inform parents about alternatives to the physical disciplining of children.[60]

2002 The New Zealand First MP Brian Donnelly places a Member's Bill to repeal section 59 in the ballot. He later withdraws his bill and it is replaced by another bill sponsored by New Zealand First MP Barbara Stewart, which seeks to amend section 59 in order to define acceptable hitting (see chapter 9).

2002 June: The Labour Government develops and launches a major child policy document called *New Zealand's Agenda for Children,* which is non-committal on the future of section 59.[61] Later, a number of non-governmental organisations publish a commentary on the policy, called *Making it Happen,* which strongly recommends the repeal of section 59.[62]

2002 June: UNICEF (United Nations Children's Fund) New Zealand and the Institute of Public Policy at the Auckland University of Technology (IPP at AUT) hold political forums in Auckland and

Wellington in the run-up to the general election. The forums focus on how to reduce violence to children. There is strong support for the repeal of section 59 among the audiences, and a number of politicians express their personal support for repeal.

2002 June: At the annual meeting of Save the Children New Zealand (SCNZ), a non-political children's rights organisation, the New Zealand Governor General, Dame Sylvia Cartwright, speaks out against physical punishment of children (see chapter 6).

2002 July: The ISPCAN Conference in Denver, Colorado, is preceded by an international meeting on *Ending Corporal Punishment* organised by Peter Newell, Co-director of The Global Initiative to End Corporal Punishment of Children. Children's rights and ending physical punishment are significant themes of the overall conference.

2002 December: Auckland church leaders from a number of denominations speak out against section 59 (see chapter 5).

2002 December: Cabinet considers a paper on the development of a national public education strategy on alternatives to physical discipline and the legislative issues surrounding the possible repeal of section 59 of the Crimes Act.[63]

2002 December: Cabinet invites the Ministry of Social Development, in consultation with the Ministries of Youth Affairs and Justice, and the Department of Child, Youth and Family Services, to develop a bid for the funding of a national media campaign and community-based education programmes on alternatives to physical punishment in Budget 2003.[64]

2003 March: A report from New Zealand non-governmental organisations, co-ordinated by Action for Children and Youth Aotearoa (ACYA), to the UN Committee on the Rights of the Child is strongly critical of New Zealand's failure to act on the Committee's earlier recommendation to repeal section 59 (see chapter 3).[65]

2003 May: The Labour Government announces $10,000,000 of funding for parent education on alternatives to physical discipline.[66] (The money is eventually used to fund the SKIP initiative, see below.)

2003 May: The Labour Government announces that a decision on section 59 will be postponed until the public education campaign has been implemented and reviewed.[67]

2003 June: Representatives at Save the Children's annual conference vote in favour of repeal of section 59.

2003 June: At the national conference of the Royal New Zealand Plunket Society, a non-governmental organisation that is the predominant provider of health services to children under five, a remit is passed calling on the Government to introduce a major public education campaign aimed at encouraging the use of positive alternatives to corporal punishment and leading to the eventual repeal of section 59 (see chapter 6).

2003 October: The International Save the Children Alliance launches a regional campaign against corporal punishment of children in South-East Asia and the Pacific.

2003 October: The UN Committee on the Rights of the Child in its country report criticises New Zealand's failure to act on section 59 and again recommends an end to corporal punishment.[68]

2003 October: The league table in a UNICEF Innocenti publication draws attention to New Zealand's poor record with regard to child deaths from abuse and makes a strong case for ending corporal punishment.[69]

2003 October: The violent beating and death of a child at about the same time as the two previous events provokes unprecedented media attention and debate about physical discipline and section 59 (see chapter 8).[70]

2004 February: The Children's Commissioner, Dr Cindy Kiro, hosts the *Children Call Symposium* in Wellington. Participants include equal numbers of children and young people as adults. The Prime Minister, Helen Clark, receives a standing ovation when she expresses personal support for the repeal of section 59.

2004 February: A group of non-governmental organisations support the publication of a pamphlet on the repeal of section 59, which is entitled *Protect and Treasure New Zealand's Children.*[71] The publication is released by UNICEF and the Institute of Public Policy at Auckland University of Technology.

2004 May 6: The Minister of Social Development, Steve Maharey, launches SKIP – Strategies with Kids: Information for Parents, which is an ongoing, comprehensive, government-funded, community-based, positive parenting initiative.[72]

2004 May: In its report to the New Zealand Government, the United Nations Committee on Torture echoes the recommendations of the UN Committee on the Rights of the Child and recommends that New Zealand repeals section 59.[73]

2004 June: The Office of the Children's Commissioner and the Children's Issues Centre publish a seminal report entitled *The Discipline and Guidance of Children.*[74] This comprehensive review of research into physical discipline receives much publicity.

2004 June: The Children's Issues Centre holds a conference in Wellington, called *Stop it – it Hurts: Research and Perspectives on the Physical Punishment of Children.* Professor Anne Smith, from the University of Otago, presents a summary of the research referred to in the previous milestone. The conference covers issues relating to ending physical punishment and includes a Māori and a Pacific perspective. The keynote addresses are later published in a special edition of *Childrenz Issues* devoted to the topic of physical punishment of children.[75]

2004 June: Associate Professor Joan Durrant from the University of Manitoba, Canada, speaks at the Children's Issues Centre Conference and other forums around New Zealand, including a breakfast with politicians and others at Parliament. She advocates strongly for an end to the use of physical discipline and the repeal of section 59.

2004 September: The ISPCAN Conference is held in Brisbane, Australia. A significant number of New Zealanders present papers on ending physical punishment.

2005 March: The New Zealand Human Right Commission publishes an *Action Plan on Human Rights*, which includes recommendations on the repeal of section 59.[76]

2005 April/May: Two significant assault cases draw attention to section 59. In one, the father is not acquitted despite invoking section 59 as a defence when charged with hitting his child on the buttocks causing bruising. In the other, the mother is acquitted of assault when she invokes section 59 in her defence during a prosecution for assault after she had struck her adolescent son with a bamboo cane and a riding crop. The cases attract significant publicity and provoke much public and media debate.[77]

2005 June: The East Asia Pacific Regional Conference under the UN Study on Violence Against Children is held in Bangkok and its recommendations include a call to end all corporal punishment of children.

2005 June: The national conference of the Royal New Zealand Plunket Society passes a remit unequivocally calling on the Government to repeal section 59.

2005 June: An international conference called *Childhoods: Children and Youth in Emerging and Transforming Societies*, held in Oslo, Norway, is attended by New Zealanders who participate in thematic sessions on ending corporal punishment.

2005 June 9: Green Party MP Sue Bradford has her Member's Bill drawn from the ballot. The Bill seeks to repeal section 59 in its entirety (see chapter 9).

2005 July 27: The first reading of the Bill occurs in Parliament and there is sufficient support for it to be referred to the Justice and Electoral Select Committee (chaired by Labour MP Lynne Pillay), which will receive oral and written submissions from the public as well as confidential ones from government departments.

2005 September: Save the Children New Zealand publishes the report *Insights: Children & young people speak out about family discipline* by the researcher Terry Dobbs.[78] This covers research into the views of children on family discipline and includes their views on physical punishment.

2005 November: UNICEF New Zealand and the Institute of Public Policy at Auckland University of Technology hold forums on section 59 in Auckland and Wellington. Included are the voices of children and young people as well as those of religious leaders supportive of repeal.

2005 November to February 2006: The Justice and Electoral Select Committee receives over 1700 written submissions either for or against the repeal of section 59.

2006 Both supporters and opponents of repeal increase their lobbying of politicians and attempts to persuade the public.

2006 Waitakere, Porirua and Auckland City Councils vote to support the repeal of section 59.[79]

2006 January: An article entitled 'On the receiving end' is published in the *New Zealand Medical Journal*.[80] It confirms that many New Zealand children experience physical punishment, and some of them, harsh discipline.

2006 February: Save the Children Sweden releases the results of research on the physical and emotional punishment of children in eight South-East Asia and in the Pacific countries, an official submission to the UN Study on Violence against Children.[81]

2006 February: The 10th Australasian Conference on Child Abuse and

Neglect (ACCAN) is held in Wellington. Discipline and guidance of children is one theme of the conference and significant papers on ending physical punishment and the repeal of section 59 are presented.[82] The attendees endorse a submission to Government calling for the repeal of section 59. Canadian Professor Joan Durrant is a keynote speaker at the conference and she also speaks at a Parliamentary Breakfast.

2006 February: A group of child advocacy agencies (Wellington Repeal 59 Network) begin meeting to coordinate the campaign in support of Sue Bradford's Bill. A similar group is established in Auckland. Barnardos New Zealand takes a strong lead in the Wellington network and provides administrative support (see chapter 6).

2006 March: A petition in favour of repealing section 59, organised by The Body Shop and signed by over 20,000 members of the public, is presented to the Bill's sponsor, Green MP Sue Bradford.

2006 March: A booklet and CD presentation developed by Rhonda Pritchard, a Wellington author, and George Hook entitled *Children are Unbeatable: 7 very good reasons not to hit children* are published jointly by the Office of the Children's Commissioner and UNICEF New Zealand.[83] The resource is launched with fanfare at Parliament and proves to be very popular. (The Families Commission later assists with funding reprints, and over 50,000 copies of the booklet are eventually printed for distribution around New Zealand.)

2006 May: The United Nations Committee on the Rights of the Child releases General Comment 8 on *The Right of the Child to protection from corporal punishment and other cruel and degrading forms of punishment*, which is sent to all politicians by UNICEF New Zealand.[84]

2006 May to August: The Justice and Electoral Select Committee hears over 200 oral submissions for or against the repeal of section 59 at various locations around the country.

2006 July: Opponents of repeal bring the Swedish lobbyist Ruby Harrold-Claesson to New Zealand to make an oral submission to the Select

Committee. She creates concern by claiming that there have been negative outcomes in Sweden following corporal punishment law reform. The Wellington Repeal 59 Network and others seek international support (including a public letter from experts in Sweden) to challenge her claims (see chapter 5).

2006 August: EPOCH New Zealand writes to the Commissioner for Police and publicises his assurances that the Police prosecution guidelines indicate that the Police would have the discretion not to prosecute in trivial assault cases if section 59 is repealed.[85]

2006 August: The *Report of the independent expert for the UN study on violence towards children* is presented to the United Nations General Assembly. It urges all states to end all forms of violence against children by 2009, including corporal punishment.[86]

2006 October: Over 60 community-based organisations sign an open letter in support of repeal, which is then sent to all politicians in New Zealand.[87]

2006 November 20: The Justice and Electoral Select Committee reports back to Parliament on the Bill after reviewing nearly 1700 submissions from the public.[88] An amended form of the Bill is recommended by the majority report. The amendments would provide some protection for parents who use force to restrain children in some circumstances, but specifically ban the use of force for the purpose of correction.

2006-07 Opponents of repeal run a highly organised and well-funded campaign. They publish advertisements in newspapers, organise street marches against the Bill, set up and maintain websites, lobby politicians, and establish a nationwide petition against repeal.

2006-07 The Wellington Repeal 59 Network prepares Briefing Sheets on the Bill for politicians, develops a media kit, and coordinates a media campaign advocating repeal.[89] A website making it easy for supporters to email messages of support for repeal to politicians is set up and heavily used. Contact with supporters throughout the country is maintained and they are kept informed of developments.

2007 February 21: The Bill has its second reading in Parliament and is referred to the Committee of the Whole House.[90]

2007 March: Marches and rallies against the Bill are held in various towns and cities in New Zealand. In Wellington there is a counter-march in support of the Bill.

2007 March 13: The Māori Party announces that it unequivocally supports the repeal of section 59.[91] Co-leader Dr Pita Sharples' assertion that 'A hit is a hit' is widely quoted in the media (see chapter 9).

2007 March 14: The Wellington Repeal 59 Network coordinates and publicises support for repeal from prominent citizens and celebrities. A banner expressing their support is presented by Deborah Morris-Travers, from the NGO coalition Every Child Counts, to politicians in Parliament's grounds.[92]

Supporters presenting the banner to Sue Bradford

2007 March 14: Parliament begins debating the Bill clause by clause. Extensive and often aggressive filibustering by opponents (particularly members of the National Party) occurs, and a prolonged debate seems inevitable. Successive Members' Days are taken up with numerous speeches until thankfully the parliamentary recess intervenes.

2007 April: Opponents of the Bill bring the American academic Dr Robert Larzelere, Oklahoma State University, to New Zealand to promote his views that there is a place for mild physical discipline in child-rearing. He also believes that Sweden and Norway have experienced negative consequences as a result of their reforms. He receives limited media attention and his views are challenged by supporters of the Bill (see chapter 5).

2007 May 2, mid-morning: In a surprise joint announcement, the Prime Minister, Helen Clark, and the Leader of the Opposition, John Key, state that both of their parties will support the Bill with the inclusion of a statement affirming that the Police are able to use their discretion and not prosecute in inconsequential cases.

2007 May 2, 11 am: Opponents gather for a major rally against the Bill in Parliament's grounds, timed to coincide with the recommencement of the debate in Parliament.

2007 May 2, midday: An ecumenical prayer vigil is held in St Paul's Cathedral, Wellington, in support of the Bill (see chapter 5). The Prime Minister and other sympathetic politicians attend the service. Later, on the steps of the Parliamentary Library, Sue Bradford and the Prime Minister accept a letter in support of reform, signed by a large number of church leaders. (The Anglican bishops had issued a statement in support of repeal of section 59 the previous day.[93])

2007 May 2, evening: The debate in the House is concluded with a vote overwhelmingly in favour of the amended Bill and speeches praising those who had helped to resolve the impasse.

2007 May 16: The Bill gains the near unanimous support of Members of Parliament (113 in favour versus 8 opposed) during its final reading in the House. The voting concludes with an unprecedented standing ovation from most MPs present and numerous long-term supporters of repeal in the Public Gallery. The applause acknowledged the role of Sue Bradford as the leading Parliamentary reformer and also the significant contributions of MPs from other parties who had supported reform.

2007 May 20: The Bill receives Royal Assent from the Governor General, Anand Satyanand.

2007 June 21: The Crimes (Substituted Section 59) Amendment Act 2007 comes into force and the defence of the use of reasonable force for the purposes of correction no longer applies. Children and young people finally enjoy the same protection against assault under the law as their elders do.

2007 November: Since New Zealand became the eighteenth state to prohibit all physical punishment of children, Portugal and Uruguay have also banned physical punishment. Another 25 states are publicly committed to doing so.[94]

Conclusion

At the beginning of this chapter we discussed the non-violent nature of child-rearing in early Māori society. After many generations of children having endured physical punishment at the hands of their parents during the two centuries since European settlers first arrived here, current and future generations of young New Zealanders are now entitled to grow up without being hit, as Māori children growing up in Aotearoa once did.

Part Two

Facets of the Journey

Chapter 3

CHILDREN'S RIGHTS

At the heart of the argument against physical punishment lie the human rights of children – their rights to human dignity and physical integrity, to safety and protection, and to equal status as human beings in the law. These children's rights are fundamental human rights. In this chapter we will explore the origins of children's rights in international law, the reluctance of many New Zealanders to accept the notion that children have rights, and how different rights-based instruments and organisations contributed towards ensuring these fundamental rights are better reflected in New Zealand law.

The Rights of Children

The rights of children are informed by international human rights instruments as described primarily in the United Nations Convention on the Rights of the Child (UNCROC).[95] The Convention adopts a rights framework and sets out a comprehensive set of civil, political, economic, social and cultural rights to which all children are entitled.

The United Nations General Assembly adopted the Convention into international law on 20 November 1989, and it came into force on 2 September 1990.[96] New Zealand signed the Convention in October 1990 and ratified it in March 1993 under the auspices of the National Government led by Prime Minister Jim Bolger.[97] Ratification requires the signatory nation to ensure that its laws and policies, as they impinge on the lives of children, are in accord with the rights set out in the Convention. The 1969 Vienna Convention on the Law on Treaties (articles 26 and 27) makes it clear that treaties must be implemented once they have been ratified and that existing domestic legislation is not an excuse for not doing so.[98] Nations are allowed though to specify reservations (exemptions) when they ratify the Convention. While New Zealand entered three reservations, none of them related to section 59. This was despite the fact that the New Zealand Human Rights Commission, an independent government–funded organisation that champions fundamental human rights, had advised the Government that section 59 might be incompatible with the Convention.[99]

The Convention attracted significant interest in New Zealand and over the years it has been influential in promoting acceptance of the view that children have individual rights. It has been an important reference point for those sectors that promote children's interests, for example, the Office of the Children's Commissioner, child advocacy organisations, child and family service providers, and some Government ministries.

A number of UNCROC articles impinge on the issue of the legality of physical punishment of children and a state's obligations to act.

- Article 3 requires that in all actions involving children, the 'best interests of the child shall be a primary consideration'.
- Article 4 requires that the state must 'undertake all legislative and other appropriate measures' to ensure the 'implementation of the rights recognised in the present Convention'.
- Article 6 requires the state 'to recognise that every child has the inherent right to life' and 'ensure to the maximum extent possible the survival and development of the child.'
- Article 19 requires the state 'to take all appropriate legislative ... measures to protect the child from all forms of physical or mental violence ...' while in the care of parents and others.
- Article 37 requires that children are not subject to 'cruel, inhuman or degrading treatment or punishment'. (emphasis added)

Compliance with the requirements of the Convention is monitored by a special United Nations committee, the Committee on the Rights of the Child (CRC). This committee issues reports on each country's performance but also issues general comments that relate to all countries. In 2006, it issued General Comment No. 8 on corporal punishment. The Committee had this to say:

> *The Committee has, from its earliest sessions, paid special attention to asserting children's right to protection from all forms of violence, ...,*

> *it has noted with great concern the widespread legality and persisting social approval of corporal punishment ...*[100]

While the terms *corporal punishment* and *physical punishment* are in fact synonymous, for many New Zealanders the term corporal punishment is likely to conjure up images of school children being beaten with a strap or cane, but the CRC made it clear that it was also talking about what most New Zealanders would call physical punishment.

> *The Committee defines 'corporal' or 'physical' punishment as any punishment in which physical force is used and intended to cause some degree of pain or discomfort, however light. Most involves hitting ('smacking', 'slapping', 'spanking') children, with the hand or with an implement – a whip, stick, belt, shoe, wooden spoon, etc.*[101]

Ever since the Committee began monitoring countries, it has consistently recommended 'prohibition of all corporal punishment, in the family and other settings.'[102] It regards the use of physical discipline as contravening the articles of the Convention.

In the aforementioned report, the Committee asserted the importance of discipline and the vital role that parents play in helping children grow into responsible citizens:

> *In rejecting any justification of violence and humiliation as forms of punishment for children, the Committee is <u>not in any sense rejecting the positive concept of discipline</u>. The healthy development of children depends on parents ... for necessary guidance and direction ...*[103] (emphasis added)

A number of countries have attempted to improve children's situation in regard to physical punishment by passing 'compromise legislation', which in one way or another limits the type or amount of physical punishment that children can be subjected to (see chapter 1). The UN Committee regards this approach as inconsistent with the provisions of the Convention. In its 2002 report on the United Kingdom's efforts at compliance, the Committee noted that:

The Committee is of the opinion that the Government's proposals to limit rather than remove the 'reasonable chastisement' defence do not comply with the principles and provisions of the Convention … Moreover, they suggest some forms of corporal punishment are acceptable, thereby undermining educational measures to promote positive and non-violent discipline.[104]

The Public's Attitudes towards the UN Convention

In New Zealand it has been the children's rights argument that has been the most difficult to convince the public about. The misconceptions persist that an appeal to 'rights' is a last resort of people pursuing an unworthy agenda, and that children's rights are really about children having their own way.[105] Children are often regarded as having to earn 'rights', by which adults mean privileges that are able to be revoked if the children do not continue to behave well, rather than entitlements inherently possessed by children by virtue of being human.

This antipathy towards the notion of children having rights can be traced back to the nineteenth century concept of children being the chattels of their parents, in particular, of the father. As children were produced and nurtured by their parents, they owed their existence to them and therefore they 'belonged' to their parents. As will be discussed in chapter 4, under English common law children did not usually acquire rights until they reached the age of majority. Historically, children were viewed as appendages of their parents rather than individuals who possessed rights by virtue of being human. The New Zealand historian James Belich describes one particular view of children in the European culture of the colonisers of the nineteenth century as the Chattel Child model.[106] According to this model, the Chattel Child was 'comprehensively subject to parental control'. The model, which did exist to some extent in Victorian New Zealand, was eventually displaced by the Cherished Child model of the twentieth century. Perhaps though, the notion of children being chattels lingered on in the sense of parents feeling that they ought to be able to bring up their 'own children' in the way they believed best, without any restrictions being placed on them by the state or by any presumed children's rights.

Many adults also believe there is an intrinsic conflict between the notion of children's rights and the right of parents to bring up children in the way they believe is best or right. They believe that the imposition of children's rights upon families through legislation would compromise parental autonomy and authority. This would undermine family discipline and result in badly behaved children growing into irresponsible adults.

Opponents of law reform capitalised on this fear, making wild claims about the impact of legalising children's rights. For example, a blogger had this to say on the Family Integrity website:

> *... (UNCROC) will become more well known. Read the whole thing. But in particular, dwell on Articles 12 through 18. These will be used to allow a child unrestricted or much less restricted access to all forms of media that the child may want to read or watch or listen to – regardless of what you, the parents, think is appropriate – because the child has rights, and these rights are to be protected by law and enforced by the Police and CYFS.*

He then urged readers to:

> *... read Article 19. They used that article to rewrite Section 59 and criminalise 'correction' even though the article talks about violence, injury and abuse.*[107]

The editor of the controversial magazine *Investigate*, Ian Wishart, claimed in a recent book that:

> *...(the) anti-smacking bill ... is virtually a cut and paste from the United Nations. ... Is it really about 'smacking', or is the real intention ... a left wing agenda to smash the nuclear family by progressively introducing laws in favour of state control of children?* [108]

Although these views appear to represent an extreme end of the spectrum of public opinion, many New Zealand parents were genuinely concerned about what they perceived to be an intrinsic conflict between the recognition of children's rights and the meeting of parental responsibilities. 'Where will it all end?' summed up the fears of many parents with regard to enshrining the rights of children in law.

Another significant factor that fed into the public debate on section 59 was a common attitude, which many New Zealanders share with citizens in other Anglosphere countries, that 'outside authorities' have no right to criticise or tell us what we ought to do. Sometimes this is based on the concept of state sovereignty, as shown in the following letter to the editor:

> *We read New Zealand is facing stinging international criticism and has consistently been criticised by the United Nations Committee. So what? Who is running this country? The Government should be accountable to New Zealand citizens and not to a pressure group from outside.*[109]

Some people regarded the recommendations of the Committee on the Rights of the Child as an unwarranted intrusion in, and/or a threat to, family life. In seeking to allay these fears, the Committee has stated:

> *The preamble to the Convention upholds the family as 'the fundamental group of society and the natural environment for the growth and well-being of all its members and particularly children'. The Convention requires States to respect and support families.*[110] (emphasis added)

Misunderstandings in some forums about the nature of children's rights and antagonism towards or apathy over the notion of children having rights meant that it was important for advocates to emphasise the link between rights and positive outcomes, rather than relying on the entitlement argument alone. In order to get politicians to even consider changing the law, the case had to be framed in terms of protecting children from assault rather than securing additional rights for them. In the end though, the law change did give them equal legal protection from assault as adults possessed, thereby affirming their rights to human dignity and physical integrity.

> ***The right of children to legal equal protection against assault is the most compelling argument for law reform but for practical reasons the case needed to be made on the basis of a range of arguments.***

The Influence of the UN Convention

In court proceedings lawyers will present arguments that are likely to give traction to their client's case, and the children's rights specified in UNCROC are now regularly raised by New Zealand lawyers and considered by the courts in relation to disputes over the care, guardianship and adoption of children, youth justice matters, and refugee and asylum seeker cases.[111]

Individual lawyers and sub-committees of the Law Society, the representative body for barristers and solicitors in New Zealand, regularly make submissions to select committees on Government and Member's bills. They frequently cite UNCROC in support of their proposals. Many of the submissions on Sue Bradford's Bill made reference to the Convention and the recommendations of the UN Committee on the Rights of the Child.

When drafting the Care of Children Bill,[112] officials from the Ministry of Justice gave prominence to children's rights issues and New Zealand's obligations under UNCROC. Many submissions on the Bill made reference to the Convention. The influence of UNCROC on the Care of Children Act 2004 is noticeable in respect of the importance given to the right of children to participate directly, or through their court-appointed lawyer, in decisions about their guardianship and care. Its influence is also clear in the Principles section:

> *(e) the child's safety must be protected and, in particular, he or she must be protected from all forms of violence ... by his or her family ...*[113]

The Influence of the UN Country Reports

Since New Zealand ratified the Convention in 1993, successive New Zealand governments have had to take their obligations under this international treaty seriously. One of the country's obligations is to prepare regular reports on 'the measures they have adopted which give effect to the rights recognised herein, and the progress made on the enjoyment of those right'.[114] In preparing its reports, the New Zealand Government consults with government departments and non-governmental organisations (NGOs). Once a report has been submitted to the United Nations, the Committee studies the report and adds its recommendations. The New Zealand Government then establishes a 'work programme' to address the Committee's recommendations. New Zealand has reported twice to the Committee on the Rights of the Child, once in 1995 and again in 2000.

In its response to both reports the UN Committee commented on New Zealand's lack of compliance with the Convention and recommended an end to physical punishment.

In the first commentary the Committee recommended:

> *... that [New Zealand] reviews legislation with regard to corporal punishment of children within the family in order to effectively ban all forms of physical or mental violence, injury or abuse.*[115]

This recommendation was influential in starting a government process to investigate what might be done with section 59 (see chapter 9). In response to various Cabinet directives, officials investigated and reported on how other countries had responded to the issue of compliance with the UN Committee's position on physical punishment, and the likely implications if section 59 was repealed.[116]

In New Zealand's second report to the UN Committee,[117] submitted in 2000, the Government referred to education campaigns to encourage the use of alternatives, and to reviewing 'other countries' steps to address this issue', but it made no promise of legal reform.

The Committee, in responding to the second report, said it was:

> *... deeply concerned that despite a review of legislation, [New Zealand] has still not amended Section 59 ... the Convention requires the protection of children from all forms of violence, which includes corporal punishment in the family ...*

and recommended that New Zealand:

> *(a) Amend legislation to prohibit corporal punishment in the home;*
>
> *(b) Strengthen public education campaigns ... aimed at promoting positive, non-violent forms of discipline and respect for children's right to human dignity and physical integrity, while raising awareness about the negative consequences of corporal punishment.*[118]

During 2002 the Government postponed making a decision on repeal and initiated work on a national public education campaign (see chapter 9) to inform people about alternatives to the physical disciplining of children.[119] Three years later New Zealand children were still not enjoying all of the human rights spelt out in the Convention.

Quite what the Government would have done about section 59 if Sue Bradford's Bill had not been drawn from the ballot in 2005 will never be known. In 2003, the Minister of Social Development, Steve Maharey, had said that the matter of section 59 would be reviewed after the public education campaign had been in operation for some years.[120]

Recommendations of the Committee on the Rights of the Child did put pressure on the Government to investigate how it might deal with section 59.

Appeals to Other Human Rights Instruments

There are several other international human rights documents that advocates used to back up their arguments when lobbying for repeal, including in the submissions they made to the Select Committee.

Universal Declaration of Human Rights (UDHR)[121]

The Declaration was adopted by the United Nations General Assembly in 1948. It does not have the same force in international law as other conventions and covenants, but legal experts consider that it forms part of customary international law. As such, it can be used to apply moral pressure to a government to change the legislation of a country.

Article 7 states that 'All are equal before the law and are entitled without any discrimination to equal protection of the law.' Under New Zealand's law, children were not afforded the same protection against assault as adults because of the provisions of section 59 of the Crimes Act 1961. As children were not being treated equally they were being discriminated against by the law. Parliament therefore had a moral obligation to repeal the law.

International Covenant on Civil and Political Rights (ICCPR)[122]

This is one of the most important and widely respected international human rights treaties. It was ratified by New Zealand in December 1978. New Zealand acceded to an Optional Protocol to the Covenant which permitted individuals who have exhausted all domestic remedies to raise complaints as to alleged breaches of ICCPR by written communication to the United Nations Human Rights Committee.

Article 24 deals specifically with children and it states that 'every child shall have, without any discrimination, ... the right to such measures of protection as are required by his status as a minor, on the part of his family, society and the State.'

Article 7 states that 'no one shall be subjected to cruel, inhuman or degrading treatment or punishment.' It is arguable that the defence of *reasonable chastisement*, which allowed New Zealand parents to use physical force to punish their children, breached these Articles but ICCPR was seldom used as a lobbying tool to challenge section 59 and no communication was ever made on this issue to the UN Human Rights Committee.

Convention Against Torture and Other Forms of Cruel, Inhuman or Degrading Treatment or Punishment (CAT)[123]

CAT was adopted by the UN General Assembly in 1984 and ratified by New Zealand in 1989. In its comments on New Zealand's third report, the Committee Against Torture recommended that New Zealand 'implement the recommendations already made by the Committee on the Rights of the Child' and amend its legislation to prohibit corporal punishment in the home.[124] (See also the section below on ACYA.)

The Implications of New Zealand's Human Rights Legislation

A law that allows children to be assaulted by their parents but which treats all other assaults as criminal acts and civil wrongs is blatantly discriminatory in that it treats children differently from, and less favourably than, adults on the basis of their age. The Human Rights Commission Act 1977 made it unlawful to discriminate on a number of grounds, but discrimination on the grounds of age was only made unlawful with the passing of the Human Rights Act 1993.[125] Surprisingly, it is only unlawful to discriminate on the grounds of age against persons aged 16 years or older in New Zealand. This creates the anomalous situation that a law designed to curb discrimination on the grounds of age, itself discriminates against the youngest and most vulnerable age group. In contrast, age discrimination laws in all Australian states and territories and in the federal jurisdiction cover all persons irrespective of their age.

The Role of the Human Rights Commission

Notwithstanding the exclusion of children from protection against age discrimination, the New Zealand Human Rights Commission has expressed disapproval of physical punishment and other demeaning forms of punishment of children.[126]

A 2001 amendment to the Human Rights Act gave the Human Rights Commission responsibility for developing a national human rights action plan.[127] In 2004, the Commission released a report entitled Human Rights in New Zealand Today (based on extensive consultation including with children and young people),[128] the conclusions of which were the basis for the New Zealand Action Plan on Human Rights released in March 2005.[129]

The Action Plan identified what should be done over the next five years so that the human rights of everyone who lives in New Zealand are better recognised, protected and respected. The report fully recognises children as human beings entitled to rights. The section Safety and Freedom from Violence lists as two priorities for action:

- *Strengthen public education programmes aimed at promoting positive, non-violent forms of discipline and respect for children's rights to human dignity and physical integrity.*
- *Repeal of Section 59 Crimes Act 1961.*[130]

With regard to the implementation of the action priorities, the Human Rights Commission plan stated only that responsibility for implementation rests with the agencies that have the relevant statutory or community mandate. However, input at the consultation stage in preparation for the plan provided another sign that despite seeming public opposition to law change on section 59, there were in fact strong voices in favour of change.

The Contribution of the Office of the Children's Commissioner

The Office of the Children's Commissioner (OCC) is an independent, government-funded body that 'promotes children's and young people's wellbeing through advocacy, public awareness, consultation, research and monitoring.' The Children's Commissioner 'speaks out on behalf of all children to ensure their rights are respected and upheld' (emphasis added).[131]

The role of the Commissioner is mandated by the Children's Commissioner Act 2003, and previously by the Children, Young Persons, and Their Families Act 1989. One purpose of the 2003 Act was:

> *To confer additional functions and powers on the Commissioner to give better effect in New Zealand to the United Nations Convention on the Rights of the Child.*[132]

The statutory functions of the Commissioner include raising awareness and understanding of both children's right and the Convention.[133]

It is an indication of the advances made in rights discourse that the functions of the Children's Commissioner specified in the foundational legislation in 1989 made no mention of rights (the legislation was drafted before New Zealand had ratified the Convention). Instead, the Children, Young Persons, and Their Families Act referred to children's welfare and 'best interests'. The Children's Commissioner Act of 2003, which replaced sections of the Children, Young Persons, and Their Families Act 1989, requires the Commissioner to act in relation to children's rights and with reference to the Convention.

Since the appointment of the first Children's Commissioner, Dr Ian Hassall, in July 1989, there have been three other Children's Commissioners – Laurie O'Reilly, Roger McClay and the present Commissioner, Dr Cindy Kiro. The Commissioners have been consistent, although not always heeded or appreciated, advocates for children's rights.

The Commissioner's Office has been very active in promoting the United Nations Convention on the Rights of the Child. It published attractive versions of the Convention in Māori and English. It made a major submission in support of the repeal of section 59 to the Select Committee, and included strong rights-based arguments.[134] Throughout the time the Bill was before the House, the Office released frequent press statements advocating repeal.

The Convention, along with the Office's statutory functions, provided an authoritative basis for Commissioners to speak out for the rights of children. Dr Kiro frequently spoke to the media and appeared on television and radio to put forward the case for repeal and to refute the arguments of opponents. In doing so she became identified by the public as one of the leading advocates.

The Contribution of Action for Children and Youth Aotearoa

When the New Zealand Government reported to the UN Committee in 1995 on New Zealand's progress in implementing UNCROC, the Committee requested a similar report from non-governmental organisations (NGOs). Action for Children in Aotearoa (ACA), a grouping of advocates, prepared the first report on behalf of NGOs in New Zealand, and submitted it to the Committee on the Rights of the Child in 1996. This report was a substantial document and included the following statement:

> *It is difficult to reconcile the Government report's assertion … that child abuse is an area of increasing concern … with the retention of Section 59 of the Crimes Act 1961. Section 59 is a provision that ignores the proven relationship between physical punishment and family and community violence and which appears to be <u>in contravention of Articles 2, 5, and 19 of the Convention</u>. Section 59 allows parents … to use physical force by way of discipline. The only limitation is that the force be 'reasonable'. No statutory definition of 'reasonable' is provided.*[135] (emphasis added)

By 2001, ACA had evolved into Action for Children and Youth Aotearoa (ACYA), a 'coalition of non-governmental organizations, families and individuals whose purpose is to promote the well-being of children and young people in Aotearoa New Zealand'.[136] The aims of ACYA in relation to the Convention on the Rights of Child include:

- promoting understanding and implementation of the Convention

- promoting action on the recommendations of the UN Committee
- providing NGO reports to the UN Committee.[137]

In 2003, after extensive consultation with a wide range of organisations and individuals (including children), ACYA published a major NGO report on New Zealand's compliance with the UN Convention.[138] The report was submitted to the UN Committee on the Rights of the Child, and members of ACYA and a young person also gave oral reports to the Committee. In addition, ACYA developed a report from a group of children and young people in the form of a video which was shown to the UN Committee.[139] In the video, young people made impassioned calls for adults to stop hitting children. Both reports included a strong recommendation to repeal section 59. (Subsequently ACYA also submitted a report to the United Nations Committee Against Torture.[140])

> ***The existence of an NGO with a specific focus on the Convention meant that the UN Committee received independent reports in addition to the Government's reports.***

In 2006, Action for Children and Youth Aotearoa also made a strongly argued submission to the Select Committee considering Sue Bradford's Bill. To illustrate the strength of rights-based arguments, we have quoted extensively from ACYA's submission in the box on the next page.

The November 2006 Select Committee report to Parliament on the Bill states in the summary of the arguments put forward by supporters of repeal 'that Section 59 provides less protection against assault for children than adults'.[141] Interestingly, nowhere in the document is there any mention of children's rights in spite of the fact that a number of submitters, including ACYA, argued the case for reform in terms of the human rights of children. There was one mention of the 'rights of parents'.

> *ACYA submits that Section 59 violates the human rights of children. New Zealand, through its ratification of numerous human rights treaties, has undertaken, in the international sphere, to promote and protect the rights of some of its most vulnerable citizens. … The rights contained in these treaties are to be extended to 'all members of the human family'.*
>
> *[The] principles of dignity, non-discrimination and equality form the cornerstone of the framework of international human rights law. The defence of 'reasonable chastisement' provided for in Section 59 is a violation of the fundamental human rights principles of non-discrimination and equality. It explicitly discriminates against child victims of assault by providing a defence to the perpetrator/parent when a similar defence is not available to other perpetrators of assault as between adults or even in terms of animal protection legislation. Furthermore, the definition of assault as contained in section 2 of the Crimes Act 1961, as it relates to an adult, can constitute the mere apprehension of 'force' whereas the determination of assault in relation to a child can only be satisfied if he or she has been subjected to unreasonable force.*
>
> *These differences in the protection against assault afforded to children do not appear to be justifiable. National and international law require that in order for differential treatment to be legitimate, and therefore non-discriminatory, such treatment should have (a) an important and significant objective; and (b) be rational and proportionate.*[142]

The Influence of the Independent Expert's Study

In February 2003, the Secretary General of the United Nations, Kofi Annan, appointed the Brazilian academic Paulo Sérgio Pinheiro as the Independent Expert who would lead a global study on violence against children. The development of the study provided both NGOs and government officials in New Zealand with the opportunity to make submissions. Delegates from UNICEF New Zealand, Save the Children New Zealand, Action for Children and Youth Aotearoa, and two young people attended the South-East Asia and Pacific Regional Consultation held in Bangkok in 2005. Two Government officials also attended. Delegates found the conference's strong focus on ending corporal punishment very encouraging. What was remarkable about the conference was the contribution that young people from around the Pacific and Asia made. In their address to the meeting the young delegates recommended that:

> *Corporal punishment MUST be banned in homes, schools and as a punishment in the justice system. Children need to be treated the same as adults.*[143]

The final report of the Independent Expert was presented to the United Nations General Assembly in October 2006 after Sue Bradford's Bill had been drawn from the ballot. Unfortunately it generated little media or political interest in New Zealand.

In his report Paulo Sérgio Pinheiro said:

> *I urge States to prohibit all forms of violence against children, in all settings, including all corporal punishment ...*[144]

With the passage of Sue Bradford's Bill into law, a significant step towards this objective was taken in New Zealand.

Conclusion

In ratifying an international treaty such as the Convention on the Rights of the Child, New Zealand incurs obligations to the United Nations and to other ratifying countries, but the specific articles of the Convention are not enforceable under our law unless they are incorporated into our statutes. (The text of the Convention is set out in a Schedule to the Children's Commissioner Act 2003, but section 36 of that Act makes a definitive statement that its inclusion is for public information only and does not give the Convention on the Rights of the Child any legal status in New Zealand.)

But international treaties cannot be ignored. They represent a solemn commitment by the signatory states to bring laws, policies and practices into line with international obligations. New Zealand's existing law (section 59 of the Crimes Act 1961) was clearly in breach of our international obligations to ensure children enjoy all of their human rights. Children did not enjoy their right to equal protection under the law, their right to physical integrity or their right to safety and protection – all of which are fundamental human rights. The repeal of that law was a major victory for children's rights in New Zealand, even if the battle was not fought primarily under the rights banner. In the next chapter we will examine in detail the origins and application of the law which allowed parents to hit their children.

Chapter 4

THE LEGAL ISSUES

In May 2005, a New Zealand mother was acquitted of a charge of assaulting her adolescent son. She had acknowledged hitting him with a bamboo cane and a riding crop, but the jury found her not guilty.[145] The mother claimed that the force used was reasonable in the circumstances (despite leaving welts and bruising) and was intended for the purpose of correcting her son.[146] She had successfully invoked section 59 (see below) as a legal defence, which meant that she was not guilty of any offence. Many members of the public were shocked and deeply offended by this verdict. Not long after the youth had been hit by his mother, he was taken into the care of Child Youth and Family, the statutory child protection agency, because of concerns about his safety and well-being.

Section 59: Domestic discipline

1. Every parent of a child and, subject to subsection (3), every person in the place of the parent of a child is justified in using force by way of correction towards the child, if the force used is reasonable under the circumstances.
2. The reasonableness of the force used is a question of fact.
3. Nothing in subsection (1) justifies the use of force towards a child in contravention of section 139A of the Education Act 1989.

In this chapter, we will explore the origins of the law that allowed parents to hit children and the limitations on its application that evolved over time. We will then consider the use and misuse of that law, and the growing conflicts between that law and other child protection laws. Finally, we will survey various opinions expressed by members of the legal profession for and against repeal before looking more closely at the implications of the new law.

The Origins of the Law

It is unusual for the law to lay down rules about sensitive and personal issues such as how parents should bring up children. It is surprising, then, that one aspect of parenting has been regulated by laws for more than two thousand years. In many countries parents are entitled to use physical force to punish their children without it constituting an assault.

New Zealand law has its roots in English common law,[147] which itself was based on Roman law. Under early Roman law, a father had the power of life and death over his children, the rationale being that a man who has given his offspring the gift of life is able to take back that gift. By the time of the codification of Roman law under Emperor Justinian in about AD 500, the father's right to punish his child had been modified but he retained the right to use reasonable force to correct misbehaviour.

Sir William Blackstone's *Commentaries on the Law of England* (1765 – 86) represented the first comprehensive survey of English law since the thirteenth century. On the issue of parental powers, Blackstone drew on Roman law in stating that:

> *A parent may lawfully correct the child, being under age, in a reasonable manner, for this is for the benefit of [the child's] education.*[148]

Blackstone's reasoning was that the power of parents over their children was partly to enable the parents to more effectually perform their duty to their children, and partly a recompense for the parents' care and trouble in discharging that duty. Blackstone also adopted the Roman law view that children naturally owed to the persons who gave them their existence a duty of subjection and obedience during childhood.[149]

Ironically, the common law defence of *reasonable chastisement* was first given statutory expression in England in the Prevention of Cruelty to and Protection of Children Act 1889.

The high water mark of fatherly authority was reached in Victorian England. One English judge thundered, 'The law of England is that the father has control over the person, education and conduct of his children until they are 21 years of age. That is the law.'[150] Another judge believed the right of chastisement was given to parents to enable them to correct 'what is evil in the child'.[151] A popular Victorian guide to the law summarised the law of parent and child thus:

> *During minority ... the father's power over his child extends so far as is necessary to keep him orderly and obedient and he may correct him reasonably.*[152]

Under English common law, children did not acquire civil rights until they attained majority at the age of 21 years. Children were seen as appendages of their parents rather than individuals with inherent rights and this perception meant that they did not have the same right to bodily integrity as was assured to adults.

Under English law physical punishment was permitted as a means of correction not only of children but of wives, servants, pupils, apprentices, criminals, as well as naval and military personnel. Since then, the power to flog, whip, cane, hit and smack has been progressively removed. With the abolition of corporal punishment in New Zealand schools in 1990, the only remaining circumstance in which human beings could be assaulted without it being an offence was the chastisement of children by parents and those 'in the place of the parent'.

During the colonisation period, British settlers imported English common law and applied it to Māori and settlers alike. Early in the development of New Zealand's legal system, English criminal law was formalised in statutes. The right of parents to use reasonable force to correct their children's behaviour was first given statutory force in New Zealand in section 68 of the Criminal Code 1893. The power of parents and teachers to inflict 'reasonable chastisement' was re-enacted in section 85 of the Crimes Act 1908 and section 38 of the Infants Act 1908, and later in section 59 of the Crimes Act 1961.

> ***The reasonable chastisement defence can be traced back to common law and behind that to deeply held beliefs about the nature of the parent-child relationship.***

Limiting the Use of Physical Punishment

In the debate over the rights and wrongs of physical punishment it is often overlooked that physical punishment is about the deliberate infliction of pain. It is based on the premise that if misbehaviour is punished by inflicting pain, it is unlikely to be repeated. It follows that if the child's behaviour is not corrected by the punishment or if the misbehaviour is repeated, more forceful punishment causing greater pain is required. The aim is to cause the child to feel pain and to fear the further infliction of pain. Arguments that most physical punishment involves nothing more than a 'loving smack' or 'the actions of a caring parent' miss the point.

Over the years, courts in Britain, New Zealand and other English-speaking countries placed some limitations on the parental power of *reasonable chastisement*.

Age of the child

Under common law, parental powers continued until the child reached the age of majority which used to be 21 years, but in New Zealand since 1970 has been 20 years.[153] Some judges have suggested that physical punishment is not appropriate for young children who have not acquired powers of reasoning and lack the ability to learn from correction or for older adolescents who have well-developed powers of reasoning.[154] In the landmark English case of *Gillick,*[155] which reached the House of Lords, the Law Lords decided that parental authority over children declines as children grow in age and understanding, and if a child has the capacity to make a reasoned decision about a matter parents cannot force their will upon the child.[156]

Motive for punishment

Punishment had to be imposed with the intention of correcting the child's behaviour: it could not be administered for revenge, spite, rage, ill-will or sexual gratification.[157] In reality, it is usually administered by angry (rather than calm and collected) parents. The boundary between anger on the one hand and rage or ill-will on the other can be tenuous.

Who can hit or smack children

Section 59 endowed parents and 'persons in the place of a parent' with the right to hit or smack children in their care. A relative, older sibling, nanny or babysitter who had sole care of the child would probably qualify as a person acting in place of a parent. Courts have held that a railway ticket inspector and a park attendant did not have a right of reasonable correction.

Nature of misbehaviour

If a parent had a genuine belief that a child had misbehaved, the courts were reluctant to scrutinise whether the child had in fact misbehaved or whether the punishment inflicted was proportionate to the misbehaviour.[158] Most physical punishment is a response to a child who is seen as disobedient or impudent. In Victorian times, when it was accepted that children were under the absolute authority and control of their parents, it logically followed that a child who defied parental authority could be corrected by the use of physical punishment.

Contemporary approaches to child-rearing suggest that discipline should involve explaining to children why certain rules apply and answering any questions they have. On this view, it is unreasonable to expect immediate and unquestioning obedience by children to parental demands. As far back as 1902, a New Zealand judge remarked that it would be unreasonable to beat a child viciously as a punishment for impudence.[159]

Method of punishment

The cases are clear that the punishment had to be carried out with a reasonable means or instrument. That said, the cases show a wide variation in what forms and severity of punishment have been considered acceptable. Blows with a fist to the head and kicks to a child's body have been considered reasonable in some cases and unreasonable in others. Juries have accepted the use of objects such as a cricket bat, tennis racquet, walking stick, stock whip, riding crop and bamboo stake as reasonable in some cases, while throwing a book or punch at a child has been held to be unreasonable in others.

It will be obvious from the above review of the limits applicable to physical punishment of children that there were significant anomalies and inconsistencies in the attitudes of judges and juries as to what constituted 'reasonable force' and amounted to 'correction'.

> ***The inconsistency of court decisions was not a useful argument for repeal because opponents countered that the issue could be resolved by defining 'reasonable force'.***

Using the *Reasonable Chastisement* Defence

The defence of *reasonable chastisement* can be raised in a wide range of criminal and civil proceedings.

Criminal cases tried by a jury

Section 59 was most commonly raised as a defence in criminal proceedings brought against a parent for assault or some more serious charge, an element of which was an assault. Because New Zealand juries have traditionally been sympathetic to parents they have often acquitted them. Newspaper reports of acquittals seldom give a full account, but parents were regularly acquitted by juries in cases where the facts as reported suggest that the punishment meted out went beyond reasonable correction. A few examples will suffice:

- a mother who slapped the face of her two-year-old son leaving red welts;[160]
- a father who chained up his 14-year-old stepdaughter;[161]
- a couple who disciplined a nine-year-old boy by hitting him with a bamboo stick;[162]
- a father who hit a 12-year-old girl with a hosepipe after she interrupted him, leaving her with a 15-cm long welt across her back;[163]
- a father who hit his daughter with a doubled-over belt;[164]
- a stepfather who hit his young stepson with a belt to stop him running out onto the road;[165]

- a father who hit his son six to eight times with a large piece of wood using considerable force.[166]

Parents typically give evidence in their defence, emphasising the child's bad behaviour. The child is rarely called as a witness, so the jury usually only hears the parent's point of view. The judgements in criminal cases are rarely published in formal law reports and as a result there has been little consistency in interpretation of what is and is not 'reasonable force'.[167]

There are other cases of serious abuse to children where a section 59 defence was raised unsuccessfully. In one case, the child had suffered a fractured skull and injuries to his testicles.[168] The defence was unsuccessful in a 2001 case where the father and stepmother of a 13-year-old had given the young person repeated beatings with their hands and with implements such as a spoon and a leather belt.[169] In another case, a parent who smacked and roughly handled a toddler in a public place was convicted of assault.[170]

Parents who have admitted charges of assault have often been given light sentences. In a 2007 case, a father who admitted hitting his 13-year-old son with a broom handle causing injury was convicted and discharged.[171]

Other Applications of Section 59

Section 59 had implications for children that went far beyond the criminal courts.

Trumping civil claims

Assault is not only a criminal offence: victims could sue the defendant in civil courts for damages for any injury suffered. While it was widely known that section 59 gave parents a defence in criminal proceedings, it was less well known that it also provided parents with a defence to civil claims for assault, battery or wrongful imprisonment. The defence applied to civil proceedings because the word 'justified' in section 59 is defined in section 2(1) of the Crimes Act to mean 'not liable to any civil proceeding' as well as 'not guilty of an offence'.[172]

Children rarely sue their parents and since New Zealand's Accident Compensation Scheme came into effect in the 1970s there are legal and procedural difficulties in claiming damages for personal injury from an assault.

While the protection afforded to parents against civil claims by a child for assault had little practical effect, the ability of a parent to rely upon *reasonable correction* as a defence in civil proceedings concerned with family violence placed children at a serious disadvantage.

Child protection and domestic violence laws are civil laws aimed at protecting children and others from family violence. It is surprising and anomalous that the Crimes Act should override provisions in civil law, and this aspect of the reasonable chastisement defence created real difficulties in civil proceedings.

Defeating protection orders

Concern about the high incidence of family violence in New Zealand led to the passing of the Domestic Protection Act 1982, aimed at reducing domestic violence, including violence towards children.[173] Broader protections from family violence were later enacted in the Domestic Violence Act 1995. A spouse could obtain a protection order against a violent partner, and a child could obtain a protection order against a violent parent through the Family Court. Once a protection order has been made, the person against whom the order is made commits a criminal offence if he or she abuses, threatens, intimidates or harasses the protected person, or enters or loiters near the protected person's property without express consent or reasonable excuse.[174]

It was not long before a father successfully raised the *reasonable chastisement* defence in opposition to an application for a protection order. The Family Court judge held that the combined effect of the word 'justified' in section 59 and the words 'not liable to any civil proceeding' in section 2(1) of the Crimes Act were wide enough to apply to applications for a protection order in favour of a child.[175] As a result, children who were hit by a parent could not obtain a protection order unless the court was satisfied that the force used against the child was unreasonable. The decision was not appealed and the ruling was followed by other Family Court judges. Later, a High Court judge reluctantly came to the view that even a parent against whom a protection order had earlier been made was entitled to rely on the *reasonable chastisement* defence.[176]

The bizarre result was that if a man assaulted his partner in the sight or hearing of their child, a protection order in favour of the child could be made but, if he hit the child, the court could not make a protection order in favour of the child unless the force used was deemed unreasonable or was not applied for the purpose of correction. A law intended to give greater protection to children from domestic violence could not override the parental right to hit children, and the safety of children was compromised.

Undermining care and contact decisions

Disputes between parents over guardianship, day-to-day care (formerly known as custody) and contact with a child (formerly known as access) are dealt with in the Family Court. For more than eighty years New Zealand courts have been required to treat the welfare of the child as the first and paramount consideration.[177] According to the provisions of the Care of Children Act 2004, a principle that must be applied by the courts in all cases is that the child's safety must be secured.[178] Section 5(e) states that the '[child] must be protected from <u>all forms of violence</u> (whether by members of his or her family ... or other persons' (emphasis added). This immediately raised the question of whether the act of a parent hitting a child for the purpose of correction qualified as a 'form of violence'.

When an adult hits a spouse, most people would view that as a 'form of violence'. If the same person hits a child, then surely the same act is also a 'form of violence'. But if a parent claimed that hitting the child was reasonable chastisement, the Family Court could be prevented by section 59 from making a protection order, despite the expressed intention of the Domestic Violence Act to provide greater protection from domestic violence, and of the Care of Children Act to protect children from 'all forms of violence'. This frustration of the intent of the law caused one Family Court judge to bemoan the difficulties that resulted from Parliament's failure to clarify whether physical punishment was still appropriate in New Zealand and the conflict between laws intended to give children greater protection from violence and the *reasonable chastisement* defence of the Crimes Act.[179]

Conflicts with child protection legislation

New Zealand's child protection legislation is set out in the Children, Young Persons, and Their Families Act 1989. The Family Court can make a declaration that a child is in need of care or protection on the grounds that the child is being harmed, ill-treated or abused.[180] The courts have never ruled definitively on the issue of whether a child who has been subjected to 'reasonable chastisement' might be found to have been thereby 'harmed, ill-treated or abused' and so declared in need of care or protection.

The case of the woman who was acquitted by a jury of assault after she had admitted striking her son with a riding crop and bamboo cane and who later had her son taken into care did not set a legal precedent because the decision of a jury in a criminal case on the evidence called by the prosecution is not binding on a civil court which must act on the evidence before it. Evidence directed to showing that a child is in need of care or protection is seldom restricted to one incident and will usually include evidence of other notifications and incidents.

> ***As section 59 was also a defence against any civil proceeding, it undermined legislation that sought to protect children from violence. This became another significant argument in the case for repeal.***

Attitudes of Members of the Legal Profession towards Repeal

Lawyers and judges are skilled in the analysis and interpretation of the law. Through their work they have a rights-focus and have traditionally been strong advocates for human rights. One might have anticipated therefore that lawyers would be in the forefront of the movement to repeal section 59.

As with other sections of the community, a broad range of opinion on physical punishment has been expressed by judges, practising lawyers, lawyers' organisations, academic lawyers and authors of legal texts. What is surprising, though, is that the views of some supporters of section 59 appear to have been influenced more by their own personal beliefs rather than a careful analysis of the relevant statutory provisions and legal principles.

High Court judges

In recent years New Zealand's High Court has seldom been asked to pronounce upon the legality or appropriateness of physical punishment of children.

In a recent decision, Justice Baragwanath was critical of an 'unexpressed sentiment' that 'like chattels and realty, children are things of their parents', observing that '[Children] did not ask to be born; and those who are responsible for their birth thereby acquire responsibilities owed to them, not rights over them.'[181] This is a complete reversal of Blackstone's view that parents are entitled to rights over their children because they had been responsible for their birth.

In an earlier case, the same judge had commented that corporal punishment involving a stick or strap would seldom be appropriate in the case of a young child or a teenager.[182] In another case, Justice Fisher expressed surprise that the Domestic Violence Act had not expressly excluded the section 59 defence, with the result that a father against whom a protection order had been made under that Act could rely on the defence of reasonable chastisement if he hit his son. The judge found that a slap to the head and two blows to the legs of a nine-year-old did not constitute reasonable chastisement.[183]

Family Court judges

Judges have to apply the law as they find it. Because of the separation of powers between the legislature and the judiciary, judges rarely make public statements critical of laws passed by Parliament.

Most cases heard in the Family Court are decided on the particular facts and the court, in making decisions about children, must treat as the paramount consideration the welfare and best interests of the child. An application for a parenting order is a civil proceeding, but, unlike an application for a protection order, it is not a civil matter arising directly out of the violent actions of a parent. The fact that one parent has used physical punishment on a child is relevant only if the court finds that this has affected the child's welfare and best interests. A study of Family Court decisions demonstrates a decreasing tolerance of any physical punishment of children. While acknowledging that the law allowed parents to reasonably chastise their children, Family Court judges often expressed disapproval of physical punishment. During the last 20 years, parents (and children) have been more likely to raise issues of physical punishment by the other parent (or the other parent's new partner) in the context of disputes over care or contact. Family Court judges have become increasingly aware of the psychological harm that can result from physical punishment. In this period, there have been at least 35 cases where a judge has expressed disapproval of physical punishment of children in a written ruling.

Legal writers

Since the early 1980s, university law lecturers and family law textbook writers have expressed reservations about *reasonable chastisement.*[184] In 1982, the authors of *Family Law Practice* stated:

> *Section 59 … derives from a time when parental authority over a child was absolute. Today we recognise that a child has individual identity and rights of his/her own. A significant minority of parents in New Zealand see physical punishment of children as undesirable and degrading. … There has in New Zealand in recent years been strong pressure to remove the protection given to parents and teachers who resort to physical punishment.*[185]

In 1989, John Caldwell, a senior lecturer at the University of Canterbury, published a comprehensive review of the laws relating to corporal punishment. He referred to modern research that physical chastisement was more likely to hinder, rather than facilitate, socially desirable behaviour and healthy emotional development.[186] He noted that Anglo-Saxon culture places more emphasis on the infliction of pain on children as a means of behavioural control than do other European societies and expressed surprise that there had not been more debate on the issue, particularly as the linkage between physical punishment and child abuse was well proven.

In 1997, academic Michael Freeman, Professor of Law at London University and an international expert on children's law, was uncompromising in his denunciation of the parental right of reasonable chastisement, describing it as 'the remnant of an uncivilised institution'.

Other academic lawyers have recently stressed that physical punishment is inconsistent with New Zealand's obligations under UNCROC and other international human rights treaties.[187]

Professor Bill Atkin of the Victoria University School of Law in Wellington made a carefully worded submission to the Select Committee that considered Sue Bradford's Bill. He supported full repeal of section 59 but suggested codifying common law provisions that applied in situations where parents needed to restrain or remove children, as a way of addressing some of the public fears about a law change. The amendment put forward by the Select Committee was influenced by his submission (see chapter 9).

Not all New Zealand academics have expressed opposition to the *reasonable chastisement* defence. Two University of Otago Faculty of Law staff members, Professor Rex Ahdar and Associate Professor James Allan, argued in 2001 that the case for the repeal of section 59 was weak.[188] As mentioned in the journal, one author, a Christian, approached the issue from a theological point of view and the other, an atheist, discussed it in secular terms. The authors were dismissive of the UN Convention on the Rights of the Child. They described proposals for repeal as paternalism and put forward the usual parents' rights arguments, labelling the views of abolitionists as 'rhetoric, fallacies and overblown sentimentality.'

The Law Society

The Public Issues Committee of the Auckland District Law Society produces discussion papers on issues of public interest. In October 2005, it released a discussion paper on domestic discipline prompted by Sue Bradford's Bill.[189] The committee expressed concern that if section 59 was repealed, any touching by a parent of a child might amount to a criminal assault. This is an odd view for lawyers to hold. There are many touchings between partners, friends, family members and carers for the sick or the elderly which may technically be assaults but which are accepted as a normal part of everyday life. Such touchings do not result in prosecutions because they are usually consensual and they do not involve violence or punishment. These everyday touchings have never been a source of concern on the part of lawyers or the general public. It was only when the right of parents to hit their children was under threat that some members of the legal profession identified it as an issue.

The Care of Children Act 2004 defines the rights and powers of parents very widely. Parental powers include the provision of day-to-day care for the child. These rights and powers are sufficient to allow parents to perform the normal tasks of good parenting, yet the Public Issues Committee made no mention of them. Nor did it mention common law powers that parents have long enjoyed.[190]

The Family Law Section of the Law Society is an influential group of lawyers who practise in the Family Courts. They are very aware of the high incidence of family violence in New Zealand society. Many of its members are appointed as lawyers to act for children in parental disputes over guardianship, care and contact.

The Family Law Section decided to consult with its members before making a statement on the issue of repeal and meetings were held around the country. At four meetings participants were unanimously or strongly pro-repeal, at four meetings there was a small majority in favour of repeal, and at three meetings members were divided. Māori family lawyers were polled separately but were equally divided in their views, with seven supporting full repeal, five supporting partial repeal, and three opposed to change. In the light of the range of views expressed, the Executive of the Family Law Section decided to further consult with members as to the option of partial reform. The outcome of this further consultation was that the majority of members favoured amendment rather than repeal.

The Law Society's submission to the Select Committee did not support the Bill, proposing instead that the right of *reasonable chastisement* be retained but that reasonable force be defined so as to ban any punishment that caused 'bodily harm' or involved the striking of children above the shoulder.

Other groups of lawyers

Youth Law Project, an Auckland-based community law centre established in 1987, consistently pressed for repeal of all legal sanctions of physical punishment of children from 1989 onwards.[191] Wellington Community Law Centre made a submission on the Bill supporting full repeal but its sister centre in Porirua, Whitireia Community Law Centre, made a submission backing the Law Society's proposal for partial reform.

Queen's Counsel

Queen's Counsel (QC) are appointed from experienced lawyers who have high standing in the profession. They are seen to be learned in the law and their views normally carry greater weight than those of other lawyers. In response to questions from *Investigate* magazine, three eminent QCs expressed their opposition to the repeal Bill.[192] In their responses, the QCs seemed to have missed the point that section 59 is about the correction of children, not about the normal incidents of child-rearing, and that repeal would not affect general parental powers to care for, protect and raise their children.

> ***Lawyers were sometimes influenced more by their own childhood experiences and personal views when commenting on the issue of physical punishment rather than a dispassionate analysis of the legal issues and implications.***

The Repeal of Section 59

When Sue Bradford's simple repeal bill was returned to the House for its second reading, the Select Committee had made some significant amendments, all of which eventually became part of the new law (see appendices 1–3 for the text of different versions).

Despite the wording of the Act's title, Crimes (Substituted Section 59) Amendment Act 2007, which implies that section 59 was amended rather than repealed, all of the old section 59 was in fact repealed. This means that the defence of *reasonable chastisement* has been eliminated from New Zealand's statutory law. The new subsection 59(2) makes it very clear that the use of force is no longer permitted as a means of correcting children's behaviour – 'nothing ... justifies the use of force for the purpose of correction.' If that were not clear enough, the Purpose section of the amendment act states that the intention is to make better provision for children to live 'free from violence by abolishing the use of parental force for the purpose of correction' (emphasis added).

The new subsections 59(2) and (3) also overturn 'any rule of common law [that] justifies the use of force for the purpose of correction'. Most legal experts believed that the common law would have come into play if section 59 had been simply repealed. The final version of the Bill was an advance on the Bill as introduced, in that it explicitly eliminated the common law defence of *reasonable chastisement*.

> ***The new law had to explicitly overturn any common law provision that might have come into play once the statutory provision was overturned.***

The Effect of the 'Parental Control' Amendment

The substitute section 59 is entitled *Parental control*, and subsection (1) is clearly intended to clarify the difference between physical punishment and parental rights and responsibilities to protect, rear and socialise their children.

The subsection sets out four situations in which parents can apply reasonable force for purposes *other* than correcting their children. Contrary to a disconcerting claim by confused TV newsreaders that this meant that parents could now hit children in order to stop them endangering themselves, committing an offence, or engaging in anti-social behaviour (see chapter 10), the legitimate application of force under the new law relates to restraining, removing or rearing children.

This is apparent if the justification for the use of reasonable force in each situation is considered:

(a) preventing or minimising harm to the child or another person

This merely enacts the common law position and allows parents to stop a child from running out onto the road or to restrain a child who is hitting a younger sibling.

(b) preventing the child from engaging ... in conduct that amounts to a criminal offence

Under section 16(1) of the Care of Children Act 2004, parents have a duty and responsibility to contribute to their child's social and personal development, and under section 283 of the Children, Young Persons, and Their Families Act 1989, parents can be ordered to pay compensation to the victim of an offence committed by their children under 16 years. It follows that parents must have the power to *restrain* their children from committing criminal offences. Under common law, parents have the right to *restrict* the liberty of their children for brief periods for their protection from harm or for other legitimate reasons. Section 22 of the New Zealand Bill of Rights Act 1990 gives all people (including children) the right not to be arbitrarily detained and the parental power described in section 59(1)(b) to prevent children from committing a criminal offence would be understood in the light of this right.

(c) preventing the child from engaging ... in offensive or disruptive behaviour

From time to time, every parent intervenes to prevent their children from engaging in anti-social behaviour. It is not in the interests of a toddler who is having a tantrum to be left free to rearrange the contents of supermarket shelves. Again, the application of force is about restraining or removing the misbehaving child – not about hitting the child to stop anti-social behaviour.

(d) performing the normal daily tasks that are incidental to good care and parenting

This provision enables parents to change nappies (diapers), place young children in the bath or bed, and move them away from situations that are harmful. This again merely gives statutory recognition to powers parents have under common law and reinforces the provisions of the Care of Children Act.

Together the amendments make a clear statement that hitting or smacking children is prohibited and the defence of *reasonable correction* is no longer available to parents. No doubt some lawyers defending criminal assault charges against parents will try to argue that their client was not hitting the child for the purposes of correction but was merely using force to prevent the child from engaging in disruptive behaviour. It is for the judge to advise the jury as to the law and to point out the clear distinction between force used for correction and force used to protect or restrain the child. While some juries may give perverse verdicts, the likelihood of this happening is considerably reduced by the clear distinction between 'correction' and 'protection and restraint'.

The Effect of the Affirmation of Police Discretion

The 'last minute' compromise amendment found in section 59(4) (see appendix 3), which was added to achieve broader political support for the Bill, did no more than confirm the discretion that the Police already had on whether to prosecute or not in any particular case. That discretion is often exercised in relation to minor assaults on adults and children and the amendment merely restates the status quo.

> ***Reformers agreed to an amendment which reassured the public that parents would not be prosecuted for minor offences because it did not compromise the purpose of the law which was to give children the same legal protection from assault as adults.***

By the time this book went to press in November 2007, the media had publicised a few cases where parents have been reported to the Police for smacking children. In most of these cases the Police have not prosecuted the parents and displayed a sensible use of police discretion. Likewise the media has reported one case of a prosecution in which a father dragged his eight-year-old son onto a bed, placed him on his knee and hit him three times with his open hand, then roughly manhandled him. His shoulder was bruised, and the Police alleged that his buttocks were also bruised and that there was a carpet burn-type injury on his back from being manhandled. The man had a previous conviction for assault and admitted that he had lost his temper and pleaded guilty to the charge. Earlier concerns had been expressed about his punishment of the boy. The complaint to the Police was made by the man's wife, who had taken photos of the boy's bruised shoulder. The man was placed under supervision for nine months with conditions that he participate in parenting and anger management courses.[193]

The national director of the lobby group Family First, which had strongly opposed the repeal bill, claimed that the prosecution was an example of how the change in the law would target good parents and that parents had every reason to be concerned. In fact, the prosecution and the orders made by the court demonstrated that the repeal of section 59 will give greater protection to children and will educate parents in non-violence methods of disciplining children.

In December 2007 the Deputy Commissioner of Police, Rob Pope, stated in a press release on the three-month review of the impact of the new law on police activity that:

> *'... claims that the repeal of section 59 of the Act would lead to the prosecution of parents and the removal of children from their homes as a result of minor acts of physical discipline have proved unfounded.* [194]

Conclusion

The criminal law sets enforceable standards for human behaviour. Section 59 was an exception to the general principles that all people should be treated equally before the law and that all people have a right to equal protection from assaults. The repeal of section 59 confers on children the same rights that adults enjoy. It recognises that children are individuals whose right to human dignity and bodily integrity should be respected and upheld.

The criminal law is more than just an instrument of punishment. It is an important symbol which sets minimum standards of acceptable behaviour. The law, therefore, has a part to play in changing adult attitudes towards children and their rights and needs. In New Zealand, we are already seeing that because prosecution, conviction and punishment of parents for minor assaults will seldom be in the best interests of children, prosecutorial discretion will be exercised sensibly. In those cases where prosecution is deemed appropriate, because of the circumstances and nature of the assault, the use of sentences that facilitate improved parenting practices are likely to be in the child's best interests.

In the next chapter, we will explore the role of religious beliefs in driving support for or opposition to law reform, as well as the contributions of particular religious groups and leaders towards advancing or hindering the campaign to protect 'all God's children'.

Chapter 5

THE ROLE OF RELIGION

On the same day that it was announced that the Bill would be passed with overwhelming support in New Zealand's Parliament, members and supporters of the Destiny Church[195] arrived in Wellington to participate in a protest against the Bill in the grounds of Parliament. This was a peaceful rally – not characterised by the black shirts and raised fists of a previous Destiny Church protest against the earlier Civil Unions Bill.[196] At the same time, a moving but dignified prayer vigil was being held at the Anglican Cathedral across the road from Parliament in support of the Bill. How was it one group of sincere Christians felt it was their Christian duty to oppose the Bill and another group of sincere Christians felt it was incumbent on them as Christians to support repeal?

Christian supporters of repeal emerging from the cathedral

In this chapter, we will look initially at the religions of contemporary New Zealanders, then briefly consider the impact of Christian religion on the child-rearing practices of indigenous peoples before discussing the biblical roots of physical punishment. After that, we will review the emergence of Christian support for repeal, which proved to be a crucial event along the journey to banning physical punishment in New Zealand. In the second half of the chapter, we will explore the nature of Christian opposition to the Bill, particularly the rise of vocal lobby groups and their use of overseas experts. Finally, we will consider how advocates were able to counter the claims of those experts.

The Religions of New Zealanders

When asked 'What is your religion?', of the 4,027,947 people living in New Zealand on the official census night of 7 March 2006, 1,297,104 said they had 'no religion' and just over two million said their religion was 'Christian'.[197] Those who identified themselves as Christian were then asked their denomination. The largest groupings by far were Anglican (584,793), Catholic (485,637), Presbyterian (385,350), and Methodist (116,622).[198] How many of these people are practising Christians, to whom faith is a central part of life, is not known. There will be many who do not regularly attend church but retain Christian beliefs and adhere to Christian values. Despite the largely secular nature of New Zealand society and the state,[199] Christianity is still regarded by many as the source of our moral values.

During the long debate over section 59, those people who publicly supported repeal from a Christian perspective were mostly Anglicans or Presbyterians, along with some Catholics and a few individuals from other smaller Protestant denominations. There were also many Christians from all denominations who opposed law reform, although their opposition was not necessarily based on Christian beliefs. Those whose opposition was firmly based on religious convictions were mostly members of socially conservative groups or churches. Both of the high profile anti-repeal lobby organisations, Family First and Family Integrity, were associated with such groups.[200] Not all Christians who opposed full repeal identified with the anti-reform stance adopted by the leading lobby groups though.

Whilst it is difficult to use the census data to identify how many New Zealanders belong to socially conservative Christian churches and groups, it is clear that Christians with those affiliations led a well-funded, co-ordinated and energetic campaign against law reform.

Christianity and Indigenous Peoples

Christianity came to the Pacific Islands and New Zealand when the British, French and German colonial powers began expanding into the Southern Pacific Ocean during the early nineteenth century. Both Protestant and Roman Catholic mission stations were established from early nineteenth century onwards. The missionaries brought with them both the religious beliefs and the cultural habits associated with child-rearing that were prevalent in their countries of origin at their time of departure.

During the period in which Māori and Pacific Island peoples converted to Christianity, indigenous spiritual concepts and cultural values were sometimes incorporated into the practices and creeds of the newly established churches, but more often the traditional religious beliefs and cultural values of the denomination dominated. Māori beliefs and values found greater expression in the creeds of new Māori Christian religions that were established by charismatic leaders in the late nineteenth and early twentieth century. These included the Rātana and Ringatu Churches which, according to the 2006 Census, were nominated as the religion of 50,565 and 16,419 people respectively.[201]

It is beyond the scope of this book to delve into what early missionaries and clergy might have taught Māori and Pacific Island converts about the role of physical punishment in the pursuit of 'godly child-rearing'. However, there is a belief among some contemporary Māori and Pacific commentators that during the 'missionary period' their peoples were subjected to strong, well-intentioned Christian messages about the vital role that physical punishment played in shaping children's moral and spiritual development, and this imperative differed significantly from their traditional child-rearing practices. As Dr Pita Sharples, co-leader of the Māori Party, explained briefly in a television interview:

> *In the olden Māori days kids were noa, they were common, and therefore they had no restrictions, and they weren't hit or chastised or anything, they were allowed to sort of run free.*[202]

In 1998, at the International Society for the Prevention of Child Abuse and Neglect conference in Auckland, there was a memorable keynote session that focused on the three principal influences on the attitudes of Pacific peoples towards children and discipline. These were tradition, religion and the modern world.[203]

Masiofo Mata'afa, a former High Commissioner to New Zealand and the wife of Samoa's first Prime Minister, spoke about the role of tradition. She was firmly of the opinion that physical punishment was not a part of the tradition of child-rearing in pre-missionary Samoa. Dr Gregory Dever from Pohnpei, one of the Federated States of Micronesia, discussed the impact on child-rearing of the modern rights-based view of children as citizens worthy of no less respect than people of other ages. The third speaker, the Reverend Tavake Tupou, a Tongan and former President of the Methodist Church in New Zealand, addressed the influence of Christian religion on disciplinary habits. He presented a pro-physical punishment perspective, putting forward the view that suffering in this world was a necessary preparation for life in the next world. Given the nature of the audience, it was hardly surprising that many were upset by his views.

The Biblical Roots of Physical Punishment

How did this belief in the moral and spiritual necessity of physically punishing children originate? In his seminal book, *Spare the Child: The Religious Roots of Punishment and the Psychological Impact of Physical Abuse*, Philip Greven, a Christian historian at Rutgers University in the United States, asserts that:

> *The most enduring and influential sources for the widespread practice of physical punishment ... has been the Bible. Both the Hebrew scriptures in the Old Testament and passages from the New Testament have sustained for centuries the defense of physical punishment and the use of the rod.*[204]

After examining the biblical roots of physical punishment, he concludes:

> *Corporal punishment is not and cannot be grounded in words ascribed to Jesus or Paul ... The practice thus rests upon only the most fragile New Testament foundation. Why, then, has physical punishment been considered 'Christian' at all?* [205]

Professor Greven considers that the fear of condemning children to an eternity in hell has been the root justification of much earthly suffering of children. He traces this back to a number of aphorisms found in the Book of Proverbs in the Old Testament,[206] such as 'Withhold not correction from the child: for if thou beatest him with a rod, he shall not die. Thou shalt beat him with the rod, and shalt deliver his soul from hell.'[207]

Hope of salvation from eternal damnation therefore included the necessity of breaking the will of the child.

> *The focal point of evangelical and fundamentalist Protestant childrearing always has been the emerging wills of children. Breaking the child's will has been the central task given parents by successive generations of preachers, whose biblically based rationales for discipline have reflected the belief that self-will is evil and sinful.*[208]

In contrast, Jesus, who was a Jewish rabbi, had a different approach to children, as epitomised by his statement 'Suffer the little children to come unto me' when his disciples wanted to drive them away.[209] Nowhere in the Gospels does Jesus speak about hitting children.

Greven goes on to make the intriguing case that the assumptions on which modern secular arguments for the infliction of physical punishment on children are based are actually derived from a religious rationale that is deeply embedded in Western thinking.

> *So embedded are these [religious] assumptions in our minds and culture, and so familiar are they to most of us, that it is often impossible to discern their actual influence on us.*[210]

It is likely that many of the New Zealand parents who used physical punishment before the law change did so more as a matter of habit rather than out of religious conviction, but as we have seen the two are not unrelated. However, as we shall also see, some contemporary Christian scholarship on the matter of child discipline does not support the use of physical punishment at all.

Although the persistence of physical discipline of children has largely been a matter of custom, it also has deep religious roots.

Christian Support for Repeal Before the Bill's Arrival

During the years preceding the Bill's unexpected arrival in the House, physical punishment and section 59 were debated to some extent in general assemblies and national church conferences. Occasionally churches or church leaders made public statements on the issues.

In 1994, in a paper entitled *Corporal Punishment*, the Joint Methodist-Presbyterian Public Questions Committee pointed out:

> *In 1986 General Assembly and Conference of our two Churches supported the abolition of corporal punishment in New Zealand schools.*

and went on to ask:

> *In two short years [since abolition in 1992] we have learnt to manage without hitting our children at school. If we can learn to do without hitting our children at school, can we learn to do without hitting them at home?* [211]

In 2002, Auckland church leaders from a range of denominations issued a media statement in which they called on the Government to repeal section 59. In their statement, they wrote:

> *The expression 'spare the rod and spoil the child' is mistakenly used to endorse hitting children, said Bishop Richard Randerson, spokesperson for the group. 'Those are not an accurate quotation of the biblical verse (Proverbs 13.24) which goes on to say "the one who loves his child is diligent in correction." Such correction does not need to be by way of physical hitting: non-physical alternatives are available.'* [212]

In 2004, Sarah Lindsell, writing in the Catholic magazine *The Tablet*, reported that the Catholic social-action agency Caritas was campaigning for a total ban on hitting children.[213]

These early expressions of support did not lead to a sustained Christian-led campaign to banish physical punishment but the input from mainstream churches did contribute a pro-repeal religious perspective to the debate that surfaced in the media and thus played a significant part in achieving change.

Collaboration with Secular Advocates

As secular advocates for repeal stepped up their efforts to gain wider public and political support during the first years of the new millennium, they sought out ministers of religion who were known to be sympathetic, and encouraged them to make their views known more widely. At public forums organised by UNICEF New Zealand and the Institute of Public Policy at the Auckland University of Technology during the run-up to the 2004 elections, two Christian speakers presented refreshingly different views on Christianity and physical punishment.

Archdeacon Glynn Cardy of St Matthew-in-the-City, Auckland, had this to say:

> *Despite what some Bible thumping Christian might tell you, there is nothing in the Christian Scriptures* [214] *to support the use of violence against children. There is no verse that says, 'If your child is disobedient, then you have a parental duty to hit him or her'. There are admonitions to children to 'obey their parents', yet the counter admonition to parents is 'not to provoke their children to wrath'. There are no verses in the New Testament about hitting children.*[215]

While the Reverend Nove Vailaau, Minister of the Congregational Christian Church of Samoa in Porirua and theologian, told the audience:

> *'Rod' is mostly used metaphorically (Ps 23) as to bring comfort in times of uncertainty. It is also used figuratively meaning Law (Torah) as guidance. Rod in the shepherd's hand is for leading, guidance and protection for sheep, not for punishing them.*[216]

Christian Support for Repeal After the Bill's Arrival

Sue Bradford's Bill was drawn out of the Parliamentary ballot on the 9th of June 2005. Towards the end of the Bill's progress through the process of law-making, Christian voices in favour of repeal multiplied and increased in volume.

Anglican and Catholic support

Support from the Anglican Church leadership culminated in a public statement issued jointly by all the Bishops of Aotearoa New Zealand on 1 May 2007, the day before the surprise announcement by the Prime Minister and Leader of the Opposition that both of their parties would support the Bill if an amendment was added. We have quoted the bishops' statement in full in the boxes on the following pages as it presents a succinct account of the Christian position in favour of repeal.

Anglican Bishops Support Repeal of Section 59

The current debate concerning the Crimes (Substituted Section 59) Amendment Bill is a crucial one as we reflect on the kind of society in which we wish to raise our children.

The proposed changes to section 59 are a further important step down the road of transforming the disproportionately high rates of violence in our country (third highest amongst OECD countries, UNICEF 2003).

There are a number of disturbing examples of the use of physical objects, belts, hosepipes and fists, which have been regarded as 'reasonable force'. Removing a loophole that has been used to justify the use of excessive force against children will reinforce the total unacceptability of violence against children. It will help break the cycle of violence, and is therefore in the best interest of our children, and of our society as a whole.

There is some debate among Christians about the use of corporal punishment and the repeal of section 59. As Christians, our primary role model is Jesus Christ. As fallible humans, we struggle with issues of power and authority, and with their use or misuse.

In the face of the abuse of power, Christ brings freedom, forgiveness, compassion, mercy, and ultimately self-sacrifice. The way of Jesus was one of non-violence. He declined to sanction violent punishment against offenders, preferring instead to look to the root causes of ill behaviour and to offer people a new start. This is how we must relate to our children.

As Christians, our reading of the Bible must always be done through the lens of Christ's teaching and life. There has been a lot of talk about 'Spare the rod and spoil the child', an attitude that can be sanctioned by scriptural proof-texts such as Proverbs 13: 24 – 'Those who spare the rod hate their children, but those who love them are diligent to discipline them' (NRSV).

However, it is inappropriate to take such texts out of their ancient cultural context, and out of the broader context of Scripture, so as to justify modes of behaviour in a modern situation very different from that for which they were given. Such texts need to be read in the light of the way Christ responded to children, placing them in the middle of the group with respect and care, as in Mark 9: 37 – 'Whoever welcomes one such child in my name welcomes me'.

We believe there is a real need to act responsibly, and to repeal section 59. It is vital to recognize that this position is held by most of New Zealand's child care and child education agencies, who work most closely with those who stand to be most affected by section 59, including: The Royal New Zealand Plunket Society Inc., Barnardos New Zealand, Parents Centre New Zealand Inc., Presbyterian Support New Zealand, and UNICEF.

It is essential that changes to section 59 go hand in hand with increased access to high quality public educational programmes, which encourage non-violent discipline and child rearing. The Anglican Church is committed to delivering and promoting high quality non-violent education and working with at-risk families through, for example, our Anglican Care Network and Te Whare Ruruhau o Meri.

This is a moment for our values to shape our laws and the future of our nation. This is a moment to make a positive difference. We believe repeal of section 59 provides an expression of hope, and we wholeheartedly support it.

Catholic bishops had earlier issued a more muted statement offering their qualified support for the Bill. They felt the legal status quo did not adequately protect children, but that the Government should not interfere unnecessarily with family decisions.[217]

Despite the strong support provided by the leadership of the Anglican church and by individual clergy in a range of other Protestant churches towards the end of the campaign, it would be wrong to assume that unqualified support came from any denomination or even a particular congregation – many congregations were not united in their views. Church-goers struggled with the personal issues that banning physical punishment of children raised. Most denominations did not get as far as debating the issues or adopting an official church-wide position by the time the Bill passed its final reading.

Wider ecumenical support for repeal

As the public and parliamentary debate became more heated early in 2007, lobbying from Christians opposed to reform became highly visible and vocal (see below). Advocates believed there was substantial mainstream Christian support for reform and sought the help of sympathetic clergy from a variety of denominations in placing a different Christian perspective before the public and politicians in a dramatic way. The response was heart-warming and effective. A number of clergy around the country engaged their colleagues in an expression of support for the Bill that involved adding their names to a formal support document. This was the document presented to the Prime Minister, Helen Clark, and the Bill's sponsor, Sue Bradford, on the steps of the Parliamentary Library on the momentous day of the 2nd of May 2007 (see chapter 9).

The document listed the names of 177 Protestant and Catholic church leaders who were prepared to publicly support the Bill. The formal statement opened with the words:

> *The Christian Leaders listed on the attached pages support the Crimes (Substituted Section 59) Amendment Bill. Their view is that physical discipline is not supported by contemporary religious scholarship and teaching and they wish to see any justification for physical force as a*

means of discipline removed from New Zealand law. They believe that this is a valuable way forward in assisting New Zealand's transition towards being a less violent society.[218]

The Revd Dr Margaret Mayman, Presbyterian minister of St Andrew's on The Terrace in Wellington, and the Social Justice Commissioner of the Anglican Church, the Revd Dr Anthony Dancer, led the initiative in the Wellington area and, with support from other colleagues, they also organised the ecumenical prayer vigil that took place at St Paul's Cathedral shortly before the support document was presented to the politicians. In Auckland, the Right Reverend Richard Randerson, the Assistant Anglican Bishop, and Archdeacon Glynn Cardy, the vicar of St Matthew-in-the-City, led efforts to publicly demonstrate Christian support for repeal, as did other clergy in different centres.

Bishop Richard Randerson being interviewed by TV journalists

Mainstream clergy provided critical leadership over a troubling public issue by putting forward a Christian perspective that fully supported repeal.

Opposing Christian Views

The conflicting views of Christians on the place of physical punishment became a major part of the public debate conducted in the media. Both Christian abolitionists and those Christians wanting to retain the status quo undoubtedly influenced both public and political opinion.

A front-page report in the *Dominion Post* on 2 May 2007 captured the polarisation of beliefs well. The headline read 'Church against Church: Groups to face off at Parliament', and the reporter went on to say:

> *Leaders of the Anglican, Presbyterian, Methodist and Catholic churches have thrown their weight behind the bill – and have accused Christian opponents of selectively misquoting the Bible.*
>
> *They will rally at Parliament at the same time as the Destiny Church-led protest against Green MP Sue Bradford's bill, which would remove the 'reasonable force' defence for parents charged with assault.*[219]

So far in this chapter we have concentrated on the pro-repeal pole of the religious debate. We will now explore the perspectives and strategies adopted by those Christians associated with the anti-repeal pole.

Christian Opposition to Repeal

Opposition to repeal from Christians was sporadic before the Bill's arrival but intensified greatly after the Bill's introduction into Parliament.

Before the Bill's arrival

Over the years of public debate on the place of physical punishment there was a variety of Christian voices raised against reform. Some espoused an extreme viewpoint that was out of touch with the modern understanding of child development.

In 1993, the Revd Graham Capill,[220] the leader of the Christian Heritage Party and a strong supporter of physical punishment, claimed:

> *Nobody has to teach [children] to be bad. It's part of their nature right from the beginning.*[221]

Other Christian opponents of reform in New Zealand were undoubtedly more moderate in their stance and, like many other New Zealanders, believed that mild physical punishment was sometimes necessary to correct children's behaviour. Mostly they were silent, which left the field free to be occupied by those with extreme views.

Throughout the early years of the debate, although not so prominently after the Bill began its progress through Parliament, the Maxim Institute was a steadfast opponent of repeal. This institute is a think-tank that has links with conservative Christian organisations in New Zealand and overseas.[222] It has a conservative social agenda that would be hard to distinguish from a conservative Christian agenda except that its objectives are expressed in secular terms. Later, in an extensive submission to the Select Committee, the institute advanced a whole raft of secular reasons why parents should retain the right to physically punish their children.[223]

Corporal punishment in schools

The strength of some Christians' belief in the necessity or efficacy of physical punishment was apparent in their willingness to defy the letter and spirit of New Zealand's law banning the use of corporal punishment in schools. The issue arose from time to time when some Christian schools asked parents to discipline their children at home for misbehaviour in school.[224] The Ministry of Education also seemed unable to prevent some Christian schools from illegally continuing the use of corporal punishment long after its use had been banned in all schools.[225] These schools tended to refuse to confirm or deny the use of corporal punishment. A national manager for the Ministry of Education responded to a question from the Children's Commissioner by saying that the Ministry's powers were limited to 'admonition' and that in the face of the school's refusal to answer questions there was little the officials could do.[226] The principal of one school was reported as saying that the prohibition on corporal punishment in schools was a 'rotten' law and 'contrary to scripture'.[227] On another occasion the principal of a Christian school attracted criticism by giving parents a pamphlet telling them how they should hit their children.[228] New Zealand's new law removes any ambiguity about the illegality of the use of force for the purpose of correction in either homes or schools.

After the Bill's arrival

When Sue Bradford's Bill was introduced into the House, repeal became a distinct possibility. During the period in which the Bill progressed through the various stages of law-making, religious opposition became well organised and funded. Full-page advertisements against the Bill were placed in major daily newspapers, a major petition seeking to initiate an official referendum on the Bill was launched (see chapter 8), and two well-known opponents from the northern hemisphere were brought to New Zealand in an attempt to discredit the evidence put forward by supporters of repeal (see below).

Leading lobby groups

The leading organisations opposed to change, at least in terms of the numbers of media releases published on Scoop,[229] were Family First, Family Integrity and the Society for the Promotion of Community Standards. These organisations were clearly committed to a socially conservative Christian agenda. Early in 2007, Family First published a list of 44 other organisations opposing repeal.[230] As is apparent from a diligent search of their websites' content and links, most of these groups also have conservative or fundamentalist connections.

One of the leading anti-repeal organisations, Family Integrity, was founded by Craig Smith. His extreme beliefs about the nature of children repelled some members of the public when his opinions were made public. In one of his publications, he claimed that:

> *Children are not little bundles of innocence: they are little bundles of depravity ... and can develop into unrestrained agents of evil ... unless trained and disciplined. Selfishness, violence, lying, cheating, stealing and other such manifestations of rebellion, are just the child unpacking some of this sinful foolishness from the vast store in his heart.*[231]

Not unexpectedly, disciplining required the use of a rod 'to drive the foolishness out.' Allies making such extreme claims sometimes proved an embarrassment to more moderate opponents of repeal.

Later in the period in which the Bill was the focus of the country's attention, the Destiny Church, a new denomination with strong Māori and Polynesian memberships, began acting as a lobby group opposing repeal and eventually became involved in organising rallies against the Bill. The church's leader, Bishop Brian Tamaki, was reported in the press as having said that the Bill:

> *... contradicted the God-given responsibility of parents to raise their children according to biblical principle, and that included administering 'Loving, proper corrective discipline in appropriate circumstances.'* [232]

However, the depth of leadership amongst the anti-repeal Christian lobby groups in New Zealand ought not to be exaggerated. The leading organisations seem to have been principally vehicles for relatively few people to advance their viewpoints.[233] Despite this limitation, the lobby groups, presumably through conservative Christian networks in New Zealand, were able to mobilise support for rallies against the Bill in a number of centres around the country.

Lobbying efforts

Opponents of repeal coordinated an extensive lobbying campaign, regularly organising members or associates to write to, email or visit Members of Parliament. They also sought and gained extensive media coverage including on television and radio where one or other of their limited range of spokespersons appeared on most interviews in order to 'balance' the views of secular or religious repeal advocates.

Despite their deeply held Christian convictions, opponents of repeal rarely justified their stance with reference to the Bible. Given the largely secular nature of New Zealand society and the political arena, it may well have been seen as inappropriate to advance arguments based on the Bible's authority. Instead, they engaged in arguments such as the right of parents to choose how they raise their children, the harmlessness and/or necessity of mild physical discipline, the potential for unwarranted State intervention in family life, the risk of criminalising good parents, and the absence of any evidence connecting child abuse with smacking.[234]

Representatives from anti-repeal Christian groups made numerous oral and written submissions to the Select Committee considering the proposed legislation. In total, 25 organisations and 1148 individuals made submissions against the Bill, but we do not know how many of those came from Christian organisations or individuals.[235]

Bringing in Overseas Experts

New Zealand has academics, such as Professor Anne Smith (who was at the Children's Issues Centre at the University of Otago during the period in which the Bill was before the Select Committee), with an in-depth knowledge of all of the national and international research on the negative consequences of physical punishment for children and the positive consequences when its use is avoided.[236] Despite this, New Zealanders have a natural tendency to turn to overseas experts when seeking to resolve matters of contention on the basis of evidence. Christian opponents of repeal therefore adopted a strategy of bringing in overseas experts sympathetic to their cause, in order to influence the public, media or political debate. Christian supporters of repeal did not do so, although secular advocates did bring in overseas experts (see chapters 1 and 2).

Religious opponents were instrumental in arranging the visits of two overseas advocates for physical discipline during the passage of the Bill through Parliament. Neither of these individuals advocated the retention of physical punishment on the basis of biblical authority. Rather they used secular arguments and research findings to back up their claims. As both of the visitors were brought to New Zealand largely at the initiative of socially conservative Christian lobby groups, it is worth exploring further the tactics involved.

Ruby Harrold-Claesson

In July 2006, Ruby Harrold-Claesson, a Jamaican-born Swedish legal advocate for parental rights, was flown to New Zealand by the Coalition section 59. This organisation described itself as 'a group of over 150[237] concerned Community and Lobby groups and families including Family Integrity, Society for Promotion of Community Standards, Family First, Sensible Sentencing Trust, NZ Centre for Political Debate, PANIC and others.'[238] The media release announcing her visit was published by the Christian lobby group Family First. While in New Zealand, the Swedish lawyer held a media conference and made a presentation to the Parliamentary Select Committee considering Sue Bradford's Bill.

In her oral presentation, she sought to promote the view that Sweden's experience since outlawing physical punishment had been negative overall. Harrold-Claesson claimed that children and young people had become badly behaved, there was unwarranted removal of children from families, and the rate of child maltreatment deaths was high.[239] To the media she made the claim that:

> *It has ruined families and ruined children. The children in Sweden are incredibly badly behaved. They have no discipline at home and no discipline in schools.*[240]

Swedish authorities were able to provide advocates for repeal with accurate statistics and peer-reviewed research findings refuting these claims.[241] Apparently solid statistical evidence for Sweden's poor state in relation to New Zealand turned out to be less than solid on close examination.[242]

Supporters of repeal were able to issue vigorous rebuttals of her claims through press releases and when interviewed by reporters seeking to express a 'balance of opinion' on the issues involved. On the whole, advocates believed that her visit back-fired – she lacked the independent expertise needed to be considered an authoritative source of information and did not interview well in the media. It is likely the sponsors of her trip did not benefit greatly from her visit, particularly in terms of convincing the Parliamentary Select Committee of the perils of reform, but 'evidence-based' claims tend to have a long 'half-life' regardless of how well they have been rebutted.

Dr Robert Larzelere

Late in April 2007, just before the momentous decision announced early in May, the lobby group Family First, with the support of For the Sake of Our Children Trust and the Sensible Sentencing Trust, brought Dr Robert Larzelere, an academic psychologist from Oklahoma State University in the United States, to New Zealand. He was brought here to promote the benefits of 'spanking' (mild physical punishment) and he also sought to discredit research findings on the negative effects of physical punishment and the positive effects of Sweden's law change.

Larzelere had earlier published a negative critique of research conducted by the Canadian academic Dr Joan Durrant into the consequences of Sweden's abolition of physical punishment.[243] His claims had been soundly rebutted by Durrant herself.[244] But, as New Zealand advocates found, the associated negative publicity made it very difficult to ensure a balanced and accurate story was reported.

The American academic advocated the use of minor forms of physical discipline, like smacking with an open hand, and advised against using physical discipline on children under two years of age or over six years of age. He called this 'normative spanking'. For many New Zealand children, 'normative' physical discipline included the use of heavy-handed force at all ages (even into adolescence) and often involves the use of implements.[245]

Larzelere's sponsors organised media conferences and meetings with Members of Parliament. His defence of mild smacking was unimpressive and he did not defend harsher forms of physical punishment. His presentation lacked relevance given that it was very unlikely that parents who used the minor forms of physical discipline he advocated would ever be prosecuted in New Zealand courts. During his visit it became clear that New Zealand's law change would receive overwhelming Parliamentary support.

Before his arrival though, repeal advocates had investigated his background, prepared rebuttals of his arguments, and circulated their material to the media and Members of Parliament. But in the end, these efforts were less critical because of the limited attention he received.

> ***The claims of overseas experts brought in to challenge research findings were able to be rebutted by advocates familiar with Swedish data and international research findings on the effects of physical punishment.***

Conclusion

Despite New Zealand being a predominantly secular country, particularly in the civil and political spheres, the actions of committed Christians played a very significant role in shaping the debate of the issues that was conducted in the media and in Parliament. Some religious opponents of law reform selectively used quotes from the Bible to buttress their beliefs, others used secular arguments to advance their cause. Religious supporters of reform were more influenced by the values reflected in the teachings of Jesus in the Gospels, and were prepared to advocate for repeal using religious as well as secular arguments.

Christian opponents of repeal engaged in a well-organised and well-funded campaign that significantly impacted upon public opinion, and which secular advocates had to find ways of neutralising. The contributions of those secular advocates is the subject of our next chapter. Towards the end of the passage of the Bill through Parliament, strong Christian support from mainstream churches, symbolically at least, stood for the rejection of more extreme views and advocated a positive change in public attitudes so that New Zealand could take steps towards becoming a less violent society. A Christian blessing was very important at that juncture.

Chapter 6

ADVOCATES FOR CHANGE

During the last half of the twentieth century, right up until the last decade, there were only a few New Zealand voices calling for the rejection of physical punishment of children. These lone voices must have felt very much like 'voices crying in the wilderness', largely ignored by the general population and their representatives in Parliament. But in the nineties and during the first years of the new millennium, an increasing number of diverse voices began calling for the repeal of section 59. Eventually, as the repeal bill progressed through the law-making process, more voices joined the chorus.

In this chapter we will discuss the distinctive contributions of different advocates and how they managed to collaborate successfully in the campaign that eventually resulted in complete repeal.

Early Advocates

There are usually a few individuals and organisations who act as the trail-blazers for social reforms, and the abolition of physical punishment in New Zealand was no exception.

Individual advocates

Anyone researching the abolition of physical punishment in New Zealand will find it impossible to ignore the contribution of the psychologists Jane and James Ritchie (see chapter 7). In the sixties and seventies they surveyed young mothers about child discipline methods and found a heavy reliance on the use of negative methods of discipline such as scolding, shouting and smacking.[246] The Ritchies expressed concern about the lack of knowledge of the undesirable consequences of physical discipline and children being subjected to regular beatings.[247]

Drawing on their research findings, they wrote a submission to a Parliamentary Select Committee hearing on violent offending in 1978. The

Ritchies argued that the level of violent offending in any society is related to tolerance of violence in that society and that 'violence breeds violence'. The pair urged the committee to 'recommend the elimination from statute of any provision that permits, to any person, the right to employ physical punishment in the correction and training of the young.' The committee declined.[248]

The Ritchies steadfastly lobbied politicians, wrote books and articles, made presentations at conferences, and campaigned for over 30 years to have section 59 repealed. Jane and James Ritchie influenced the thinking of many other advocates.

Another early campaigner for the repeal of section 59 was Robert Ludbrook, a children's lawyer with a long-standing interest in children's rights. He worked with Peter Newell (see below) at the Children's Legal Centre in London in the early 1980s. In 1986, he founded the Youth Law Project in Auckland, which evolved into YouthLaw Tino Rangatiratanga Taitamariki in the mid-nineties. Throughout the following decades, Robert strenuously promoted children's rights in New Zealand, including their right to legal protection from physical punishment.[249]

Peter Newell and Robert Ludbrook in 1999

The abolition of corporal punishment in schools

In the 1980s a group of school teachers and other individuals formed a lobby group called Campaign Against Violence in Education (CAVE). This organisation, along with other child advocates such as Rae Julian, a Human

Rights Commissioner, argued for the abolition of corporal punishment in schools. Their advocacy resulted in heated public debate.

In the late 1980s, the Labour Government led by Prime Minister David Lange, who was also the Minister of Education, proposed a series of school reforms, and the abolition of corporal punishment was to be one of them. But the new Education Act in 1989 did not include a ban on the use of corporal punishment in schools, in fact it made the situation worse because by-laws that had limited the extent to which corporal punishment could be used in schools had been revoked in anticipation of reform. Perhaps taking advantage of a temporary gap in the law, one principal opposed to repeal actually started caning girls.[250]

In 1990, the Labour MP Anne Collins introduced an amendment to the Education Act that removed the right of teachers to use corporal punishment. As the amendment was put forward in a Supplementary Order Paper,[251] this meant that it was not considered by a Select Committee and submissions from the public were not called for. The Labour Government supported the amendment and extended it to include private schools and early childhood centres as well as state schools. The Bill was put to a conscience vote in Parliament and passed with a small majority. As a result, teachers were excluded from the list of persons in section 59 of the Crimes Act who could apply 'reasonable force' for the purpose of correction.

The children's movement

The 1980s saw the beginning of organised child advocacy in New Zealand, inspired in part by the 1979 International Year of the Child and sustained by the work of the New Zealand Committee for Children, which was established in 1980 to carry on the work begun the previous year. This committee opposed the use of physical punishment.[252]

The New Zealand Government's ratification of the United Nations Convention on the Rights of the Child in 1993 helped raise public awareness of children's rights. Interest in child advocacy began to blossom during the 1990s when it became apparent that the neo-liberal economic reforms imposed upon New Zealand by the Labour Government during the mid to late eighties, and the ideologically linked National Government welfare reforms of the early nineties were impacting negatively on families with young children.[253]

The application of simplistic managerialist thinking to the functioning of government departments and government-contracted service providers during the nineties unintentionally undermined the early development of child advocacy. Government funding, upon which many non-governmental organisations (NGOs) relied, now required a close definition of the services to be provided – the outputs. Advocacy, which had formerly been undertaken as a matter of course but not named as such, was not recognised as a funded activity.[254] In response, some NGOs with general or specific interests in advocating on behalf of children, such as Plunket and Barnardos, as well as professional organisations, such as the Paediatric Society and the Public Health Association, formally included advocacy as one of their primary functions.

Child advocacy has since become firmly established as a distinct, respectable and effective activity in New Zealand, and child advocates played a vital role in securing the abolition of legally sanctioned physical discipline.

As different organisations and individuals took up child advocacy, they found common causes and were able to provide a unified voice for children in campaigns. Over time, they became sufficiently organised and effective to warrant the name *children's movement*. The existence of this grass-roots movement enabled effective campaigns advocating the repeal of section 59 to be mounted from time to time. One example is the *Protect and Treasure New Zealand's Children* campaign of 2004, whose primary resource was a pamphlet, endorsed by 24 leading child-focused organisations, that was widely distributed throughout New Zealand.[255]

> ***The growth of the children's movement enabled child advocates expressing similar messages to become influential players.***

Leading Advocates

A number of organisations displayed effective and critical leadership on the issue of ending physical punishment and repealing section 59 over the years, both in the public sphere and within their particular spheres of interest. However it is appropriate to place special emphasis on the work of two organisations whose roles as leading advocates commenced in the 1990s and were sustained until the Bill became law in 2007.

> ***The continuity of committed leadership was a critical factor in engaging and sustaining support for law reform from a wide range of organisations.***

The Children's Commissioners

During the 1980s a variety of organisations, including the National Council of Women, lobbied successfully for the establishment of a children's ombudsman.[256] In 1989, the Children, Young Persons, and Their Families Act established the role of the Commissioner for Children, with a range of functions including the promotion of children's welfare. In 1992, Dr Ian Hassall, the first Commissioner for Children, began speaking out publicly against the use of physical punishment. His conviction was partly based on the arguments put forward by Peter Newell, the international children's rights advocate and world-leading campaigner for ending the corporal punishment of children. But Ian's viewpoint on physical discipline was also a response to his concern at the level of violence towards children that existed in New Zealand and his belief that physical discipline was inconsistent with the children's rights specified by the United Nations Convention on the Rights of the Child.

The three subsequent Commissioners were all staunch in their opposition to physical punishment and actively supported the repeal of section 59. They widely promoted the use of positive, non-violent discipline as an effective, safe alternative. The Commissioners advocated ending physical discipline in innumerable public presentations, in newspaper and magazine articles, as well as on television and radio. They lobbied politicians and government officials many times over the years. They were greatly assisted by the legal mandate of the Children, Young Persons, and Their Families Act 1989 by which their office was established and later by the Children's Commissioner Act 2003, which now requires them 'to give better effect in New Zealand to the United Nations Convention on the Rights of the Child' (see chapter 4).[257]

Being the advocates with the highest public profile, the Children's Commissioners bore the brunt of angry or threatening letters from the more extreme opponents of repeal, and were sometimes ridiculed in the media for their advocacy. Dr Cindy Kiro, a tireless advocate for children's rights, who was the Children's Commissioner throughout the period in which the repeal bill progressed through Parliament, had to face the most intense criticism from the public, press and politicians.

Cindy Kiro (second from the right) with Rosie Williams, Keegan Bartlett and Kawiti Waetford, members of her Young People's Reference Group, who met with politicians to express their support for repeal of section 59

Opposition MPs sometimes criticised the stance of the Commissioners,[258] while government ministers, at best, expressed ambiguous support for proposals from the Children Commissioners to repeal section 59, at least up until the time that Sue Bradford's Bill arrived on the scene (see chapter 9).

While the Office of the Children's Commissioner has statutory independence, it has to report annually to the minister responsible for Social

Development on the exercise of its statutory functions. It also has to respond to sometimes intense or adversarial questioning from members of the Social Services Select Committee during its annual financial review. In these kinds of situations, subtle pressures can be brought upon an independent, government-funded body not to embarrass the Government in power by being too strident in its criticism of Government policy, but commissioners continued to criticise the failure of successive governments to repeal section 59.

> ***An independent statutory voice for children steadfastly advocating the banning of physical punishment added to the pressure for reform.***

EPOCH New Zealand

Early in 1997, a group of Wellington women, led by child advocate Beth Wood, established EPOCH New Zealand. This organisation was inspired by the work of the international organisation EPOCH Worldwide (later replaced by the Global Initiative to End Corporal Punishment) and sought to support the efforts of the Commissioner for Children. EPOCH's aims included both the promotion of positive parenting and full repeal of section 59. It was set up as a charitable trust but never had any paid staff or even an office. Fundraising for its mission was always a challenge because the cause was, initially at least, not a popular one. Despite its lack of resources, during the early years of the twenty-first century EPOCH played an increasingly important role in the campaign.

EPOCH's activities initially included providing positive parenting information to organisations that worked with children and families, but other organisations, such as Plunket and Parents' Centres, had a much greater capacity to do this and over time this role became less prominent. Members of EPOCH also lobbied politicians in successive governments, in person and through letters, and later by email. EPOCH regularly promoted repeal through presentations at national conferences and local meetings, as well as in journal and newspaper articles. In 1998, it began publishing its own newsletter, which was distributed widely to interested organisations and individuals. A website was set up to provide easy access to information that related to the campaign to repeal section 59.[259] This website now functions largely as a repository of historical resources.

From 1999 onwards, EPOCH played a vital role in achieving repeal by engaging the support of a wide range of NGOs. The organisation did this by establishing an informal network of supportive organisations, recruited through personal contact, letters, telephone calls and, later, email. These organisations had no formal link with EPOCH, nor were they required to pay a membership fee or subscription. Network members were kept informed of developments through regular newsletters, bulletins and newsflashes.

When repeal became a real possibility with Sue Bradford's Bill being drawn from the ballot in Parliament, it was possible to demonstrate to politicians that over 140 organisations supported repeal – a significant number in a country the size of New Zealand. (Appendix 6 shows the range of organisations involved.) These NGOs included major child and family service delivery agencies, professional organisations, family violence prevention services, as well as some Māori and Pacific organisations. Political opponents found it difficult to deny the substance of a cause supported by organisations with this collective credibility.

EPOCH members found that maintaining an email-based network was challenging and involved constant updating of addresses and contacts. However, engaging support from and communicating regularly with other organisations and individuals in this way was undoubtedly an important factor in demonstrating growing support for reform.

The strengths of EPOCH lay in its primary focus on law reform and its ability to create and sustain a network of supportive organisations without requiring formal membership.

Having an independent organisation building up an informal coalition of supportive NGOs and sustaining it through networking proved invaluable.

Significant NGO Advocates

NGOs are not-for-profit, non-governmental organisations working within the community. Some NGOs are funded by the Government to deliver specific services to the community, but their governance lies outside of the control of Government, residing rather in elected boards or trusts. NGOs also seek funds from private donors, corporations and philanthropic trusts. Numerous NGOs, both large and small, took a public stance in favour of repeal. At the Select Committee stage, 185 organisations made oral or written submissions supporting the Bill, although not all of them were necessarily NGOs.[260] The wider contributions of some of those NGOs are explored in this section.

International children's rights organisations

The two major international children's rights organisations that have offices in New Zealand – Save the Children New Zealand and UNICEF New Zealand – met their obligations to advocate or lobby for the rights of children admirably.[261] Their chief executives took leading roles in lobbying politicians and speaking to the media.

Save the Children, which has a nationwide membership, worked hard to secure the support of its membership for repeal by highlighting the issue of physical punishment at its June 2003 national conference and later holding regional meetings with its membership. The Governor General of New Zealand, Dame Sylvia Cartwright, a former judge, gave the opening address which focused on violence towards children and challenged the use of physical discipline by parents. In her speech she said:

> *We must ask ourselves whether the right to smack children is so precious a right, so necessary to parenting, that we are willing to sacrifice [names of children killed], and the many, many children who are assaulted in the name or using the excuse of discipline who survive.*[262]

The speech not only inspired many members of Save the Children to support repeal but also provoked a great deal of public discussion and debate.[263]

In 2005, Save the Children commissioned and published research by Terry

Dobbs, an independent researcher, in a report entitled *INSIGHTS: Children & young people speak out about family discipline.*[264] This ground-breaking report effectively injected the voices of children into the debate on physical punishment. The research into the views of children on family discipline, particularly physical discipline, revealed that children believed that a significant motivation for hitting them was parental anger rather than a desire to correct their behaviour.

> *Children knew that parents' reactions were sometimes motivated by parental need for anger or stress relief.*[265]

This had already been admitted by New Zealand parents in research done forty years earlier,[266] but in the current debate the reality of parental anger being a prime motivator for smacking children was often obscured by adult self-righteousness. The report also gave an indication of just how many children in New Zealand were experiencing heavy-handed physical discipline (see chapter 7), for example:

> *You get a smack on the mouth. (7-year-old boy)*
>
> *Parents whack them (children) that's what happens to me. (14-year-old boy)*
>
> *Yeah, we get hit, we dirtied the washing the other day and we got the triple cane the next morning. (13-year-old boy)*

UNICEF held a number of forums that focused on ending physical punishment of children, and in 2004 it coordinated widespread NGO support for a publication entitled *Protect and Treasure New Zealand's Children,* which aimed to increase public understanding of the need to repeal section 59.[267]

In June 2005, UNICEF and Save the Children facilitated the participation of two young people, Michael Bendall and Casey Haverkamp, in the East Asia and Pacific Regional Consultation under the UN Study on Violence against Children. Both held strong convictions that all physical punishment of children was unacceptable. Michael subsequently attended the official launch of the report of UN study on violence towards children held in Bangkok during October 2006 (see chapter 10), where he took part in a joint presentation and made reference to ending all forms of corporal punishment of children.

In 2006 UNICEF, along with the Office of the Children's Commissioner (and later the Families Commission), funded the publication of a booklet and CD developed by Rhonda Pritchard and George Hook called *Children are Unbeatable: 7 very good reasons not to hit children.* Rhonda, a long-time advocate for repeal, argued a convincing case for parents to desist from hitting their children. Her reasons included mixed messages, children's rights, emotional distress, physical harm, religious imperatives, as well as the ineffectiveness and superfluousness of physical punishment. The booklet and CD were designed as resources for organisations involved in parent education as well as for parents themselves.

Dame Sylvia Cartwright launching the booklet
Children are Unbeatable: 7 very good reasons not to hit children

Major service providers

Strong leadership also came from two of New Zealand's largest non-governmental child and family service providers – Barnardos New Zealand and the Royal New Zealand Plunket Society. Barnardos provides child and family support services along with early childhood education. Plunket provides extensive preventative health care for young children. Both of these organisations were early supporters of repeal. They have large numbers of staff throughout New Zealand, and Plunket in particular provides services to a large proportion of young families. The Plunket Society has a huge membership and an extensive volunteer base. It was inevitable in organisations of this size that not all people associated with them would support repeal. Both organisations worked hard to encourage staff, members and clients to support repeal and kept them well informed about progress towards repeal and the benefits of positive parenting. The governance boards of both organisation were supportive, and the chief executives and senior staff spoke out in favour of repeal. Murray Edridge, the chief executive of Barnardos, had this to say:

> *I am confident that future generations will find it grotesque, even bizarre, that we have spent all this energy trying to preserve an outdated right to hit vulnerable children entrusted to the care of adults.*[268]

Deborah Morris-Travers (Every Child Counts), Kaye Crowther (Plunket Society), Sue Bradford (Green Party MP), Murray Edridge (Barnardos), Lynne Pillay (Labour Party MP) and Beth Wood (EPOCH NZ) at a joint media conference

Mike Coleman, a highly experienced child advocate employed by Barnardos, was an indefatigable political lobbyist and, along with Beth Wood, he acted as an adviser to Sue Bradford during the passage of the Bill through Parliament. Many other non-governmental organisations gave generously of staff time in various ways and worked with their communities to promote law change and reduce public anxieties and opposition to change.

Mike Coleman and Beth Wood handing out pamphlets

The repeal of section 59 was a highly contentious and divisive issue. The public advocacy role engaged in by these service organisations sometimes came at a cost, including a loss of donations and verbal attacks on, or threats to, the leading voices as well as disparagement by some sectors of the media.

> ***The support of well-regarded NGOs that served the community made it difficult for opponents to dismiss those in favour of repeal as being outside of 'mainstream New Zealand'.***

International advocates

The existence of a strong international movement to end the corporal punishment of children inspired New Zealand non-governmental organisations and citizens who were advocating for repeal. The website of the organisation Global Initiative to End Corporal Punishment of Children proved a very valuable source of information.[269] Other international websites, such as Children are Unbeatable, provided access to useful advocacy and parent education material.[270]

Other New Zealand Advocates

A wide range of other organisations and individuals advocated either formally or informally for repeal.

Commissions

In New Zealand, Commissions are independent, government-funded bodies with statutory functions. The Office of the Children's Commissioner, as we have already seen, advocated strongly and effectively for repeal. Later the Families Commission, which was established by the Families Commission Act in 2000, also came out in support of full repeal. The Families Commission put out media releases advocating repeal and made a submission to the Select Committee. The Human Rights Commission also made a submission to the Select Committee stating that 'enacting legislation that outlaws corporal punishment is a significant step in promoting the message that violence towards children is unacceptable.'[271]

Government departments

Government departments involved in child welfare, health or education were not free to advocate repeal because repeal was a policy matter for the Government to decide on (see chapter 9). This led to the strange situation of officials working for Child, Youth and Family Services (CYF), the statutory child protection agency mandated to protect children from harm, being unable to express an opinion on the desirability of banning physical punishment, even though their social workers frequently had to deal with cases involving its excessive application. Despite this, CYF demonstrated leadership by expressing its opposition to smacking in its website advice and in the resources supplied to parents:

> ***Smacking is not okay.*** *Hitting damages children. It can hurt them physically and hurt their feelings.*[272]

Public servants who supported repeal were entitled under the New Zealand Public Service Code of Conduct to express their personal opinions, but the possibility of a perceived conflict of interest occurring if they spoke out publicly or went into print meant that opportunities for their voices to be heard were limited.[273]

Some Government departments, such as the Police and CYF, were consulted by the Select Committee considering the repeal bill in confidential sessions but their contributions focused on outlining the possible implications for their departments if section 59 was repealed.[274]

Academics and professionals

Concerned individuals within government-funded institutions were free to advocate repeal and a number, particularly some paediatricians and academics, did so strongly. In New Zealand, universities have a legal mandate to act as the 'conscience and critic of society',[275] so academic experts speaking out on an issue are viewed by most members of the public as exercising a legitimate role. Some of those experts who did speak out publicly in favour of repeal included Professor Anne Smith and Dr Nicola Taylor from the Children's Issue Centre of the University of Otago in Dunedin,[276] Dr Emma Davies and Dr Ian Hassall who were senior researchers at the Institute for Public Policy at the Auckland University of Technology (now AUT University),[277, 278] and Dr Clair Breen from the Law School at the University of Waikato in Hamilton.[279]

Local bodies and communities

Interestingly, some local government bodies decided to come out in favour of repeal. During 2006, Porirua, Auckland and Waitakere City Councils all voted to support the repeal of section 59.

In 2004, in an intriguing community initiative, a Māori organisation Te Whare Hauora O Ngongataha and the James Family Trust (a non-governmental child and family support agency with an affiliation to the

Presbyterian church) formed a partnership to develop a project aimed at making their small central North Island community around the township of Ngongotaha the 'first smack-free community in New Zealand and the safest place in the world to bring up children.'[280] In addition to gaining support for smack-free zones in local retail outlets they worked with leaders of local marae (meeting places) to make their environments smack-free as well. The project also involved providing parents with information on positive, non-violent parenting methods. Financial support came from the SKIP Local Initiatives Fund (see chapter 9).[281]

Commercial organisations

Another unique initiative came from The Body Shop, which was the only commercial organisation to become involved in advocating publicly for repeal. Staff at the Body Shop organised a petition in favour of repeal, with sign-up forms and information about physical punishment and law reform in all of their shops throughout New Zealand. The managing director of The Body Shop chain in New Zealand, Barrie Thomas, presented a petition with over 20,000 signatures in support of repeal to Sue Bradford just before the second reading of the Bill commenced in Parliament.

Individual citizens

Over the years a significant number of individuals independently challenged public attitudes about the use of physical punishment, advocated for the adoption of positive parenting approaches or lobbied for the repeal of section 59. Some of those individuals were professional child advocates but others acted as private citizens.

Pacific peoples

New Zealand is a country with a significant number of migrants and their descendants from Pacific Island countries. Over 250,000 identified themselves as being connected to Pacific Island cultures, according to the 2006 census.[282] Pacific peoples have strong ties to their churches and many hold a deep belief in the importance of physical discipline. Despite this, a few Pacific groups registered with the EPOCH network, including in 2005 the organisation Pacifica, a large women's group concerned with Pacific women's well-being and development.

The minister of the Congregational Christian Church of Samoa in Porirua, the Reverend Nove Vailaau, has been a significant Christian voice within the Samoan community advocating the rejection of physical punishment. He also presented papers at forums on section 59 outlining the biblical basis of his stance (see chapter 5).

Another significant Pacific advocate for repeal was Fa'amatuainu Tino Pereira, a Wellington-based Samoan community leader and former broadcaster, who consistently stood up for not hitting children. In 2004, Tino wrote:

> *There is nothing in our pre-missionary history to suggest any evidence of physical punishment as a way of raising children.*
>
> *Instead we say in Samoa:*
>
> *E fafaga tama a manui fuga o laau, ae fafaga tama a le tagata I upu ma tala e fau ai le fa'autautaga. (The young of birds are fed on fruits and berries, while the young of human beings are fed on words so they could grow strong and wise).*[283]

He also called on church leaders to become part of the quest for a solution.

Pacific voices in support of repeal were also present in the media, notably that of Tapu Misa, the *New Zealand Herald* columnist (see chapter 8).

Māori

There are many Māori community organisations that focus on the needs of Māori children and their families. These agencies work in ways that reflect Māori cultural values and are often iwi-based (tribal) organisations. Some Māori organisations, for example, the Māori Women's Welfare League, joined the EPOCH network.

However, it was not until late in the campaign that visible, organised support for repeal emerged from the Māori community. One group of iwi in the north of New Zealand declared themselves fully in support of Sue Bradford's Bill and made a powerful submission to the Parliamentary Select Committee. In a press statement concerning their submission, it was stated that:

> *Iwi leaders from Te Tai Tokerau have made a strong statement in support of repealing S59 at a Select Committee hearing today. Chief executives of 7 iwi authorities – Te Aupōuri, Te Rarawa, Ngāti Kahu, Whāingaroa, Ngāpuhi, Ngāti Wai and Ngāti Whātua made a joint submission to the Justice and Electoral Reform Select Committee, arguing that attitudes to violence within the community are influenced by existing law.*
>
> *'We want to dispel the myth that violence against children is normal or traditionally mandated, and work towards removing opportunities for violence to take place.' said Naida Glavish, Chairperson of Te Runanga o Ngāti Whātua. 'Our number one responsibility is manaakitanga, the care of our people, and our children need to be protected from physical punishment', added Allan Pivac, Ngāti Whātua Chief Executive.*[284]

After considerable reflection on the issues involved, the Māori Party voted unanimously for the Bill at every stage of its progress into law, despite reports that many Māori were opposed to the Bill and anxious about the possibility of Māori parents being unfairly targeted for prosecution.[285] This apprehension can be at least partially explained by research that has shown Māori and Pacific over-representation among offenders and victims of violent crime.[286]

The Māori Party co-leaders, Pita Sharples and Tariana Turia, set out during a parliamentary recess to explain their position at hui (gatherings) held around the country and won the support of many Māori. (See chapter 9 for a fuller discussion of the Māori Party's role in achieving repeal.)

> ***Māori feared that repeal of section 59 would increase their vulnerability because it would provide another reason for unfair Police attention.***

On the day before the surprise accord that assured the Bill would be passed by a huge majority in the House, the Māori Anglican Church bishops came out in support of repeal. The Venerable Dr Hone Kaa said:

> *It's about our children who are entitled to the same legal status as everyone else. ... We strongly support the creation of a society that is completely free from violence, and it's simple: adults should not be allowed to hit children.*[287]

Advocates' Submissions

Many advocates made a very significant contribution to the Bill's passage by presenting oral and written submissions to the Parliamentary Select Committee considering Sue Bradford's original bill (see chapter 9). Both the Families Commission and the Children's Commissioner made written and oral submissions, as did many NGOs, a number of professional and academic institutions, and some private citizens. The submissions that the authors have seen were well researched and carefully referenced as well as being clearly written and logically argued.[288] The arguments put forward in these submissions were often based on children's rights and research findings on the negative outcomes of physical discipline for children. The review of international research into the disciplining of children conducted by the Children's Issues Centre at the University of Otago in 2004 proved a valuable source of information for many submissions.[289]

> ***Submissions in favour of repeal often used evidence found in publications reporting the key findings of international research on physical punishment.***

Coordinating Advocacy

From the time that Sue Bradford's Bill was drawn from the ballot until the Bill became law, representatives from key non-governmental organisations and from the Office of the Children's Commissioner and the Families Commission met regularly in Wellington and Auckland to coordinate the campaign for repeal. The objectives of the campaign were:

- to increase public support for repeal
- to counter misinformation being circulated by opponents of repeal
- to lobby politicians in order to gain sufficient parliamentary support to secure the Bill's passage
- to support sympathetic politicians.

The activities (see appendix 7) of this informal coalition of many leading advocates and NGOs included:

- coordinating contact with politicians in Wellington
- encouraging concerned citizens to meet with politicians in their electorate offices or email or write to them
- preparing and distributing briefing sheets for politicians that communicated relevant information at each stage of the debate[290] (These were appreciated by sympathetic MPs and sometimes used as a source of information for speeches in Parliament.)
- developing an effective media strategy to ensure supportive views were regularly aired in newspapers, on the radio and on TV

> ***An effective communication strategy was required to counter opposition claims, support political reformers, and meet media demands.***

- preparing and distributing a comprehensive media kit that addressed myths, misunderstandings and misinformation relating to law reform[291]
- ensuring that the views of opponents were challenged in the media (see chapter 8)
- ensuring a significant presence in the public gallery at every parliamentary debate on the Bill
- liaising closely with supportive politicians

- engaging and publicising the support of sympathetic celebrities and Christian organisations (see chapter 5)
- keeping supporters informed of the current issues and providing them with evidence of the positive consequences of repeal overseas
- establishing a website with a facility that made it easy for supporters to send messages to politicians. (Before this was set up politicians reported that the number of emails opposing the Bill far exceeded the number in favour – this trend was reversed when supporters were provided with an easy way of contacting politicians.)

The reach of the campaign was greatly enhanced by electronic technology. The use of email for distributing information and appealing for action, the provision of a blog site for supporters to express opinions, and the previously mentioned 'Write to your local MP' facility, all helped to increase the effectiveness and impact of the campaign.

Making it easy for people to email politicians was essential for demonstrating the extent of public support. Providing succinct arguments for inclusion helped as well.

In Reflection

Over the years the work of NGOs and others supporting law reform had two aims – influencing the views of the public, including parents, and influencing politicians. As far as the law was concerned, the repeal of section 59 was the ultimate objective and clearly political support was needed for this. Before Sue Bradford's Bill was drawn from the ballot, NGOs lobbied politicians sporadically, and attempted to influence public opinion through the media (see chapter 8) and by distributing materials within their spheres of influence. Efforts tended to be opportunistic, such as when a conference presented an opportunity for making a presentation, or project-driven, for example in the development of newsletters or the organisation of a forum. Some collaboration occurred between agencies but not on a sustained basis.

After the Bill was introduced into Parliament, which made the repeal of section 59 an imminent possibility, NGOs developed and implemented a well-coordinated strategic campaign targeted at politicians and the public as described above. At this juncture public interest was at a high point. Various restraints had curtailed the development of this type of campaign earlier, including the fact that law reform seemed a long-term rather than imminent possibility, limited funds, and competing demands on the advocacy efforts of most agencies.

> ***NGO organisations working together in a collaborative and organised fashion after the Bill's arrival greatly enhanced advocacy efforts.***

Conclusion

New Zealand is a small nation in which most child advocates know each other and most community-based agencies working with children have good working relationships. The value of these individuals and organisations working together closely, particularly when advocating for children's rights, was amply confirmed throughout the events associated with the campaign to repeal section 59. It provided an excellent opportunity to put the principles of collaboration to the test. The goal was clear, there were no competing agendas, and there was passion for the cause.

Leading advocates were very effective in expanding the support base to include many professional organisations and NGOs. This resulted in informed and influential pressure from different sources being applied to politicians. NGOs, professional organisations, the Children's Commissioner and the Families Commission were responsible for many of the high quality submissions made to the Parliamentary Select Committee considering Sue Bradford's Bill, and for putting forward the positive case for reform at every opportunity. However, as we shall see in the next chapter, changing public opinion remained a formidable task – the general public were hard to reach, except perhaps through the media whose reporting was not always sympathetic or accurate, and many members of the public were constrained by deeply held convictions or fears.

Chapter 7

PUBLIC ATTITUDES

In this chapter we will explore the attitudes of New Zealanders towards hitting children as revealed in academic research and by opinion polls. We will see that research showed that over time there was a progressive movement away from the use of more severe forms of punishment, and also increasing doubts about its efficacy. In contrast, opinion polls as customarily framed in terms of parental rights showed that a consistently large majority opposed banning physical punishment. But when questions were framed in terms of the impact on children, law change was more likely to be favoured. Finally, we will survey the human factors that lay behind people's unwillingness to change, and how some of them were responded to.

Twentieth-century Child-rearing Habits

Physical punishment has long been regarded by most New Zealand parents as a normal and necessary part of child-rearing. James and Jane Ritchie, the modern pioneers of research into child-rearing practices in New Zealand, interviewed 151 mothers in 1963 and 1964 and concluded:

> *Methods of control are the key to the mother-child relationship and it is here that the New Zealand pattern is sharply defined. Control by smacking is its chief characteristic and for many mothers virtually the only control consistently employed.*[292]

After asking about their use of non-violent ways of changing their children's behaviour, the Ritchies reached the depressing conclusion that New Zealand mothers:

> *... have thrown away some of the most potent reward techniques; praise is thought by many to be inappropriate; tangible rewards are castigated as 'bribery'; holding up other children as positive and negative models is thought to be an antisocial technique; very few families use a credit-point reward system; most think isolation of the*

> *child cruel (or find it impossible to achieve); many regard reasoning as a waste of time. What is left for them to use? Only punishment, threat of punishment, and occasional praise.*[293]

The researchers found that the mothers were willing to speak freely about their use of physical punishment and regarded it as being 'as necessary to child-rearing as the mid-morning cup of tea.'[294] At the two extremes of their sample (1% of each), there were mothers who administered severe and regular beatings to their children, and mothers who did not use physical punishment at all. In between were 35% who used it less than once a month, 40% who used it once a month to once a week, and 23% percent who administered daily spankings.

Jane and James Ritchie with Jenny Hassall in the background

Attitudinal Changes

There has been much public discussion since that ground-breaking survey in the sixties. Numerous public opinion polls and media articles have tracked the New Zealand public's views on the role of physical punishment in bringing up children, although few polls ever asked children their opinions. There are signs of evolution of opinion but no revolution yet.

Evidence of a gradual shift in public opinion can be found in successive surveys of parental attitudes and practices that were initiated by the Ritchies. There has been a steady reduction in the number of people who believe that there are circumstances in which it is all right to 'thrash' or 'beat' a child, from 11% in 1981[295] to 3% in 1993.[296] During the same period, the proportion of parents believing there are certain circumstances in which it is okay to 'smack' a child has remained steady at around 80%.[297]

Forty-three years later, there were echoes of the findings of the Ritchies' original survey in the parliamentary debate of 14 March 2007 on the Bill. During the debate, some Members of Parliament loudly expressed satisfaction or pride in having struck their children.[298]

> *I am happy to say they got a smack. It was not a hard smack; it did not make any marks, leave any welts, or draw any blood, but it actually started to put a boundary in place.*
>
> *I certainly smacked my son when he was a toddler. I did so in a loving way, in a responsible way, and in a caring way, because I do not know how one can reason with a 3-year-old. I am proud to say that my son is now a responsible young adult. I am proud that I exercised my responsibilities of fatherhood in the way that I did.*
>
> *I smacked my child and I am damned proud of it, because I have a good kid, and I am really pleased about it.*[299]

Perhaps, though, this was not so much confidence in the rightness of what they had done as bravado in the face of the inevitable, as the smacking of children was about to become legally indefensible.

The 'Anglo Connection'

The Ritchies' considerable body of research portrayed a society in which hitting children was commonplace and in which authoritarian attitudes ruled.[300] They considered that New Zealand shared this orientation with the other, so-called, 'Anglo nations' – Britain, America, Canada and Australia. The populations of these countries believe, to a greater degree than those of many other Western countries, in the efficacy of punishment in dealing with disobedience and wrongdoing. All have high rates of imprisonment of adult offenders as well as legally sanctioned physical punishment by parents.[301]

In such societies, physical punishment of children is held to have a salutary effect, and there are social pressures to administer it.

> *The objective of all this is thought to be the development of 'character'. A person who lacks 'character' has been 'spoilt'. 'Spoiling' results when parents are indulgent, give way to the wishes of the child, have not taught their children patience, consideration for others, respect for elders, respect for property, to be seen and not heard.*[302] (emphasis added)

There have been voices raised against this rationale for physically punishing children over the years. Its futility, injustice and brutality have been recognised and the prevailing view of its normalcy challenged. The internationally acclaimed New Zealand writer Katherine Mansfield was one such voice. In her 1921 story *Sixpence*, she evokes the feelings of betrayal, helplessness and regret in a father who is coerced by his wife into administering physical punishment to his son.[303]

Children's Experience of Physical Punishment

Common threats heard by New Zealand children during the latter half of the twentieth century were 'I'll tan your hide!' or 'You'll get a good hiding when your father gets home!' or the more recent rephrasing, 'You'll get the bash!'

Recent mainstream New Zealand literature is replete with accounts of severe punishment, abuse or humiliation of children. Keri Hulme's Booker prize-winning novel *The Bone People*,[304] and Alan Duff's book *Once Were Warriors*,[305] which was made into an internationally acclaimed film, described brutality towards children and held up a disturbing mirror to New Zealand society.

Contemporary New Zealanders have written or spoken of the use of severe physical punishment in their own childhood. Colin Crump, brother of the popular comic novelist Barry Crump, recalled brutal beatings that Barry had received at the hands of a parent.[306] As a child, the most famous and universally admired of New Zealanders, Sir Edmund Hillary, was taken repeatedly to the woodshed and thrashed by his father for misdemeanours, as Sir Edmund recalls them, that many would judge as being minor.[307]

Not every New Zealand child is treated like Barry Crump or Edmund Hillary. The severity with which New Zealand parents punish their children varies from beatings to no physical punishment at all.

The two large-scale birth cohort[308] studies that commenced in New Zealand in the seventies indicate the widespread use of physical punishment and the not infrequent use of severe or excessive punishment.

The Dunedin cohort, born in 1972–73, were questioned at 26 years of age in 1998–99. Of the 962 interviewed, 20% reported receiving no physical punishment, 29% had been smacked as the most severe form of punishment, 45% had been hit with an object, and 6% reported extreme physical punishment involving injury or lasting bruises.[309]

The Christchurch cohort, born in 1977, were questioned at 18 years of age in 1995. Of the 1025 with a complete interview record, 11% reported that their parents had 'never used physical punishment', 78% that they had seldom used it, 8% that it had been used regularly, 2% that it had been used too often and too severely, and 2% that they had been treated in a harsh and abusive way.[310]

Doubts about Motives and Efficacy

The belief that in certain circumstances it is all right for a parent to smack a child is not the same as a belief in its efficacy. The Ritchies surveyed samples of New Zealand parents in 1963 and 1977, and in 1979 questioned 12- and 13-year-olds in a Hamilton intermediate school. They found that both the parents and the children agreed that physical punishment was an ineffective way of changing behaviour.[311]

Many parents have been willing to admit that hitting their children was a consequence of their own state of tiredness, frustration or anger rather than part of a deliberate policy aimed at improving their children's behaviour.[312]

> ***Many New Zealand parents regard hitting children as a normal part of child-rearing, but acknowledge it can be in response to their own tiredness or exasperation as well as to their child's misbehaviour.***

New Zealand parents have more recently expressed their lack of confidence in the effectiveness of physical punishment. A UMR Insight mail survey of 1367 readers of the magazine *Tots to Teens* was conducted in 2005.[313] Respondents were asked to rate seven ways of guiding children to behave well, using a five-point scale from 'highly effective' to 'not at all effective'. The seven ways of guiding children encompassed all of the commonly used methods of guidance, including 'smacking when they do things wrong'. Smacking was considered 'effective' by only 9%, while 71% of the respondents believed it to be 'ineffective'. Smacking was also considered the least effective of all seven strategies by a wide margin.[314]

In 2005, the Ministry of Social Development sponsored a survey that was conducted by Gravitas. It included 612 parents and 539 caregivers with children aged five and under. Encouragingly, 49% said they had not smacked their children in the past three months or used physical discipline as a way to handle misbehaviour.[315]

Children can be forthright in telling of their parents' motives for smacking them and perceptive about how it influenced their own behaviour. In 2005, Terry Dobbs, a social science researcher, questioned 80 children about their experience and views on discipline. She found that children believed that anger was often the reason why parents hit them rather than trying to make them behave better. Children said that smacking made them 'feel angry, upset and fearful' and didn't help them do the right thing.

> *I think it makes them [children] do it again because they get angry with their parents for doing it [smacking], so they do it again. (12-year-old girl)*[316]

The study also indicated that many children in New Zealand are likely to be experiencing heavy-handed physical discipline.[317] For example, 40% of the 5- to 7-year-olds reported being smacked or hit around the face and/or head, and 25% had been struck with implements, including belts, canes, tennis racquets and spatulas.[318] This is what some of those children said:

> *I get smacked in the back of the head with a hand, or I get smacked on the arm with a spoon. (9-year-old girl)*

> *It makes you feel sad and you cry. (6-year-old boy)*
>
> *You feel real upset because they are hurting you and you love them so much and then all of a sudden they hit you and hurt you and you feel like as though they don't care about you because they are hurting you. (13-year-old girl)*[319]

Opinion Polls

As is to be expected, the framing of the survey questions in public opinion polls significantly influences the findings that emerge. This well-documented effect is very apparent in New Zealand surveys that asked questions about attitudes towards physical punishment, as can be seen in the following three examples of statistically valid public opinion polls.

A 1995 Heylen poll conducted for the *Listener* magazine surveyed the opinions of 1000 randomly selected New Zealand residents, aged 15 or above, from major populations centres and small towns. They were asked 'Is corporal punishment at home acceptable?' In relation to boys, 54% said yes, 35% said no, and 11% didn't know.[320] In relation to girls, 49% said yes, 40% said no, and 11% didn't know. The use of the expression 'corporal punishment', with its connotations in the New Zealand idiom of officially sanctioned strapping or caning in schools, as opposed to the term 'physical punishment' or 'smacking', may account for the low percentages in favour of punishment when compared with some other studies.

By way of contrast, a 2001 Ministry of Justice telephone survey placed questions firmly in the customary domestic context of parental rights when children misbehave. A thousand adults, aged 18 or over, were asked if they agreed or disagreed with the following viewpoint: 'A person parenting a child should be allowed, by law, to smack the child with an open hand if the child is naughty.' This time, not surprisingly, 80% of respondents said that physical punishment should be legal,[321] a figure much more in line with the Ritchie-initiated studies, which also framed the questions in terms of parental practice.

In a 2006 telephone survey commissioned by the Office of the Children's Commissioner,[322] 750 adults aged 18 and over were asked if they 'strongly agreed', 'somewhat agreed', 'somewhat disagreed' or 'strongly disagreed' with a number of statements about section 59. Only 37% percent agreed with the statement 'Section 59 of the Crimes Act that allows parents to use physical punishment to correct children should be ended.' But 71% percent agreed with either the preceding statement or the following, 'Section 59 of the Crimes Act should be ended providing guidelines were developed to prevent prosecutions for mild slaps and smacking'.

Questions posed in opinion polls were nearly always framed around the right of parents to smack their children and hardly ever around providing better legal protection for children who were at risk of significant abuse. If the questions had been framed differently, pollsters might have found that many more people would have favoured repeal.

Public Opinion of the Bill

During the two-year period in which the repeal bill was before Parliament, a large number of formal and informal polls sought either to ascertain or to make claims about public opinion on the issue. Most of them were not statistically valid measures of the opinions of all New Zealanders, because the respondents were self- rather than randomly selected. They were based on individuals choosing to go to a particular website or choosing to text, email or telephone in their opinion. Typically, people with strong opinions on an issue tend to look for opportunities to express their views, resulting in a biased sample. Some self-selected surveys can also be vulnerable to multiple submissions being made by individuals wishing to advance their cause.

Two examples of self-selected, on-line surveys follow. A Fairfax Media Stuff webpoll, active on 16 February 2006, found that nearly 84% of 5322 respondents said 'no' when asked the question 'Should smacking children be outlawed in NZ?' A TV1 webpoll that had been live for seven months since the Bill was introduced showed that by February 2006, 93% of participants (number not known) were in favour of parents being 'allowed to use reasonable force to discipline their children'.[323]

The views of children who might have participated in self-selected polls are not known to us (they were not included in the statistically valid polls discussed below), but it appears that no poll conducted during this period specifically sought the views of children on the banning of smacking.

There were several statistically valid public opinion polls conducted by reputable polling companies during the period of the Bill's passage through the House, although two of them were framed in terms of parental rights. A Digi-Poll survey conducted for the *New Zealand Herald* around the time that the Bill was introduced into Parliament (July 2005) found that 71% of respondents wanted 'parents to keep the right to use "reasonable force" to punish their children ...'; 21% did not want this to occur.[324] A Colmar Brunton poll conducted for One News near the end of the law-making process (March 2007) surveyed 1002 randomly selected adult New Zealanders and found that 83% of the respondents thought that '... parents should be allowed to smack their children when they are naughty'. Only 15% disagreed.[325]

With one exception, all of the polls conducted between the Bill being drawn out of ballot and becoming law consistently showed that the large majority of respondents were not in favour of 'repealing section 59' or 'banning smacking'. The exception was the 2006 survey sponsored by the Children's Commissioner, which was also the only one during this period to frame the questions in terms of the impact on children. It found a 64% majority in favour of the repeal of section 59 'if research showed that removing it would decrease child abuse'.[326]

Poll questions framed in terms of parental practice and rights consistently evoked opposition to repeal but questions framed in terms of child-impact evoked support for law reform.

Defying the 'Will of the People'

In some of the debates on the Bill in the House, the poll results in favour of the status quo were brought up by anti-repeal MPs. How could supporters justify imposing a law on the country when the large majority of people in poll after poll opposed the change, and only a slim majority of MPs in the House supported repeal?

Protesters against the repeal of section 59

Unfortunately, MPs who responded to this challenge often failed to come up with a convincing answer. Had the case for repeal been framed more often as a human rights issue, then perhaps they would have made a more effective response. The logic of a human rights response is as follows:

> It is a fundamental human right that all humans are entitled to equal protection under the law. Children are humans, therefore they too are entitled to equal protection. Section 59 denies them equal protection. Human rights are universal and are not subject to the whim of the majority. Therefore section 59 should be repealed even if the majority of adult New Zealanders oppose it.

A Digi-Poll survey conducted for the *New Zealand Herald* immediately after the law was passed may have been of some comfort to those MPs who were brave, or foolhardy, enough to defy 'public opinion' and the intense lobbying against repeal from voters. According to that poll, 44% of respondents were satisfied with the new law. Only a slim majority of 53% was dissatisfied (see below). It will be interesting to see how public opinion shifts over time as the new law is applied by Police and the courts, and New Zealanders begin to see themselves as progressive in the context of other English-speaking nations. Perhaps this new law will eventually be seen as part of the New Zealand tradition of passing innovative legislation, such as becoming the first country in the world to give women the vote and banning visits by nuclear powered or armed ships.

Influences on the Public Debate

Since the Ritchies challenged the necessity and efficacy of parents physically punishing their children, there has been sporadic public debate of the issues. It intensified as public awareness of the reality of violence towards children grew, but has been sustained only since Sue Bradford's Bill was introduced into Parliament in July 2005.

Since then, a wide range of viewpoints has been forcibly expressed by those seeking to influence the debate. Arguments in favour of law change have been put forward by children's advocates, spokespersons for non-governmental organisations, some mainstream church leaders, and politicians of a variety of political persuasions. Arguments against have been expressed by socially conservative Christians, as well as by non-religious individuals of a libertarian or conservative persuasion (see chapter 5).

Framing the public debate was important in determining its course. When the repeal bill became a public issue, journalists sought a dramatic and easily remembered label. They were, perhaps unwittingly, influenced by the Bill's opponents who sought to alarm the public with the idea that it would criminalise 'good parents' who were just doing what most New Zealanders considered trivial and normal. The popular label became 'the anti-smacking bill'. The use of this term continued in spite of the fact that the cases which had aroused public concern were ones in which parents had successfully used section 59 as a defence in prosecutions for assaults that involved much more than what is usually meant by the term 'smacking'. A more fitting title might have been 'the anti-child assault bill', although this does not have quite the same populist ring.

Nearly six months after the new law had come into force, *New Zealand Herald* commentator Tapu Misa wrote:

> *Language matters, it seems. How much smoother the passage of Sue Bradford's bill might have been if those opposed to it hadn't got in first and framed it as an 'anti-smacking bill' which would usurp the rights of parents to lovingly discipline their children, rather than a long overdue attempt to stop abusive people hiding behind the law when they seriously hurt their children.*[327]

As the debate spread into every corner of New Zealand society and into most homes, it became impossible to get an opinion on repeal that was not clouded by the person's beliefs about the Bill's purpose or effect if passed, and some beliefs were based on misinformation. More often than not, people mistakenly believed that repeal meant taking away an existing legal right to smack, rather than providing better legal protection for children abused by parents, let alone safeguarding children's right to physical integrity.

> ***Naming and framing the issues inevitably influenced the course of the public debate, and the media played the lead role.***

Eventually, the trivial 'anti-smacking bill' label began to rebound. If the word 'smacking' was to be used to cover actions that were defensible under section 59, then it would have to include some harsh physical punishments. Since this was beyond what most members of the public regarded as acceptable hitting, the word 'smacking' began to be seen as a euphemism for a range of assaults on children, with a meaning more akin to the phrase 'getting smacked around'.

A variety of events was significant in swaying public opinion towards repeal at times. One such was the case of a Timaru woman who was acquitted despite admitting that she had beaten her adolescent son with a riding crop and a bamboo cane.[328] The fundamentalist religious affiliations of some of the Bill's opponents also affected public opinion, particularly since there had been considerable concern during the 2005 general election campaign at the secretive attempts of members of the Exclusive Brethren church[329] to influence the vote in favour of the National Party.[330]

The Human Factors Underpinning Opposition to Change

During the period the Bill was before the House, advocates experienced what appeared to be a significant lack of success in increasing public support for repeal, as judged by opinion polls and other expressions of popular opinion in the media. (In contrast, they were very successful in gaining the support of important NGOs, significant professional associations, and highly respected individuals, who were then willing to speak out in favour of repeal.) To our knowledge, none of the numerous formal and informal polls conducted during this period explored the reasons why people opposed the law change. The pollsters were, on the whole, far more interested in the numbers for and against. But newspapers around the country did receive hundreds of letters to the editor opposing repeal. Those that were published often revealed the human factors that underlay people's reluctance to change. These factors are explored in the following section, which is by necessity speculative in nature, since the research has yet to be done.

Power of custom

National, communal and family customs are powerful forces. International research has shown that there is a significant tendency for parents to approve of the same type of physical and emotional punishment that they experienced as children.[331] Historically, in New Zealand's case at least, the type of punishment used to control children's behaviour has largely involved striking the child. This custom, inherited from child-rearing practice in the British Isles, was passed on through the generations since British settlers first arrived, and remained strong right up to the twenty-first century (see chapter 1). Many parents believe that since this was how they were brought up and it never did them any harm, there is no reason to change that custom.

Strength of habit

Some parents were concerned that even if smacking was banned, their practice of using physical discipline to control their children's behaviour would be difficult to alter. Old habits die hard, even when there is a desire to change. Force of habit would result in them doing illegal acts, so they preferred the law to remain unchanged.

Pressure to conform

A potent pressure on parents to physically discipline their children comes from the fear of being shown up by their misbehaviour in public, such that parents will appear either weak or foolish when they are unable to control their children. This social pressure, whether real or imagined, implies permission for decisive control measures including force and intimidation if alternatives are unknown or unclear.

The 'supermarket tantrum' was frequently cited during the public debate as a representative tableau of the issues. The parent feels the disapproval of surrounding shoppers. Entreaties, bribes and threats have had no effect. Being tired and distressed, the parent eventually strikes the screaming child. Some shoppers inwardly applaud the action, others silently condemn it. As such, it functions as a good illustration of how fear of disapproval and expected shame can lead to actions that are later regretted.

Fear of inadequacy

Being a good parent is a demanding role that throws up many difficult challenges. Few parents would claim to have met them all well. Many parents are willing to acknowledge this and have come to an acceptance of their limitations. This idea is acknowledged in the concept of 'good enough parenting'.[332] Even so, adults often feel they are not good enough parents when, through frustration or tiredness, they lose control and hit their children. Banning physical punishment would make them feel more inadequate, especially if the hitting was observed by critical relatives or acquaintances.

Resentment of experts

Many parents express resentment at being told that there are better ways of disciplining children than hitting them. They particularly resent being told what to do by so-called child-rearing experts, whom they see as not sharing their values or life experience and pursuing an agenda which is foreign to them. This view has special resonance in New Zealand where people claiming to be experts are often regarded with suspicion or scorn. The 'do-it-yourself' aspect of our national psyche extends to parents believing that they can figure out the best way to raise their own children.

Resentment of criticism

Many parents felt that if physical punishment of children was banned then their previous parenting habits would now be judged as being wrong or bad. Actions that they believed were normal, socially acceptable and good for their children, would suddenly become the opposite. 'Good parents' felt that the law change would unfairly label them as 'bad parents', a situation that naturally led to resentment.

Anger at intrusion

Parents naturally object to the unnecessary intrusion of the state into the private realm of home and family. Vocal opponents of repeal sought to turn this into anger by using phrases such as 'home invasion' and 'the nanny state'. The latter phrase encapsulates the view that the law change would involve an unnecessary and unwarranted interference in family matters that are best left to the family.

Anxiety about control

Related to social pressure to exercise effective control over children who are misbehaving in public is the anxiety that adult authority and standing will be undermined by real or imagined challenges from children. Some adults were anxious that banning physical punishment would take away a vital disciplinary tool, and result in an out-of-control generation of young people.

Anxiety about 'softies'

There is a common apprehension, particularly among fathers, that children will grow up 'soft' if they do not experience and learn to cope with some physical pain in their lives. That attitude is often reflected in statements such as 'It never did me any harm' and 'It made me the man I am today.'

Apprehension about biblical injunctions

Some parents were concerned about what the Bible appeared to advise on how to bring up children (see chapter 5). For many, this was summed up in the proverbial saying 'Spare the rod and spoil the child', and consequently they were apprehensive that their children would grow up badly if they were denied the experience of physical punishment.

Failing to meet obligations

Another factor contributing to resistance to change was the duty that some strongly principled parents felt they had to raise well-behaved children who conform to society's models of proper behaviour. The banning of physical punishment would make it more difficult for them to bring up children who would respect and obey their elders.

Fear of prosecution and conviction

Some parents feared that if they lightly smacked their children, they would be prosecuted by the Police, and if convicted under the new provisions of the Crimes Act, they would then become criminals. Most people would find conviction, or even being prosecuted, a shaming experience. This fear persisted despite repeated reassurances from politicians that the Police had discretion not to prosecute in trivial cases. Practically speaking, it was clear that the habit of hitting children cannot be given up overnight, and it was a certainty from the beginning that the Police would have to exercise their discretion in deciding whether or not to prosecute. Eventually this discretion was affirmed in an amendment to the Bill.

Fear of 'criminalisation'

Related to the fear of successful prosecution was a more widely held fear based on a misconception. Opponents of the Bill sometimes claimed that once section 59 was repealed, any parent who smacked his or her child would be committing a criminal action. This failure to distinguish between breaking the law and being prosecuted and convicted led many parents to believe erroneously that they would now be categorised as criminals without having been near a court.

> ***Fear that parents would be prosecuted for minor assaults was a major obstacle to gaining public and political support for law reform.***

Fear of losing children

Some parents feared that the statutory child welfare agency, Child, Youth and Family Services (CYF), would intervene to remove the children of parents who were convicted of smacking them. Despite reassurances that CYF would 'consider removing children only if they are at serious risk of harm,'[333] this fear was not easily allayed, particularly as vocal opponents kept raising it. The fear was unintentionally inflamed again after the new law was passed when the new Police practice guide implied that people who repeatedly smacked their children lightly would be notified to CYF.[334]

Responding to the Human Factors

Identifying the human factors behind resistance to change is much easier than addressing them. Most of the human factors relate to deeply experienced emotions or beliefs, and are therefore not particularly susceptible to the power of carefully reasoned arguments. Finding ways of addressing those fears or dealing with resentments was not an easy task, particularly when some opponents were doing their best to intensify those emotions.

> ***Understanding the nature and origin of resistance to change was helpful when it came to considering how to increase support for change.***

Interestingly, the amendment that affirmed Police discretion, which emerged out of the last-minute accord between Labour, National and the Greens, combined with the public support offered by John Key, leader of the conservative National Party, may well have played a significant role in allaying the fears of a large numbers of New Zealanders at that point in time. As mentioned previously, in the Herald Digi-Poll held immediately after the Bill was passed, 44% of respondents expressed satisfaction with the new law, as compared with the large majorities (typically around 80%) of respondents who opposed repeal in numerous polls taken throughout the passage of the Bill through Parliament.[335]

> ***Addressing a specific fear that the public had about a possible consequence of repeal did increase public support when the Bill was finally passed.***

Conclusion

Although the strength of public opposition to law reform may have been exaggerated by opinion polls that focused solely on parental rights, resistance to change was undoubtedly strong. Such resistance is not difficult to understand given the deeply held feelings and beliefs that we have discussed. As was the case in earlier progressive social developments that involved huge social change (such as the abolition of slavery and women's suffrage), law reform was aimed in part at facilitating that change. In relation to physical punishment of children, we believe that changing public attitudes and parental behaviour without law reform would have been a very slow process. In New Zealand, where we now have the benefit of a legal ban, that process of social change is gathering momentum.

It may be that in passing the new law in 2007, New Zealand is experiencing a *tipping point* phenomenon in which social change appears to take place suddenly, although preparedness for that change has in fact been slowly building over time, albeit reluctantly for some.[336] It may be that growing preparedness for change amongst the public was disguised by the assiduous framing of the issue by those opposed to change.

At the very least, there is reason to believe that many New Zealanders have reached a point of acquiescence with regard to the new law. Since its passage, there has been only limited public and media interest in it. As we will see in the next chapter, this contrasts strongly with the intense media interest that accompanied the prolonged passage of the Bill through Parliament.

Chapter 8

THE ROLE OF THE MEDIA

Hundreds protest anti-smacking bill [337]

Bradford's law will save our children [338]

These headlines exemplify the intensity and polarisation of the public debate that accompanied the passage of the Bill and the media's high level of interest in the issue.

In this chapter we will explore the attitudes of the media towards child discipline and also its link with child abuse before the Bill focused the nation's attention. Then we will look at how the media responded during the passage of the Bill, and the key themes that emerged while the media ran with the public debate. Next we will consider briefly the impact of the media on public opinion and politicians, and then finally reflect upon the challenges and opportunities that interacting with the media presented for advocates.

The Media

The media played a very influential role in shaping public and political responses to repeal. Sometimes the media took an oppositional stance, sometimes it was supportive of repeal, and at other times it sought to act as a neutral umpire. But whatever the stance adopted in a particular medium, the issue rarely experienced a low profile once it had entered the political arena.

Advocates for repeal conscientiously collected newspaper and magazine articles, editorials, cartoons, opinion pieces and letters to the editor throughout the period in which the Bill progressed through Parliament. Their filing boxes bulged with the sheer volume of words devoted to the topic. Still more words were expended on the issue in other less 'collectable' media, such as radio and television.

> ***The media played a critical role in the public debate by reporting the arguments put forward by proponents and opponents and by publishing the views of commentators.***

Public and private media

The events and issues surrounding repeal were reported and debated extensively, sometimes in depth, in newspapers and magazines. TV reporting and commentary was less extensive and the exploration of the issues was naturally shallower given the nature of the medium. Some current affairs programmes took a sensationalist or ill-informed approach to the issues.[339] Radio stations, particularly the state-owned broadcaster National Radio, devoted much time to exploring the issues in interviews, commentary and panel discussions. Commercial radio stations also paid close attention to the issues, although some broadcasters adopted populist stances that merely comforted opponents of repeal.

The public media also offered many opportunities for citizens to contribute to the debate through writing letters, posting opinions on newspaper blogs, emailing and faxing responses to current affairs programmes on TV and radio, and of course vocally expressing their views on talkback radio.

Private media such as blog sites set up by individuals or organisations opposing repeal were also involved in the debate.[340] These blogs mostly attracted people of like mind, and because of this limitation were unable to influence uncommitted public opinion significantly. Non-partisan blogs, including those hosted by the public media (newspapers, radio stations and TV channels), had greater potential for shaping the issues.

Public functions of the media

Most public media in New Zealand are in private ownership, with the exception being the state-owned but editorially independent broadcasters Radio New Zealand and Television New Zealand. In general, mainstream media in New Zealand perform the following public functions:

- reporting events

- providing commentary from different perspectives
- expressing editorial opinion
- providing a forum for the public to express their views.

In fulfilling these public functions, most media aspire to reflect the widely accepted public media principles of accuracy, balance and fairness.[341] Later in this chapter we will explore how these principles were applied by the media in their treatment of the issues surrounding repeal.

Media Interest Before the Bill's Arrival

Prior to Sue Bradford's Bill being drawn from the ballot, media interest in the repeal of section 59 was sporadic, and it proved difficult for advocates and political reformers to consistently increase public awareness of the issues. That said, there was some media focus on child discipline issues and strong periodic interest in the issue of child abuse.

The disciplining of children

The idea that children should not be subjected to physical punishment at home had surfaced intermittently in the media during the last two decades. Ripples of media interest were triggered by campaigns initiated by the academics Jane and James Ritchie, successive Children's Commissioners, and EPOCH New Zealand (see chapter 6). The issue was discussed in articles on child-rearing practice in general-interest women's magazines such as the *New Zealand Woman's Weekly*.[342]

The topic of law reform had also surfaced in the media, particularly during the heated debate over the abolition of corporal punishment in schools in the late eighties and early nineties (see chapter 6).[343]

From an early stage, those advocating the ending of physical punishment also called for section 59 to be repealed.[344] The legitimisation of physical 'correction' of children was seen to be a major barrier preventing the development of more humane and respectful relations between parents and children. Over time the two issues, ending physical punishment and law reform, became closely associated in the media. After the introduction of the Bill into Parliament in

2005, repeal rather than changing parental behaviour became the main media focus.

Physical punishment and child abuse

The physical punishment of children was accorded greater media attention as public awareness of child abuse increased and the two issues became linked in people's perceptions.[345] Considerable media attention was devoted to the 2003 UNICEF report which stated that New Zealand's high rate of child homicide placed us among the worst-performing OECD nations.[346] In its wide-ranging discussion of forms of violence towards children, the report considered physical punishment, bullying and domestic violence, as well as homicide. Media interest was heightened because the report's release coincided with the discovery of the body of a yet another murdered child.[347]

The connection between child homicides and the practice of physically punishing children was variously reported and debated in the media. Although a connection between the two was never universally accepted, it was increasingly assumed in much media commentary.

The media's focus on child deaths by maltreatment helped generate an elevated public concern for the safety of children, which led to demands for better protection of children. This also encompassed curtailing abusive disciplinary practices described in assault prosecutions brought against parents. There were frequent calls by the media and the public for the Government to find ways of reducing the levels of violence in society, particularly within families. In some cases this involved commentators arguing that New Zealand parents needed to stop hitting their children.[348]

Editorial comment increasingly recognised the intergenerational transmission of violence. When the killer of a six-year-old girl was finally brought to justice in 2002 after 15 years, it was discovered that as a child he too had been the victim of abuse. The editorials of the country's two leading newspapers, the Wellington-based *Dominion Post* and the Auckland-based *New Zealand Herald*, revealed two distinct responses that recurred throughout the media coverage of child homicides during the next five years. One editor called for increased surveillance by neighbours, family and members of the public, together with more severe punishment of the offenders.[349] The other advocated greater support for parents and, where that failed, alternative care for endangered children.[350]

A few days later, when the Government's response to the renewed outcry against ill-treatment of children included a consideration of whether to repeal section 59 or not, New Zealand's third major newspaper, the Christchurch-based *Press* asserted a connection between New Zealand's legally sanctioned physical punishment of children and the risk of lethal or damaging assault, and so advocated repeal of section 59.[351]

Intense public and media reactions to the death of children by maltreatment led to a wider concern about the possible consequences of physical punishment for children and the two issues became linked.

The Public's Views as Expressed in the Media

In 2004, Beth Wood from UNICEF and Dr Emma Davies from the Institute of Public Policy at the Auckland University of Technology reviewed items relating to physical punishment of children that had appeared in a selection of leading newspapers published over a period of 40 days during 2003. This period was chosen because three events in quick succession drew intense media interest. These were the release of the UNICEF Innocenti report into child maltreatment deaths mentioned above,[352] the highly publicised death of a child by maltreatment, and the release of the report of the UN Committee on the Rights of the Child on New Zealand's compliance with the Convention.[353] Items located included reports, editorials, cartoons, opinion pieces and letters.

Letters to the editor tend to reflect the views of citizens who feel strongly about an issue, in this case those strongly for or against physical punishment and law reform. Newspapers usually receive more letters on an issue than they care to publish. Which ones see the light of day will depend on editorial policies, such as presenting a balance of views, and on the quality of the letters themselves. The 42 letters that touched on the issue of physical punishment were reviewed, and of these, nine correspondents wanted the law changed and/or were against physical punishment. The remaining 33 writers supported the use of physical punishment on grounds such as: the state should not interfere in family life; moderate physical punishment does no harm; smacking is good for children; physical discipline is essential for control; and that there is no proven connection between physical punishment and child abuse.

One correspondent wrote:

> *If the law is changed, children will take advantage of it, and it will breed children ... who have no respect for authority. Mothers and fathers must be allowed to smack their children if they are unreasonable.*[354]

Another said:

> *Why is healthy physical discipline being confused with child abuse? A violent society is not the result of smacking. It is the result of poor discipline ...* [355]

Media Responses to the Bill

The media had a tremendous impact on the public debate of the issues surrounding the repeal of physical punishment.

The intensification of the debate

Predictably, once Sue Bradford's Bill was drawn out of the ballot on 9 June 2005, media interest increased dramatically. Given the deeply polarised opinions of many New Zealand citizens and their representatives in Parliament, the issue naturally shot to the forefront of live media topics and stayed high in the rankings right up until the day the Bill was passed by Parliament some 23 months later. (A Google search carried out 9 October 2007 using the words 'repeal' and 'section 59' and 'New Zealand' registered about 32,000 hits on public and private media websites!)

Previously, physical punishment had been reported primarily as a social or welfare issue, but now that it had become a political 'hot potato', political journalists were assigned to it as well. The issue surfaced in lead articles on the front pages of newspapers, at the top of the evening TV news, in panel discussions on the radio, as the subject of numerous blog discussions, and endlessly on radio talkback shows.

Reporters from a variety of media attending a press conference

After the Select Committee stage, once it had become apparent that the Labour Party was going to back the amended bill, public reactions further intensified because of the increased likelihood that the law change would occur. This in turn encouraged journalists to focus more closely on the political ramifications. At a later stage, a leading political journalist and commentator, Vernon Small of the *Dominion Post*, described some of those ramifications:

> *The public is giving the Government a caning over Sue Bradford's bill outlawing physical punishment of children. … The opposition is gleefully reporting that its tracking polling has it an unbelievable number of streets ahead … [It] may be that the bill has become a lightning rod for disaffection with the Government as its third term wears on …* [356]

The framing and headlining of the debate

Before the Bill's arrival, the media had dubbed the debate over physical punishment of children and law reform as the 'smacking debate'. Advocates feared that this trivialised the issues and fed public anxiety. The labelling also suggested that those who wanted to change the law were concerned solely with the trivial end of the assault continuum rather than protecting children from serious harm. When the Bill first came to Parliament's attention, the media quickly labelled it the 'anti-smacking bill' and the name stuck despite efforts by its political sponsor and others to have it referred to as 'the child discipline bill'.[357]

The framing of the issues as the 'smacking debate' and the Bill as the 'anti-smacking bill' provided reporters and sub-editors with many opportunities for wordplay in headlines:

> *Why you just can't beat a good caning* [358]
>
> *Hands off* [359]
>
> *Smacking bill's time out* [360]
>
> *Reasonable force or unreasonable Bradford?* [361]
>
> *Bill will not take the heat out of smacking* [362]

Some headlines captured the essence of issues, others trivialised them.

The impartiality of reporting and interviewing

The TV Code of Broadcasting Practice states that 'News and current affairs … must be truthful and accurate on points of fact, and be impartial and objective at all times' (emphasis added).[363] At times, advocates expressed concern about the inability or unwillingness of reporters to check the accuracy of some of the claims being made by opponents. Another concern was the subtle lack of impartiality implicit in the 'naming and framing' of the issues. Either TV reporters and newsreaders were unaware of the bias implicit in their labelling or they were aware and chose to ignore the bias, perhaps for the sake of a catchy label.

> ***The framing of the debate proved to be the media's prerogative and the bias implicit in its labelling was rarely acknowledged.***

The Charter of Television New Zealand states that in fulfilling its objectives it will 'provide independent, comprehensive, impartial, and in-depth coverage and analysis of news and current affairs in New Zealand' (emphasis added),[364] but the impartiality of some interviewers was not always apparent. A good example was a *Breakfast Show* interview of Dr Pita Sharples, the co-leader of the Māori Party, which had just announced its support for full repeal. The interviewer, Paul Henry, consistently projected pro-smacking views into his questions and constantly disagreed with the interviewee's responses. We believe this style of interviewing, while perhaps intending to be provocative, displays a lack of impartiality. Eventually, Dr Sharples responded with a telling statement that was widely quoted in the media 'A hit is a hit.'[365]

Presenting opposing viewpoints

One of the key principles of both the radio and television codes of broadcasting practice is that of 'balance'. The principle states that 'when controversial issues of public importance are discussed, reasonable efforts are made … to present significant points of view.'[366] Complaints about print articles are subject to review by the New Zealand Press Council. Its first principle states that 'publications (newspapers and magazines) should at all times be guided by accuracy fairness, and balance'.[367]

This admirable objective was reasonably well met in most mainstream media reporting on the issue, but there was an unintended consequence stemming from simplistic applications of the principle. When reporters responded to initiatives of repeal advocates, they invariably sought to present other 'significant points of view' in their reports. But in doing so, instead of presenting the range of alternative opinions, they sometimes sought brief responses from well-known opponents of repeal.[368] This approach oversimplified, polarised and added nothing new to the debate.

The diversity of editorial opinion

Editorials play a significant role in shaping public opinion and influencing the positions that politicians adopt. Newspaper editorials are usually considered to provide thoughtful, well-reasoned opinions that carry greater weight than the musings of media commentators.

The three leading New Zealand daily newspapers enjoy sizeable circulations: the *New Zealand Herald* prints about 200,000 copies, the *Dominion Post* nearly 100,000, and the *Press* around 90,000.[369] The editor of the *Press* took an early stance in favour of simple repeal and eloquently advocated for repeal throughout the period in which the Bill was before the House. Early on, the editor of the *Dominion Post* wrote that 'good parents don't hit their children'[370] but later he expressed unhappiness with the final form of the Bill. It was his contention that if the real intention of the Bill was to ban all smacking then Parliament should be upfront about it.[371]

The *New Zealand Herald* editorials reveal a fascinating opinion trail. The editorials may not have been written by the same editor but the journey nevertheless reflects an illuminating process of developing awareness.

- 10 May 2001: *Repealing section 59 would, in fact, promote only confusion.*[372]
- 24 September 2003: *[Repeal] would amount to a ban on smacking. Is it necessary to go that far? Probably not.*[373]
- 13 June 2005: *What is needed is not the repeal of section 59 but a substantial rewriting of the Crimes Act.*[374]
- 23 November 2006: *There is, however, the welcome possibility that the Bill will send a latent message to some parents who cross the line ...*[375]
- 2 April 2007: *Yet it could send a message to parents who do not understand the meaning of reasonable force, and as such could be a catalyst for a change in attitude.*[376]
- 3 May 2007: *Now it is important that the concluding agreement leaves no doubt that the law will no longer allow children to be beaten by anyone.*[377]

The opinions of the commentators

Much of the highly charged debate on the repeal of section 59 was conducted in opinion pieces put forward by regular newspapers commentators.[378] Some provided thoughtful insight; others were dogmatic in their stance. During the passage of the Bill through the House, numerous opinion pieces were written, some of which generated more heat than light. Some commentators took a consistent stance against repeal and nothing would convince them otherwise. One commentator who was unconvinced to start with but eventually came to support repeal was Tapu Misa of the *New Zealand Herald*. In 2005 she wrote:

> *The first time I tackled the subject of smacking in this column, it started out as a defence of a parent's inalienable right to smack ...*
>
> *But in the midst of what had seemed to me unassailable arguments ... I had a change of heart.*
>
> *It became clear to me that I was defending the indefensible.*
>
> *Could there really be anything right about accepting a lesser standard of protection in law for children than we would for adults and animals?*[379]

Themes in the Media

A number of significant themes emerged in the protracted 'media dialogue' that occurred during the Bill's passage.

The 'criminalisation' of parents

One of the challenges that had to be addressed in the proposed law reform was how to ensure that the use of force for the purpose of correction would be banned and at the same time reassure parents that they would not be dragged into court every time they were observed committing a minor transgression (see chapter 9). The risk of 'good parents being criminalised' if section 59 was repealed was the argument that most frequently surfaced in editorials, commentary and letters to the editor.

For example, in July 2005 the editor of the *Dominion Post* wrote:

> *It may be that Ms Bradford's bill proves unworkable in its present form. There is no benefit to anyone in making a criminal of a parent who warns a young child against reaching for a jug cord with a light smack on the hand, or who, in a moment of stress, smacks an older miscreant.*[380]

In contrast, the editor of the *Press* had this to say:

> *This claim that parents would become criminals is simply scare-mongering, because the Police would become involved only if there was a serious fear of child abuse occurring. But for those who do subscribe to this view, the obvious way to avoid the threat of being made criminals would be to stop smacking their children.*[381]

Children's rights versus parental authority

Media discussion on the place of physical punishment in bringing up children inevitably gravitated towards a consideration of children's rights versus parental authority. Reference to children's rights often provoked an outraged response from talkback hosts and columnists who subscribed to the old dictum 'children should be seen and not heard'.[382]

Some commentators appeared to think that children did not possess any inherent rights by virtue of being human but had to earn them by behaving well. Others believed that parental and children's rights were fundamentally incompatible:

> *Children's rights are increasingly usurping parental rights, which is clearly seen in the debate over whether to repeal section 59 of the Crimes Act.*[383]

However, each time these arguments were put forward, there were politicians, social scientists and NGO representatives among others whose support for law reform was well known, and to whom journalists seeking balance in their reporting could turn to for other 'significant points of view'.

A few sympathetic editors and commentators argued the case for repeal on the basis of the human rights of children to physical integrity, safety, and equal treatment under the law, one example being the *Press* editor who wrote that 'Politicians need to recognise that the bill is about the rights of children above all else.'[384] The case for banning physical punishment was usually made on the basis of children's needs (for better protection) rather than their *rights* (to equality under the law).

The consequences of not smacking

The debate conducted in the media frequently focused on how children would behave if their parents could no longer smack them. Advocates for repeal claimed that life would carry on as normal as there were other more effective and safer ways of disciplining children; usually they were referring to *positive parenting*.[385] Case Avery, a commentator for the *New Zealand Herald*, described another approach:

> *If we make smacking kids illegal what do we risk? Will they run amok and behave like monsters? Only if we let them. But how will we stop them? Now that's a good question.*
>
> *How will we raise kids who can make their own choices about consequences and accountability?*
>
> *How will we raise kids who will understand other people's needs in relation to their own and make empathetic choices?*
>
> *Easy, by being those people ourselves.*[386]

Some opponents of repeal claimed that children would soon be out of control, creating havoc at home and eventually in the community. A few went so far as to predict that it would ruin families or undermine civil society.[387]

The link between physical punishment and child homicide

This contentious theme continued to be given prominence in the media during the Bill's progress through Parliament. The arguments advanced by commentators for and against this linkage were the same ones that had been canvassed prior to the Bill's arrival (see above) but the evidence put forward in the media failed to resolve the issue one way or the other.

> ***Issues on which members of the public had polarised views were accorded a high profile in media coverage of the debate.***

The Media's Influence

The views expressed in the media often sought to influence the attitudes of the public and politicians towards the repeal of section 59 and the banning of physical punishment. In the absence of any research, it is not possible to make any comment on how successful the media's efforts were in terms of shaping public and political opinion. Given the strength of feelings that people often expressed when asked about the issue, it is more likely that emotional appeals had a greater effect than appeals based on well-reasoned arguments.

There is, though, another way of considering the influence of the media. Politicians relied on the media to gauge the public mood. The collective wisdom of editorials in articulating the concerns of the country, along with the results of numerous formal and informal public opinion polls conducted by a wide variety of newspapers, magazines, TV channels and radio stations (see chapter 7), must have influenced individual politicians with their finely tuned antennae, particularly those whose stances were not necessarily based on deeply held convictions. Those parties supporting the Bill would have been acutely aware that in accepting the weight of well-reasoned arguments by opinion leaders and backing the Bill they were going against the apparent tide of public opinion.

> ***Both advocates and politicians regarded the media as an informal way of monitoring the mood of the country over the issue.***

Media Interest Post-repeal

Once the Bill passed its final reading in Parliament on 16 May 2007, media interest in the issue seemingly evaporated. Perhaps exhaustion had set in after the tens of thousands of words spoken or written on the issue in the preceding 23 months. There was very little reflective media analysis of the course the debate had taken, the issues involved, or what the future might hold for children and parents. The *New Zealand Herald* editor may well have been speaking prophetically in February 2006 when writing the words:

> *Like the anti-smoking law, the repeal of the parental defence to assault will be hotly debated until the day it is enacted. Thereafter it will seem so right and sensible we will forget the issue.*[388]

However, at the time of this book going to print, the media had reported several cases in which the Police had allegedly inappropriately interviewed a parent who had been reported to the Police for smacking a child. Although such details as were available did not appear to support those allegations, the issue is still of interest to the media. There was also one case which received a lot of media attention in which the Police prosecuted and the judge convicted a father for smacking and bruising his son (see chapter 4). This case did attract some sensationalist reporting such as the 'Three smacks and he's "guilty"' article of the *Dominion Post,* although a report published a few days later did present a more balanced view.[389] It is also apparent that when such cases do occur that some people who are still vehemently opposed to the new law will continue to issue alarmist media statements.[390] Eventually editorials in the *Herald on Sunday* and the *Press* condemned the tactics of critics of the new law.[391]

Media Opportunities and Challenges

The media spotlight on the Bill created significant opportunities and challenges for repeal advocates. From an advocate's perspective the attendant publicity was a positive opportunity to provide the public with accurate information on the issues involved and to communicate the case for repeal to a very wide audience. The negative aspects of the intense media focus included issues being trivialised or sensationalised, misinformation becoming accepted as fact, and advocates being misreported.

In the competitive world of mainstream media though, it is inevitable that controversial, high profile issues will be presented in attention-grabbing ways, including the use of provocative headlines and commentary, and by injecting extreme dissenting views that serve to polarise rather than illuminate the issues.

Building relationships

Advocates were well aware of the power of the media in influencing public opinion, but the media were wary of advocacy groups attempting to influence them. The high level of media interest did provide a golden opportunity to inform the debate, so considerable effort went into developing good working relationships with respected political and social reporters as well as with commentators who were sympathetic to the cause. Where it was known that an event was coming up that would be of interest to the media, advocates sought to prepare the ground by briefing selected reporters beforehand.

Communication strategies

Over time, the efforts of advocates became more sophisticated and the advice of communication consultants was sought. Campaigners developed clear communication plans with timelines and responsibilities; they monitored newspapers around the country and encouraged local supporters to respond to section 59 items. Supporters were encouraged to write letters to the editor, especially in response to editorials, opinion pieces or letters opposing law reform. As supporters were not always confident about communicating through the media, sample letters or key points to expand on were sometimes provided. The child advocacy group Every Child Counts published a helpful media kit that identified common items of misinformation circulating in the media and provided factual information for countering them.[392]

> ***As the campaign for repeal intensified, advocates became highly organised and therefore more effective in their responses to media interest.***

Advocates issued press releases on current developments. The effectiveness of this strategy of course depended on whether reporters referred to them in their articles. Most of the releases were posted on an independent news website called Scoop, which published them in full without editorial comment.[393] This website also proved a useful source of information on the current assertions and tactics of opponents.

Wherever possible, spokespersons with a known public identity and appropriate media presentation skills were promoted to the media and they made themselves available for interviews and panel discussions. Opinion pieces were regularly offered to major newspapers and were sometimes published.[394]

Early in the campaign, advocates had decided to present the case for reform dispassionately in the media, basing their arguments on research and reason (see chapter 6). They strove to speak persuasively rather than rhetorically. Advocates made a conscious decision to avoid polarising the debate further. On reflection, adopting this policy was a critical decision – it avoided provoking needless criticism by the media; it was consistent with the image that respective organisations wished to project; and it encouraged the media to treat the issues more thoughtfully.

> ***Arguing dispassionately for a cause that advocates felt passionate about, counter-intuitively proved very worthwhile.***

Talkback radio

This form of media attention was the most difficult for advocates to respond to effectively. No formal monitoring of talkback radio programmes took place and so it is not possible to say whether all talkback interest in the issues was reactionary. Nevertheless, it seemed that way, with talkback hosts often offering conservative views on the use of physical discipline and callers directing their anger at supporters of reform. Informal monitoring was time-consuming as was attempting to respond on air. It was never clear how wide an audience a particular talkback show had or whether the investment of time was productive.

The use of the media by opponents

Undoubtedly, those opposing reform adopted similar strategies. The significant difference between proponents and opponents of repeal was that the latter appeared to be very well funded compared to the former. Opponents regularly purchased expensive, eye-catching advertising space in newspapers. Many of the advertisements engaged in scaremongering, particularly by pushing the 'criminalisation of good parents' canard, in order to provoke opposition to law reform.[395] A major petition seeking a Citizens Initiated Referendum[396] on repeal was also promoted in full-page advertisements in major daily newspapers.[397] According to the promoters of the petition, over 220,000 of the required 300,000 signatures had been collected by November 2007.[398]

Conclusion

On reflection, the media mostly hosted the section 59 debate well. All aspects of the debate were presented at various times and relevant issues got a substantial airing so that very few people would not have known something about the proposed law change. The media play an important role in a democracy and in this case they largely fulfilled that role in a responsible way.

Supporters of reform were challenging a deeply ingrained parenting habit that a large proportion of parents had previously used and a lesser proportion currently did. It was inevitable that efforts to change parental attitudes and behaviours as well as reform the law would be controversial and divisive, and therefore eminently newsworthy. Most of the public debate about the place of physical punishment and the desirability or otherwise of law reform therefore occurred in the mainstream media.

Once the issues became intensely political, the penetration of the controversy into a greater range of media and the much increased visibility of the issues provided welcome opportunities for advocates to reach a much wider audience. At the same time, the move into unfamiliar, sometimes hostile, media territory and the sheer number of journalists and media organisations engaging with the issue, made being responsive difficult. Advocates also relied on media reporting to gauge the public mood and to monitor the activities of opponents.

Much of the attention that advocates paid to interacting with the media related to their desire to influence public opinion in favour of reform, but it was also aimed indirectly at influencing politicians, in whose hands the fate of the Bill resided. This is the subject matter of our next chapter.

Chapter 9

THE POLITICAL SPHERE

On reflection, it seems likely that the growing pressure exerted by New Zealand's repeal advocates, combined with the recommendations emanating from the United Nations Committee on the Rights of the Child, and significant changes to the political scene, would eventually have been sufficient to achieve the repeal of section 59. How soon this might have occurred without Green MP Sue Bradford having the good fortune of seeing her Member's Bill being drawn out of the ballot on the 9th of June 2005 will never be known.[399] It is clear, though, that the repeal of section 59 would not have occurred when it did without the strongly principled and determined political leadership of Sue Bradford.

Sue Bradford at a media conference (courtesy of the Dominion Post*)*

There was a period of nearly two years between the Bill being drawn from the ballot and the new law finally coming into force on the 21st of June 2007. The

Bill's fraught passage through the various stages of law-making stirred many into action and strengthened support for repeal in many quarters.

Initially, some advocates feared that the arrival of Sue Bradford's Bill was premature, that there would be insufficient public support to allow the Bill to succeed at that point in time. Fortunately, this did not prove to be the case. In hindsight, it is apparent that it would not have been possible to generate the massive publicity that occurred, or the extensive public, media and political airing of the issues involved, without the question of whether to repeal or not having been forced upon New Zealanders by the luck of the draw.

> ***The enforced publicity associated with the surprise arrival of the Bill proved invaluable in generating heightened public interest.***

Political Aspects Favouring Reform

Different aspects of New Zealand's political system favoured a change in the law, or at least eased the passage of the legislation repealing section 59.

The single House of Parliament meant that the debates would not have to be conducted and won a second time in an Upper House.

- Political parties sometimes allow MPs to exercise a 'conscience vote' rather than expecting them to toe the party line.
- New Zealand has a mixed-member-proportional (MMP) representation system for allocating seats in Parliament. Members of the public cast two votes, one for the local member they support and the other for the party they favour. Thus, some politicians are elected and others gain a seat owing to their position on a party list – the numbers of the latter depending on the proportion of the party vote their party gained. List members do not have electorates. Sue Bradford is a Green Party politician. At the time her bill was drawn, all seven Green Party MPs were list members and not beholden to a geographically based electorate. Green Party politicians could therefore unite in their support for the Bill without coming under

direct pressure from opponents out in electorates, as occurred to many other electorate MPs.

- The introduction of the MMP system in 1996 gave significant political power to smaller parties. During most of the two-year period in which Sue Bradford's Bill progressed through Parliament, the Labour Government, which came to support repeal, held only a very slender majority over the main opposition party, National, which up until the very last stage of law-making opposed repeal. Minor parties, such as the Greens and the Māori Party, as well as individual members of other minor parties, played a vital role in ensuring that the Bill remained 'alive'. (See appendix 5 for more information on the composition of Parliament.)
- In New Zealand, lobbyists and members of the public can access politicians with relative ease. While this benefited both supporters and opponents of repeal, it did mean that advocates could work closely with Sue Bradford and other key politicians who wanted the law changed. This involved information sharing and mutual support, as well as coordinating campaigns aimed at increasing public and political support for repeal.

> ***Close working relationships with key politicians were essential for effective advocacy and achieving the eventual change in the law.***

Pressures on Politicians

All politicians were inevitably drawn into the debate on the place of physical punishment in New Zealand families once Sue Bradford's Bill made law change a real possibility. They were subject to various pressures and influences coming from lobbyists, constituents, the media, and in the case of the party in power, advice from officials.

Members of Parliament, like most other New Zealanders, had strongly held personal views on the place of physical punishment in child-rearing and on the law relating to it. The issue of physical discipline became a political one in New Zealand as internal and external pressures for change built up. Indications were that at no point in time in the years preceding law reform did a majority of voters support repeal according to most well-publicised polls (see chapter 7). MPs supportive of repeal were understandably anxious about their future political careers as well as the fortunes of their party and were cautious about displeasing some of their voters. The extent to which law reform presented politicians with challenges and dilemmas should not be underestimated. Members of Parliament who personally supported reform experienced a very real tension between what they believed was best for children and what the majority of the public and/or their political colleagues might have believed.

> ***Lack of majority public support for law reform in the polls inevitably meant that politicians sympathetic to reform faced the challenge of displeasing some of their voters.***

Before the New Millennium

The political story extends at least as far back as the late 1990s when advocates became increasingly vocal about law reform and regularly lobbied politicians. MPs were generally not interested, although one Labour MP, Dianne Yates, had publicly supported repeal of section 59 since 1994. Her early support resulted in one disgruntled voter in her electorate starting a public petition against her stand.[400]

In 1998 EPOCH New Zealand sent a questionnaire to MPs asking about their attitudes to repealing section 59.[401] Only 21 of 120 politicians responded. Thirteen responses were completed questionnaires and five were letters of acknowledgement. Only seven Members of Parliament were fully supportive of repeal, three of whom were also supportive of the aims of EPOCH (the others were non-committal). Only one MP opposed to repeal bothered to reply.

The 1997 recommendation of the United Nations Committee on the Rights of the Child, which advised the New Zealand Government to reform the law in order to meet its international obligations, was strongly opposed by at least one political hopeful. The Revd Graham Capill, the then leader of the Christian Heritage Party, was outraged that New Zealand would even consider repealing section 59. He warned:

> *Thou shalt smack thy child and any attempt to take that right away will be met with widespread civil disobedience.*
>
> *Any politician who wants to take this on is buying a big fight and it may cost them their office at the next election – that's the sort of gravity of this sort of interference.*[402]

In November 1999, during the last days of a National Government, the Minister of Social Services, Roger Sowry, responded to a letter from EPOCH New Zealand by writing:

> *You have asked for the Government's position regarding section 59 of the Crimes Act 1961. The Government has* *<u>no current plans to repeal section 59</u>*. *It is committed to working to change societal attitudes in New Zealand to physical punishment of children, through campaigns such as the 'Breaking the Cycle' campaign.*[403] (emphasis added)

In 1998, the statutory child protection agency, Children, Young Persons and their Families Agency, ran a public education campaign entitled *Breaking the Cycle*, which aimed at reducing child abuse and included a section designed to decrease the use of physical discipline in the home called *Let's beat smacking – hands down.*[404]

Opposition to legal reform remained party policy after the National Government lost the election in November 1999. The then National Party leader, Jenny Shipley, was later reported as saying that parents had the right to smack their children in certain circumstances but should not injure them.[405]

From the Start of the Millennium till the Arrival of the Bill

When a Labour-led coalition came into power late in 1999, it took the recommendation of the United Nations Committee seriously enough to instruct officials to begin investigating the feasibility of repeal. Over the next few years section 59 was the subject of various Cabinet briefing papers and decisions. Early in 2000, Cabinet directed officials to:

> *... report on how other comparable countries, particularly in the European Union, have addressed the issue of compliance with UNCROC including educational campaigns that have preceded legislative change.*[406]

In summary, the subsequent report, dated 23 March 2000, stated:

- *Many European countries ... have enacted laws to ban physical punishment. They have tended to do this by making changes to legislation in the form of new child protection laws or other amendments to civil laws.*
- *Some countries that have Westminster-based systems ... are either taking no action or considering placing restrictions in law on when the use of physical punishment is appropriate.*[407]

But at the same time that this confidential activity was going on, in public the Labour Government was non-committal on the repeal of section 59. EPOCH had written to all MPs in April 2000 urging repeal. On 19 May, Phil Goff, who was also the Minister of Justice, replied:

> *The Government supports the use of alternative forms of discipline to physical chastisement but believes this is better accomplished by encouragement and parenting programmes. It has <u>no plans to repeal section 59</u> ... in a way that would suggest that it is illegal and a criminal offence to smack a child.*[408] (emphasis added)

In April 2000, the same Minister of Justice, in responding to a letter from University of Waikato Professor Jane Ritchie, stated:

> *It remains Government policy that section 59 ... does not sanction any form of violence or abuse against children, or protect a parent ... from the consequences of using force other than for correction or which is not reasonable in the circumstances. Therefore, in New Zealand's second report on compliance with the Convention, the Government will be reporting ... that <u>in its view s.59 does not come within the scope of review</u> ...*[409] (emphasis added)

Meanwhile, officials continued to respond to further Cabinet directives to report on the likely outcomes if section 59 were repealed and how these could be addressed; and to report on educational measures that could be undertaken.[410]

In November 2002, a briefing paper went to the Cabinet Policy Committee, entitled *Physical Discipline of Children: Public Education and Legislative Issues*. Notably the paper reported:

> *There are already significant safeguards in the justice system to minimise the risk of parents being prosecuted for trivial offences if section 59 were repealed.*

and:

> *Officials do not consider it is feasible or necessary to develop a specific mechanism to try to manage the risk of parents … being prosecuted for trivial offences …*

and also:

> *Officials agree that public education to lead attitudinal and behavioural change is required regardless of any decision concerning repeal of section 59.*[411]

In response to that report, Cabinet directed the Ministries of Social Development and Youth Affairs, and the Department of Child, Youth and Family Services to develop a proposal for a national public education strategy. The Ministry of Social Development was also invited to prepare a bid for funding of a national media campaign and community-based education programmes in Budget 2003. Officials were also asked to give further consideration to the legislative issues associated with section 59.[412]

The public education component of these directives led to a successful bid by the Ministry of Social Development in Budget 2003. As a result, in May 2004, the Labour-led Government launched the SKIP initiative – *Strategies with Kids: Information for Parents*.

SKIP resources, such as pamphlets and videos on positive parenting for parents and early childhood educators, promote a greater awareness of alternatives to physical punishment, but avoid making any direct reference to the shortcomings of physical discipline. SKIP also contracts with national providers to deliver SKIP programmes, and funds local initiatives. The local fund is contestable and successful applicants receive funds to support community-based initiatives that promote greater awareness and use of alternatives to physical discipline.

During the early 2000s, there was ongoing political interest in repealing section 59 from outside of the Government benches. In August, New Zealand First MP Brian Donnelly announced his intention to draw up a bill to repeal section 59.[413] He later placed a bill calling for complete repeal in the ballot of Member's Bills. In 2001, National's spokesperson on Social Services, Bob Simcock, put forward a Member's Bill to amend section 59 that would have defined the meaning of 'reasonable force'. Neither bill was ever drawn from the ballot. Brian Donnelly later withdrew his bill, and it was replaced with a bill sponsored by New Zealand First MP Barbara Stewart, which sought to amend section 59 in order to limit the degree of force that could be used by parents. This was never drawn either. In 2004, United Future MP Murray Smith proposed the Crimes (Parental Discipline) Amendment Bill, in which he tried to define the difference between acceptable force and child abuse. This bill too was unsuccessful in the ballot.

Other Members of Parliament also expressed public support for repeal. Alliance Party MP Laila Harré, who was Minister of Youth Affairs in the 1999–2001 Labour-led Government, was a steadfast supporter of repeal.[414]

> *She [Laila Harré] said the Alliance wanted the law allowing smacking repealed as countries that had done so had reduced violence to children.*

And, of course, Green MP Sue Bradford herself was a vocal parliamentary supporter of repeal. In a letter to EPOCH in October 2001, she wrote:

> *The Green Party stands firmly behind every one of your key recommendations. I look forward to continuing to work with your organisation and others towards the strategic goal of total repeal.*[415]

In December 2001, the Labour-led Government released the results of a survey of 1000 adults who were asked about their attitudes to section 59 and its possible repeal.[416] Over 80% of those surveyed believed that light smacking should be legal. Phil Goff, the Minister of Justice, said the Government supported education programmes over law change, although he added:

> *It is likely that eventually public attitudes will move towards repealing legal sanctioning of smacking as has now happened in most European countries.*[417]

Others politicians were strongly opposed to reform, including ACT MP Stephen Franks. In an address to a forum on section 59 organised by Barnardos in October 2001, he made an impassioned case against changing the law on the grounds that the rationale for repeal was poorly thought through, that repeal would not lead to less violence, and that the result would be bad law.[418] In October 2002, Labour MP John Tamihere, then Minister of Youth Affairs, told reporters that he would not support the repeal of section 59.[419]

But by the end of 2002, the Government felt it needed to reassure New Zealanders that it had not backed off repeal of section 59 altogether. In a press release, Social Services Minister Steve Maharey said:

> *The assumption at large in the media that the Government has 'backed off' repeal ... is wrong. The truth is that the Government is working through the issue and has <u>not yet arrived at a conclusion</u>.*[420] (emphasis added)

He advised the media that Cabinet would review its options in 2003 and expressed his personal support for repeal. Shortly after that, Prime Minister Helen Clark said that a public education campaign would be run before any law changes were considered.[421] In May 2003, when Steve Maharey, now Minister of Social Development, announced the funding for that campaign, he also announced that the Government would consider changes to section 59 once early evaluations of the public education campaign were available.[422]

However, by early 2005, the same Labour-led Government was still postponing making a decision on what to do with section 59, at least that was the impression it conveyed in response to queries. In a letter to EPOCH, Phil Goff, the Minister of Justice, wrote:

> *Whether changes to the law on the physical discipline of children are*

> *necessary will only be considered after evaluations of the programme (SKIP) are available.*[423]

and, in response to lobbying from a private citizen, he wrote that 'The Government did not believe that an immediate law change was desirable.'[424]

Without any inside information, we can only speculate whether Labour was procrastinating in order to avoid incurring the inevitable political costs of supporting repeal in a country where the majority of adults favoured retaining physical punishment of children, or patiently waiting to see whether the outcome of the SKIP initiative would eventually mean that law change was unnecessary or at least supported by more parents.

But before the Government had to face up to making a decision one way or the other, Sue Bradford's Bill intervened. She had first announced her proposed bill in October 2003 in response to the United Nations Committee's report.[425] Her bill, entitled Crimes (Abolition of Force as a Justification for Child Discipline) Amendment Bill,[426] was drawn from the ballot of Member's Bills on the 9th of June 2005, and had its first reading 48 days later.[427] The thrust of the Bill involved a simple repeal of section 59 (see appendix 1).

Progress of the Bill through Parliament

In New Zealand, proposed laws must pass through a series of stages that ensure that members of the public can express their views and that the text is closely scrutinised by MPs (see appendix 4).

First reading

When Sue Bradford presented her bill to Parliament on 27 July, she said that it was '... a chance for Aotearoa New Zealand to take a step into the future and rid ourselves of an archaic law that legitimises the use of quite serious force against our children'. She ended her speech with the plea:

> *For the sake of all our futures, I call on MPs here tonight to think seriously about allowing this bill to go to select committee, and to consider the possibility that full repeal of section 59 would actually benefit all parents and children in this country rather than create some*

> *of the totally absurd scenarios currently being put forward in some quarters.*[428]

The 'absurd scenarios' she was referring to were that:

> *... parents will suddenly be subject to arrest, prosecution, and conviction if they lightly smack their child. There is no way the Department of Child, Youth and Family Services will abruptly abandon its huge current caseload to remove children from parents who smack them, ... nor will Police, all at once, start arresting parents who put their child in a room for a bit of time out ... Goodness knows, they have enough other work to do.*[429]

But these scenarios were to gain more traction than Sue Bradford might have anticipated, as they shaped many of the public, political and media-fuelled debates that occurred during the next 23 months.

After heated debate, the Bill passed its first reading with 63 votes for and 54 against. It was supported by all 51 Labour MPs, 2 New Zealand First MPs, all 9 Green Party MPs, as well as the sole Māori Party MP. It was opposed by all 27 National MPs, 11 New Zealand First MPs, all 9 ACT MPs, and all 7 United Future MPs. The Bill was then referred to the Justice and Electoral Select Committee. During the debate, Marian Hobbs, the Minister for the Environment, described the reasoning behind Labour's initial support of the Bill. Sending it to a select committee would provide a 'forum for argument, a forum for listening to submissions from the community, a forum for examination. It is hoped that some clarification will result.'[430] She also indicated that Labour's continued support for the Bill in its current form was not assured. Labour had supported the Bill so that '... a full range of options can be identified and carefully considered.'

A general election intervened before the closing date for submissions arrived. After the vote on 17 September 2005, Labour was eventually returned to power but with two seats less in Parliament. As a minority Government, it was even more dependent on its formal and informal coalition partners to secure a workable majority with which to govern. In terms of passing legislation in the House, sufficient support would have to be garnered from different parties on a bill-by-bill basis.

Select Committee hearings

After the election, submissions from the public were accepted by the Select Committee up until 28 February 2006. Those who chose to make an oral submission were heard during June, July or August at several locations around of the country. The committee, which was chaired by Labour MP Lynne Pillay, received 1718 written submissions – 247 from organisations and 1471 from individuals. Seventy-six submissions were from children or young people. The Committee also heard over 200 oral submissions. The committee read and heard submissions for and against the Bill – the great majority of organisations which made a submission supported the Bill while a majority of individuals who made a submission opposed it.[431]

The chair of the Select Committee, Labour MP Lynne Pillay
(courtesy of the Dominion Post*)*

The Select Committee was required to make a written recommendation to Parliament by November 2006. Before then, it had become clear to the committee that in order for the Bill to gain majority support in Parliament to continue its passage through the remaining stages of law-making, some changes would need to be made. The purpose of these amendments would be to reduce public anxiety about parents being criminalised for acts that were a normal part of parenting such as removing a child from danger or restraining a child, which technically could be considered to be assaults.

The committee therefore sought the advice of the New Zealand Law Commission, an independent, government-funded body that reviews laws that need updating, reforming or developing. With its help the Crimes (Substituted Section 59) Amendment Bill was drafted (see the full text in appendix 2). The work of the Law Commission played a critical role in ensuring majority support from the Select Committee for the repeal of section 59, and Labour Party support for the amended version of the Bill.

The amended bill would also repeal section 59 with its statutory defence, but it would replace it with a new section, entitled *Parental control,* which would allow parents to apply a force to a child in certain circumstances such as lifting a child away from danger (see chapter 4). The Bill would override any common law rule that might have justified the use of force for the purpose of correction, and in doing so it would introduce an explicit ban on the use of force for the purpose of correction. It thus went further than Sue Bradford's original bill by introducing a ban and overturning common law.

Even with the amendment drafted by the Law Commission, the Select Committee was divided in its decision. Most members of the Committee supported the revised bill, although two National members did not. They stated in a minority view that their concern was still the risk of prosecution of parents for trivial assaults. Nevertheless, support from the majority of members of the Select Committee enabled the Crimes (Substituted Section 59) Amendment Bill to progress to the next stage.

Second reading

This debate took place on 21 February 2007. After several hours of debate on the nature and implications of the amendment, 70 MPs voted for and 51 against the Bill proceeding to the next stage of law-making – the Committee of the Whole House. Prior to the vote, National MP Chester Borrows had made public his intention of introducing an amendment to the Bill at the 'Whole House' stage, which would ensure a statutory defence still existed in cases of 'transitory and trifling' assault. Accordingly six National Party MPs voted to keep the Bill 'alive', so that he could eventually introduce his amendment.

Actual supporters of the Crimes (Substituted Section 59) Amendment Bill as it currently stood included all Green Party MPs, all Labour MPs, three

New Zealand First MPs, all four Māori Party MPs, one United Future MP, and the sole Progressive MP.

Members of the Labour caucus were required to vote for the Bill. In Westminster-style governments, this practice is referred to as 'whipping' – an unfortunate term in this context as National MPs taunted Labour for having to 'whip' its MPs to vote for a bill opposing corporal punishment.

Some contrasting views were expressed during the debate:[432]

> *The Judeo-Christian tradition ... [has] held that for millennia children are not born virtuous; that they are designed to be trained to be virtuous.* Gordon Copeland (United Future Party)

> *I will vote for the amended bill because it is the best way to ensure that we make some progress ... I believe in the persuasive power of this House otherwise I would not have been here for as long as I have.* Jim Anderton (Progressive Party)

> *I was raised firstly by my grandmother. At no time did she raise her hand or her voice in taking care of me or my cousins, who were all loved, nurtured and cared for by her. ... I hope that is what my children, grandchildren and great-grandchildren remember about me when I am gone.* Tariana Turia (Māori Party)

Evolving political positions

In the September 2005 election, the recently formed Māori Party gained an additional three seats, giving them four of the seven *Māori electorate* seats in Parliament.[433] Although the first Māori Party MP, Tariana Turia, had voted in support of the Bill at its first reading in July, it was by no means certain that the Māori Party as a whole would support the Bill in its second reading. The MPs were concerned that the provisions of the Bill would result in Māori families being unfairly treated by the Police or the statutory child welfare agency. The party held a number of hui (gatherings) around the country to discuss the issues with their Māori constituents. Despite conflicting feedback, the four MPs courageously decided to support full repeal (see chapter 6). In a press statement released before the second reading debate, they stated:

> *We believe that Parliament has an important role in dispelling the*

illusion that violence is normal and acceptable. We believe that statements of aspiration are important in encouraging whānau to create and maintain violence-free homes.[434]

Maori Party co-leader Dr Pita Sharples (right), along with MPs Hone Harawira (left) and Te Ururoa Flavell (middle), explain their position on section 59 (courtesy of the New Zealand Herald*)*

As discussed earlier, at the first reading stage the Labour Government was non-committal on whether it would support full repeal as the best option. By the time the Select Committee's report was debated during the second reading, Labour's position had firmed up considerably. Mark Burton, Minister of Justice, said that he was pleased to speak on behalf of '... a unified Labour caucus, and, indeed, a unified Government ...' that now supported the Bill.[435]

What brought the Labour Party and Government to a point of conviction about the need to repeal section 59? Perhaps the recommendation of the Select Committee convinced those who were hesitant beforehand, perhaps it was felt that the time was now right to back repeal, perhaps it believed that the political fallout would not be as bad as had been anticipated earlier, or perhaps the Prime Minister, Helen Clark, convinced her colleagues that they too must have the courage of their convictions. It may be some time before we know what actually happened behind closed Cabinet and caucus doors. What we do know, though, is that section 59 would not have been repealed if the Labour Party had not decided to become official backers.

Committee of the Whole House

This stage commenced on 14 March with the amended bill being debated line by line. As amendments could be now be introduced by any MP, a number of them took advantage of this for genuine or vexatious reasons. Both major parties were by now 'whipping' their members – Labour for the Bill as it stood and National for the Borrows' Amendment.

Within Parliament there was extensive filibustering, often involving either trivial or turgid speech-making, mostly by National Party MPs who kept leaping up in unison to catch the attention of the chair. This tactic promised to delay the final decision for several months as debate of Member's Bills was allocated only a few hours every second week that Parliament was in session. A number of MPs proudly boasted of smacking their children (see chapter 7), while others warned of the criminalisation of 'good parents' or claimed that families would have their children removed by the state under the new law. This approach was sustained throughout the sessions on 14 and 28 March, and looked set to continue on 2 May when Parliament returned from a three-week recess. Repeal advocates, on their way home from listening to the evening debates in the House, undoubtedly felt dispirited at the level to which debate had sunk.

Reaching a compromise

During the recess, the Leader of the Opposition, John Key, made public his intention of negotiating a compromise amendment with Sue Bradford.[436] He took the first step by offering to meet with both Sue Bradford and Helen Clark. The Prime Minister did not meet with him at this stage but the Green MP did. The initiative failed when Sue Bradford resolutely refused to agree to any compromise that would describe in law how children might be hit. At the select committee stage she had already demonstrated her willingness to consider amendments that would reassure the public, but at the same time she would not compromise her stance that the law must not endorse any justification of the use of force for correction. She had also stated a number of times that she would withdraw her bill if such an amendment was forced upon it.

Even though the Bill as it stood had sufficient committed support to be passed eventually, private conversations continued behind the scenes with the aim of developing a form of wording that would gain wider parliamentary support. This time, the Prime Minister worked with Geoffrey Palmer, ex-Prime Minister and President of the Law Commission, to develop an amendment that would further address public and political anxieties. This involved adding a clause that 'affirmed that the Police have the discretion not to prosecute' in cases where the force used on the child was 'inconsequential'. Helen Clark then approached Sue Bradford, who was receptive to the amendment. After briefing Cabinet and the Labour Caucus, the Prime Minister then spoke to the Leader of the Opposition to see if he was prepared to back the amendment, which he indicated he would. Then on the 2nd of May 2007, the historic press conference to announce the accord took place.[437]

John Key and Helen Clark shaking hands over the compromise (courtesy of the Dominion Post*)*

When the Committee of the Whole House reassembled in the afternoon following the surprise morning announcement, the compromise amendment was put forward by the leader of United Future, Peter Dunne. The debate in the House eventually concluded with a vote overwhelmingly in favour of the amendment, and speeches praising those who had cooperated in resolving the 'impasse'. The Bill could now progress to the last stage of law-making.

Explaining the accord

Why did Labour seek an accommodation with National and why did National suddenly reverse its opposition to the Bill at the last minute?

Despite the sometimes acrimonious debates in the House, National did share with Labour a common desire to provide better legal protection for children who were at risk of being beaten by their parents. That said, the political manoeuvrings involved were also likely to have been driven by other considerations.

The National Party appears to have adopted a strategy at an early stage in the select committee process, if not before, of at some point introducing a compromise amendment that would allow it to support the legislation and take credit for addressing the public's concerns. John Key may also have wanted to adopt a 'statesman-like' stance on this issue, as he had recently done over several other contentious issues.

Cartoonist Mike Moreu illustrates the initial disbelief that many experienced on hearing the news of the surprise accord (courtesy of Mike Moreu)

The majority of the Select Committee had already decided against simple repeal and had put forward an amended bill that responded to public and media fears that parents would get into trouble with the law for actions such as restraining of a child, which technically qualifies as an assault. This had made the position of the National Party more problematic – did they support a law change that would provide better legal protection for children or not?

During the Committee of the Whole House stage, National decided to mount a filibuster to delay proceedings and embarrass the Labour Party, which had chosen to 'whip' their MPs to vote en bloc for the Bill. National hoped that it could persuade some Labour MPs, known to have doubts about the Bill as it stood, to reject the 'whip' and vote for the Borrows' Amendment. Events during the first evening of filibustering were publicised on national television. To the public, the amendment being put forward by National seemed little different in effect from the existing law, and the party now appeared to be supporting the status quo. Its position was becoming less tenable.

The Labour Party was not gaining public support for its stand. In fact, for some months it had been hammered in public opinion polls, and no doubt wanted to bring the issue to as rapid a conclusion as possible. So Helen Clark was looking for a solution that would take the heat out of the situation for her party. John Key was still hoping to put forward a statesman-like solution, and found it handed to him on a plate by the Prime Minister. In the surprise accord, a minor addition to the wording of the Bill was publicised as addressing the public's concerns, but the compromise amendment was essentially cosmetic in effect as it only affirmed what was already the case.

Some commentators believed that the protests organised by the Destiny Church had the unintended consequence of encouraging National to change its oppositional stance. Destiny Church's public posturing had alarmed many New Zealanders as it echoed the role that another minority religious group, the Exclusive Brethren, had played in attempting to influence the outcome of the 2005 election.[438] They had provoked intense public criticism for aligning themselves with the National Party in an expensive campaign, which may have cost National the opportunity of becoming the Government. As one political commentator wrote:

As with the Exclusive Brethren, National is finding your staunchest allies can be your biggest liabilities.[439]

The third reading

In its final reading on 16 May 2007, the Bill was passed with the support of an overwhelming majority of MPs. The 113 MPs who voted in favour included all Labour, National, Green and Māori Party MPs, as well as four New Zealand First MPs, one United Future MP, and the sole Progressive MP. Only eight MPs voted against the Bill.

The voting concluded with an unprecedented standing ovation from most MPs present and the numerous long-term supporters of repeal in the public galleries. Supporters were elated and the applause acknowledged the role of Sue Bradford as the leading reformer and also the significant contributions made by other MPs.

Sue Bradford being congratulated by Green MP Metiria Turei during the standing ovation (courtesy of the Dominion Post*)*

The role of minor parties and individual MPs

Throughout the protracted law-making process, minor parties and individual MPs played a critical role. Their votes were essential for keeping the Bill 'alive' in the early stages, and for making it clear that the Borrows' Amendment would not succeed in the final stages. The Greens, of course, all supported the Bill at every stage. Just before the second reading stage, in a crucial decision, all Māori Party MPs agreed to back the Bill. Both New Zealand First and United Future allowed their MPs to exercise conscience votes throughout. Staunch supporters of the Bill included Brian Donnelly, Doug Woolerton and Peter Dunne. But for United Future, the price of Peter Dunne's support for the Bill was the defection of an MP, Gordon Copeland, from the party. There were also reports of disharmony in New Zealand First's ranks.[440]

Over the years a few National Party MPs expressed their personal support for repeal. Most National MPs were willing to support Chester Borrows' proposed amendment to limit the statutory defence. But the sole National MP who steadfastly supported repeal throughout the years of public and political debate was Katherine Rich. Although she voted with her party when 'whipped', her personal support for repeal was respected and valued by reformers both inside and outside of Parliament.

The Prime Minister's role

The strength of Helen Clark's leadership and the influence she wielded as Prime Minister were undoubtedly a critical factor in the final outcome. Her contribution was based on a deep personal conviction:

> *In all conscience there is no way I could have led a party that didn't support a change. The change was about trying to stop the appalling toll of death and injury for children in homes in our country. When you have the opportunity to do something about it you can either take that opportunity or curse yourself for the rest of your life that you didn't act.*[441]

Conclusion

The passing into law of the Crimes (Substituted Section 59) Amendment Bill, which resulted in full repeal of the old statutory defence and a ban on the use of force for the purpose of correction, came about when it did through the luck of the draw, pressure from credible advocates, leadership from strong and principled politicians, the desire of many politicians to reduce the amount of violence towards children, as well as complex political manoeuvrings.

It is fitting here to pay tribute to Green MP Sue Bradford, who has a long history of courageously standing up for less powerful members of society, and whose strengths include a willingness to work closely with community-based organisations. At the time of writing, she was listed in the *Listener* magazine in eighteenth position on a list of 50 powerful people who have shaped New Zealand recently.[442] Rebecca Mcfie, one of the panellists compiling the list, described the passing of the Bill as 'a fundamental shift in the moral climate for New Zealand families ... a decision that penetrates every home.' In our final chapter we will review the forces for and against that shift and look to the future for New Zealand children.

Part Three

Journey's End?

Chapter 10

THE WAY FORWARD

Many who advocated for the repeal of section 59 had as their ultimate goal a New Zealand in which everyone would know that it is wrong to hit children and would not do so. They saw law reform as a critical step towards achieving this long-term goal but at the same time it would also achieve the more immediate goals of providing children with better legal protection against assault and increased recognition of their human rights, including equality under the law.

Although it is still early days under the new law, it is important to consider how the repeal of section 59 will impact on families and children. In this final chapter of the book, we briefly recap the changes that have occurred in the law, then look at how the public, media, Police, courts, government departments and social agencies are responding. We will touch on some of the emerging issues and how they might be addressed. Finally, we will focus on the longer term goal of a future in which all children live their lives free of violence.

The New Law

Sue Bradford's original bill simply called for the full repeal of section 59 but along the way it was modified several times to ensure sufficient and then later overwhelming Parliamentary support for the Bill passing into law (see chapter 9). In summary, the new law has five significant elements:[443]

1. Children have the same legal protection against assault as adults do.
2. All physical punishment is banned.
3. Parents are allowed to restrain or remove children.
4. Police have the discretion not to prosecute.
5. Officials will monitor the impact of the law.

At the time of writing, the new law had been in effect for only five months. Any consideration of responses to the law is by necessity exploratory.

Interpreting the New Law

What do the words of the new law actually mean? When the *Parental control* section was added, there were criticisms of the terms used and the wording. Would it create confusion about what parents were allowed or not allowed to do?

The public's understanding

Given the sustained media attention devoted to the Bill over a period of nearly two years, it is unlikely that many adults or school-aged children would have been unaware of its existence. When it was finally passed, the public would have been left in no doubt that the new law banned the use of smacking to correct or punish children. This was due in no small part to the efforts of opponents and of media reporters who had dubbed the proposed legislation the 'anti-smacking bill'. Despite this, there is likely to be a significant number of people who believe that the new law allows parents to smack their children in certain circumstances (see below).

The media's misinterpretation

The public relies on the media to keep it in touch with changes in the law and what they might mean. When the Bill was finally approved by Parliament, most mainstream media simply reported that it was no longer legal for parents to hit or smack their children. About a month later, two days before the new law came into force, the Police released their practice guide on how officers ought to apply the new law.[444] TV journalists and newsreaders from both major channels expressed erroneous interpretations. In 'top of the news' items they asserted that the Police had indicated that it was okay for parents to hit their children in order to prevent them from running out on the road or committing a criminal offence or engaging in anti-social behaviour.[445] But nowhere in the guide was there any mention that the Police considered it 'okay to smack' or 'okay for parents to use physical discipline'.[446] How did TV journalists and newsreaders come to that conclusion?

It may be a reflection on New Zealand's linguistic assumptions that the television commentators believed that references to 'using force' must mean 'smacking the child' rather than the much more obvious meanings in the context of the whole Act of *removing* a child from danger or *restraining* the child to prevent others being hurt or a crime bring committed.[447] More likely though, the media's mistake was due to the inclusion of a highly charged phrase in the guide – 'reasonable force'. The phrase is a legal relic from the old section 59 where it clearly referred to striking children.

Those two news items may have been the last thing that some members of the public heard about what the new law meant, as media interest in the new law surfaced only sporadically after that. If this misunderstanding has gained a foothold in some people's thinking, it might prove difficult to shift.

The Police Practice Guide

In order to further reassure the public, the 'last minute' compromise amendment to the Bill had inserted a clause which 'affirmed that the Police have the discretion not to prosecute ... where the offence is considered to be so inconsequential that there is no public interest in proceeding with a prosecution.'[448] Interest then focused on how the Police might exercise that discretion. In their practice guide, an effort was made to clarify the meaning of the new law by referring to case law and dictionary definitions.

Cartoonist Tom Scott injects a little humour into the issue of what the new law means (courtesy of Tom Scott)

One task was to clarify which cases might be considered *inconsequential* and therefore did not warrant prosecution. Descriptions such as 'minor', 'trivial', and 'unimportant' may or may not prove helpful for frontline police officers facing a decision on whether to prosecute or not. The Police practice guide was, however, clear about what were *not* inconsequential actions:

> *The use of objects/weapons to smack a child, strikes around the head or kicking would not be considered inconsequential assaults.*

One significant consequence of the law change is to lower the threshold for Police to initiate prosecutions of parents who have significantly assaulted their children.[449] Police no longer need to consider whether the *reasonable chastisement* defence would make pursuing a prosecution a waste of time. The number of prosecutions brought against parents for assault could rise initially, as might the percentage of convictions. Because of the newness of the legislation it has not been possible to confirm whether this is happening.[450]

The view of the courts

Not surprisingly, given the time it takes for prosecutions to proceed through the criminal justice system, we have yet to see any legal rulings on the meaning of the new law (see chapter 4).[451] Some defence lawyers will no doubt claim that section 59 allows parents to hit their children for the purpose of preventing injury, criminal offence or anti-social behaviour. But the new law 'abolish[es] the use of parental force for the purpose of correction',[452] and it is obvious that hitting is not necessary when restraining or removing a child.

Case law will inevitably develop and be of assistance to judges and juries in future cases.[453] It will also lead to revisions of the Police practice guide.[454] We would anticipate that any future legal ruling on what the law means will reflect the basic intention of the Act, which is 'to make better provision for children to live in a safe and secure environment free from violence ....'[455] The effectiveness and impact of the legislation is due to be considered by Parliament two years after it came into force (see below). This would provide an opportunity for our lawmakers to amend the wording of the law if its intent was being frustrated in the courts.

Informing Families and Children

Those who advocated for law reform believe that parents and children are curious about the new law and what it might mean for them. They would also argue that New Zealand families are entitled to accurate information about a law that impacts on everyday family life.

Although the Government has no legal duty to inform the public about new legislation that directly affects them, it often does so. The responsibility for informing the public is usually undertaken by the relevant government department which, for this law, would be either the Ministry of Justice or the Police.[456] The Police indirectly informed the public about their interpretation of the law but, as outlined above, this resulted in some misinterpretations being advanced in the media.

Shortly after the Bill passed into law, the Ministry of Social Development consulted with non-governmental organisations on how information for parents might be framed and widely distributed. No information has been distributed so far but, given the possibility of some public confusion, it remains important that the law's implications are succinctly communicated to families. Now that some distance has been gained from the heated public debate during the passage of the Bill through the House, it may prove easier to do this without re-igniting the controversy.

Various non-governmental organisations, such as Barnardos and EPOCH as well as the Office of the Children's Commissioner, developed information sheets on what the new law meant for children and their families.[457] These information sheets make it clear that the new law specifically bans the use of force for the purpose of correcting children but also inform parents of the discretion that Police have with regard to prosecuting parents for minor offences. But these initiatives are limited in their capacity to inform all New Zealand families.

Assisting Parents to Make a Change

As a consequence of the law change, there will be some parents who just stop using physical punishment and others who struggle to do so. In this section we will look at some of the issues relating to the provision of services by government and non-government agencies.

Resources for parents who want to change

For parents wanting to change their approach to discipline there are a number of NGOs such as Plunket, Barnardos and Parent Centres that offer online resources covering alternatives to physical discipline, particularly the *positive parenting* approach.[458] Some provide parent education courses and/or support groups to assist parents in making the transition.[459] Resources on positive parenting are also available through the Ministry of Social Development's SKIP programme.[460] (Their paper resources are also widely available in the community.) There is an issue of how readily parents can locate this information if they are not sure which website to visit or what search terms to use, and what they can do if they don't have access to the Internet.

Responding to parents who are reluctant to change

Administering the law will pose some challenges for the Police. The practice guide indicated that when they respond to complaints about a parent hitting a child, Police will use a graduated series of responses ranging from warnings over mild misdemeanours through to criminal prosecutions for serious assaults.[461] For repeat 'mild misdemeanours' the likely step will be diversion, where the parent has to attend a parenting course in order to avoid prosecution. How successful compulsory attendance might be in terms of changing parental behaviour remains to be seen.

Responding to parents who are struggling to change

There will also be parents who want to stop hitting their children but have difficulty in 'staying their hand' when their children are behaving badly, particularly in stressful situations when parents are under duress. The habit of hitting will not stop overnight, nor will parental education reach all parents effectively. Supportive arrangements for those parents who are struggling to change will be important. Access to effective family support services such as home visiting, parent education and child-care support, as well as adult support services for parents experiencing mental illness, domestic violence or addiction will continue to be critical if outcomes for children are to improve.

The role of the statutory child protection agency

Parents who find it difficult to stop hitting their children are likely to come to the attention of CYF, as Police officers have been instructed to notify CYF in cases where non-inconsequential assaults have occurred.[462] Concerned members of the public can also notify Child, Youth and Family directly. In December 2007, the Ministry of Social Development confirmed that there had been 'no significant increase in care and protection notifications to Child, Youth and Family since section 59 of the Crimes Act was amended in May 2007'.[463]

The role of CYF involves responding to cases of child abuse by ensuring that children and young people are protected from harm. In cases involving a serious assault, CYF social workers are able to apply to the Family Court for a warrant to remove the child from the family. At the time of writing, Peter Hughes, the chief executive of MSD, stated that the repeal of section 59 had not affected CYF's intervention theshold. [464] Other strategies for securing the safety of the child within the family would be employed first before social workers would consider removing the child, unless the risk was high.

CYF already has to cope with an increasingly large number of notifications. It assesses each case on the basis of risk and confines its statutory responses to more serious cases of alleged abuse. If in future a relatively large number of parents experiencing difficulties in rearing children without hitting do come to CYF's attention, how would it respond? An investigative response would not be appropriate when what is required is a family-support response. Investigations can be intrusive and frightening and are likely to cause a further loss of confidence in child-rearing abilities.

Child, Youth and Family is currently developing responsive systems that will enable it to refer families experiencing these kinds of difficulties to locally based NGOs that are working in partnership with CYF. The NGOs are more likely than CYF to be able to provide the kinds of supportive interventions that parents need to make progress towards the goal of no longer striking their children. The success of this strategy will depend on how effectively the Government can build capacity in the NGO sector, as most community agencies currently report being overloaded and under-resourced.

Monitoring the New Law

One of the difficulties that advocates of law reform experienced during the public debate conducted in the media was obtaining relevant data on the impacts of law reform in countries that had already banned physical punishment (see chapter 8). Hopefully, in the future, advocates seeking to repeal similar laws in other countries will find an abundance of relevant data on the impact of New Zealand's law change thanks to the compromise amendment and the findings of academic researchers.

Monitoring the impact of the Act

Under the provisions of the new law, the chief executive of the Ministry of Social Development (MSD) must 'monitor ... the effects of the Act, including the extent to which the Act is achieving its purpose', which is 'to make better provision for children to live in a safe and secure environment free from violence'.[465] At the time of writing, officials from the Ministries of Social Development, Justice and the Police were considering a range of mechanisms for monitoring the impact of the Act, including the use of data that is currently collated as well as initiating supplementary research.[466]

Parliamentary review

There is also provision in the new legislation for Parliament to receive a report after two years on the extent to which the Act is achieving its purpose and on any additional impacts. This provision was introduced largely to reduce public anxiety about the risk of trivial prosecutions. If there is a spate of prosecutions for minor infringements of the law, or if the intent of the legislation is being frustrated in the courts, then the wording of the law can be revisited. MSD is required to review the available data and identify trends, then report the findings to the Minister who will present the report to the House. Such reporting is likely to be a useful source of information about whether the new law is beginning to make a difference for children.

Research

Not only does the application and interpretation of the new law need monitoring, but so too does its impact on adult attitudes and behaviour. Impact research in most countries that have banned physical punishment remains underdeveloped. Sweden is the exception as officials and academics there have extensively documented the trends.[467] Longitudinal research on attitudinal and behavioural change would be extremely useful; perhaps it could form part of the new longitudinal research study into New Zealand families and children that the Ministry of Social Development is developing.[468] Academic researchers could also extend the in-depth, interview-based research programme initiated by Jane and James Ritchie in the sixties (see chapter 6). Repeated interviews with children and parents in conditions of trust and confidentiality would be the only way of gaining an accurate picture of whether the use of physical punishment within families is diminishing over time.

Children's advocates

At this stage it is not clear what roles advocates and NGOs might chose or be invited to play in monitoring the impact of the new law on children and their families. Such activities might include informal monitoring of inappropriate applications of the law, researching public perceptions about the new law, and establishing and maintaining a research programme into changes in attitudes and behaviour over time.

Making a Success of the New Law

Shortly after the new law was passed, some leading advocates sat down together and thought about what might be required in the future to make a success of the new law, both in terms of its immediate goal of providing better legal protection for children and its longer-term aim of ensuring that all New Zealand children could live lives free from any form of violence. The advocates came up with an action plan that captures most of what remains to be done.[469] With their permission we have adapted their plan below and offer it as a useful summary to focus the thoughts of all those concerned with, or having responsibility for, the welfare of New Zealand's children.

Priorities for Action

The development of a strategic implementation plan would greatly enhance the chances of all New Zealand children experiencing the full benefits of the new law. The plan would need to be developed by government agencies working in partnership with non-governmental organisations. The following objectives would form the basis of such a plan.

1. **Accurate public information**

   How can parents and children be provided with accurate, straightforward, easily accessible information about what the new law means?

2. **Accessible parental education**

   How can all parents, wherever they live, have access to high quality, practical resources on effective *positive parenting* methods?

3. **Effective support services**

   How can stressed parents who are struggling to stop hitting their children be supported with appropriate family and/or adult services?

4. **Constructive policing responses**

   Are prosecution rates falling after the initial expected increase? How effective are other Police responses in changing parental behaviour?

5. **Appropriate legal interpretation**

   How are the courts interpreting the *Parental control* section? How might Parliament need to amend the law if its intent is being frustrated?

6. **Purposeful impact monitoring**

   How can the law's impact be monitored to see if its primary purpose is being achieved? Are children living safer lives, free from violence?

7. **Useful social science research**

   How are the attitudes of parents towards physical punishment evolving over time? What kinds of discipline are children experiencing at home?

Promoting a 'Violence-free' Environment for Children

Law reform is a fundamental underpinning of attitudinal and behavioural change. Without it, other measures such as public education will struggle to succeed. Many of the constraints that made changing the law difficult also come into play when seeking to change opinions and habits. These constraints include:

- a lack of respect for the human rights of children
- the needs of adults trumping those of children
- the power of traditional cultural customs
- a lack of knowledge of the negative effects of physical discipline
- insufficient information or resources on positive parenting
- religious convictions that it is right/necessary to hit children
- beliefs in the effectiveness of physical discipline
- reluctance to change old habits
- public opposition sustained by well-organised groups
- resentment over perceived state intrusion into family life
- the political risks of supporting change initiatives
- confusing media comment
- continued fear of parents being criminalised.

Despite this somewhat daunting list of constraints, in New Zealand there were, and increasingly are, many critical factors that aid change. These factors will provide opportunities for advocates and government agencies to positively influence public attitudes and private practices. These supportive factors include:

- robust international evidence confirming the negative effects of physical discipline and its lack of effectiveness
- convincing research findings on the effectiveness and safety of positive parenting
- evolving public attitudes towards the use of physical discipline, particularly among the younger generation of parents
- public disquiet over the disturbing persistence of child abuse and its transmission from one generation to the next
- the existence of a loose network of well-informed groups advocating for children's rights and needs – the children's movement
- the coordinated efforts of advocacy groups – in public education campaigns, in engaging the media, and in political lobbying
- public support for change provided by respected voices within the community, particularly those of religious and secular leaders
- the existence of principled politicians willing to exercise leadership and take political risks in order to secure the rights of children
- legal obligations to prohibit all corporal punishment under the United Nations Convention on the Rights of the Child
- an explicit recommendation in the United Nations Study on Violence to Children to end all corporal punishment.

We would hope that many if not all of these supportive factors might be harnessed by advocates who are seeking to repeal similar laws in other countries or to change the child-rearing habits of a new generation of parents. Social and legal approval of physical punishment of children is a persistent and highly symbolic reflection of children's low status as 'possessions'. The abolition of physical punishment is a huge step towards fully recognising children as individual human beings and rights-holders.

Enhancing Children's Rights

Family violence, including child abuse, continues to make the headlines in New Zealand despite the law change. It causes public outrage and inspires protest marches that demand further action from the Government. Breaking the cycle of violence, which operates from one generation to the next, involves changing the ways in which we regard and treat our children. In New Zealand, the task of fully protecting children from all forms of violence, including physical punishment, is still a work in progress. We need to build on the clear break with the past that the law change represents and build on the opportunities that the new law presents. The focus of much of the journey towards banning physical punishment of children in New Zealand was on reforming the law – this in itself consumed almost all of the resources and energy of advocates and political reformers. Yet it is important that we do not to lose sight of the fact that the struggle was also about enhancing the human rights of children – their rights to physical integrity, to protection from harm, to equal protection under the law, and to human dignity.

As one step towards a wider recognition of children's human rights, we need to attend to the right of children to know what the new law means for them. According to the United Nations Convention on the Rights of the Child the Government has a duty to inform children of their rights.[470] Surely this can be done in a thoughtful way that does not give rise to a series of unwarranted complaints to the Police, but rather simply explains to them what their newly acquired legal right is and where to go for help if that right is being seriously breached.

Conclusion

In the last chapter we mentioned the view of one commentator, Rebecca Mcfie, who said that the passing of the Crimes (Substituted Section 59) Amendment Act in 2007 represented a 'fundamental shift in the moral climate for New Zealand families.'[471] Such a seismic shift does not occur in isolation. We could place this one in a series of societal and statutory changes that have progressively brought different groups making up our population into full citizenship. There is reason to hope that the intense public debate and the dramatic final passage into law of a small and seemingly innocuous bill were indeed the gestation and birth pangs of our children's emergence into full citizenship.

EPILOGUE

I was influenced in my resolve to change Aotearoa New Zealand's physical punishment legislation by my own personal convictions, by my experiences as a mother, and through my political commitment to the core Green principles of non-violence and social responsibility. Physical punishment harms children and is unnecessary. It also affronts my personal values about how human beings ought to treat each other.

I was stirred into political action by the recommendations that the UN Committee on the Rights of the Child made on two occasions encouraging New Zealanders to repeal our law legitimising smacking and hitting. Of course other things added impetus to my resolve, including research findings, New Zealand's high levels of family violence, and the urgings of the many advocates who work with children and families in the community.

It was fortunate that my Member's Bill was drawn from the ballot when it was, and I am still amazed by the fact that in the end, nearly all Members of Parliament saw fit to vote for it. This level of agreement within Parliament is rare. I believe it reflected, among other things, a recognition that children need positive guidance in their upbringing and better protection from violence than they had experienced in the past.

The law change was preceded by a prolonged and sometimes shameful debate but in the end the rights and interests of children prevailed. I acknowledge my colleagues from nearly all parties in Parliament for their support for the new law.

I also honour the work of all those advocates in the community who worked so hard to change hearts and minds, with the goal of convincing the public and Parliament alike that our children would be better served if they were not physically assaulted in the name of discipline.

Over the last few decades there has been very visible growth in community support for a better deal for children, and for their becoming more central to political decision making and resource allocation. I hope that the children's movement will continue to grow from strength to strength and that its voice will be heard and acted on at all levels of Government and society in the years ahead.

Before the Bill was drawn from the ballot, one of my parliamentary colleagues described the repeal of section 59 as an iconic issue, something that would symbolise a change in the way we view and treat children, something larger than outlawing the hitting of children – and indeed it is. This law change is not about persecuting parents; it is about encouraging social change and growing our humanity.

Despite the years of debate about the place of physical punishment in child-rearing, there are still some people who fear or even resent the law change. However, I believe that it will not be long before the vast majority of people in our country will feel confident that Parliament did children a great service in 2007.

Sue Bradford, Green Party MP

CHAPTER ENDNOTES

Chapter 1: **SETTING THE SCENE**

1. A recently established Christian church with a strong Māori and Pacific following and conservative values opposed to social reforms such as repealing section 59.
2. *Hansard* record of the debate, retrieved 2 September 2007 from http://www.parliament.nz/en-NZ/PB/Debates/Debates/3/f/6/48HansD_20070502_00000954-Crimes-Substituted-Section-59-Amendment.htm
3. *Crimes (Substituted Section 59) Amendment Act 2007*. Retrieved 13 September 2007 from http://www. http://www.legislation.govt.nz/browse_vw.asp?content-set=pal_statutes (See appendix 3 for the full text.)
4. The term 'physical punishment' is more commonly used in New Zealand than the more internationally used term 'corporal punishment'.
5. In 1979, Sweden became the first country in the world to ban physical punishment of children.
6. *2006 Census*. Retrieved 12 September 2007 from http://www.stats.govt.nz/census
7. Ibid.
8. Salmond, A. *Two Worlds: First meetings between Māori and Europeans 1642–1772*, Viking, Auckland, 1991, p. 422.

   and: Elder, J.R. (ed.), *The Letters and Journals of Samuel Marsden*, 1932, p. 128.
9. Makereti, 'The way it used to be' in: Ihimaera, W. (ed.), *Growing up Māori*, Tandem Press, Auckland, 1998, p. 24. (Abridged from *The old time Māori* published in 1938. Makereti, also known as Maggie Papakura, was a famous guide at Rotorua.)
10. Pivac, A. *Submission from Amokura Family Violence Prevention Consortium to the Justice and Electoral Committee of Parliament*, 2006.
11. Young, A. 'Survey may force Māori Party shift on Bradford bill', *New Zealand*

Herald, 30 April 2007. Retrieved 14 November 2007 from http://www.nzherald.co.nz/topic/story.cfm?c_id=146&objectid=10436902

12. Metge, J. *New growth from old: The whānau in the modern world*, Victoria University Press, Wellington, 1995, p. 265.

13. Fanslow, J. and Robinson, E. 'Violence against women in New Zealand: Prevalence and health consequences', *New Zealand Medical Journal*, Vol. 117 No. 1206, 26 September 2004. Retrieved 24 October 2007 from http://www.nzma.org.nz/journal/117-1206/1173

14. UNICEF. *A League Table of Child Maltreatment Deaths in Rich Nations: Innocenti Report Card No. 5*, Innocenti Research Centre, Florence, 2003. Retrieved 14 November 2007 from http://www.unicef-icdc.org/publications/pdf/repcard5e.pdf

15. Connolly, M. and Doolan M. *Lives cut short: Child death by maltreatment*, Office of the Children's Commissioner, Wellington, 2007, pp. 20–22.

16. Ministry of Social Development. *Te Rito: New Zealand Family Violence Prevention Strategy*, Ministry of Social Development, Wellington, 2002. Retrieved 14 November 2007 from http://www.msd.govt.nz/publications/te-rito/

    Te Rito described a strategy for the prevention of family violence, including 18 'areas of action' ranging from mechanisms 'to promote cross-sector commitment and consistency and to monitor progress', to strategies that will 'expand and improve home, community, pre-school and school-based services and programmes'. It has been a guide to the development of violence prevention projects and programmes.

17. Ministry of Social Development. *Taskforce for Action on Violence Within the Family: The First Report*, Ministry of Social Development, Wellington, 2006. Retrieved 14 November 2007 from http://www.msd.govt.nz/documents/work-areas/sector-policy/te-rito/taskforce-report-action-on-violence.pdf

    The Taskforce Report involved 'a significant commitment by the government and non-government sectors, independent Crown entities and the judiciary to work together and provide leadership to end family violence and promote stable, healthy families'. The effectiveness of the former has not been ascertained and the public campaign associated with the latter had just commenced at the time of writing.

18. For example: Office of the Commissioner for Children. *The Report into the Death of James Whakaruru*, Office of the Commissioner for Children, Wellington, 2000.

19. Gil, D.G. *Violence Against Children: Physical Child Abuse in the United States*, Harvard University Press, Cambridge, 1970, pp.126-32.

    Crittenden, P. and Craig, S.'Developmental trends in the nature of child homicide', *Journal of Interpersonal Violence*, 5, 1990, pp. 202–16.

20. Smith, A.B., Gollop, M., Taylor, N.J. and Marshall, K. *The Discipline and Guidance of Children: A Summary of Research*, Office of the Children's Commissioner, Wellington, 2004. Retrieved 14 November 2007 from http://www.occ.org.nz/media/files/discipline_guidance

    Smith, A.B., Gollop, M., Taylor, N.J. & Marshall, K. (eds.) *The Discipline and Guidance of Children: Messages from Research*, Office of the Children's Commissioner, Wellington, 2005. Retrieved 14 November 2007 from http://www.nzfvc.org.nz/PublicationDetails.aspx?publication=12285

21. Gershoff, E.T.'Corporal punishment by parents and associated child behaviours and experiences: A meta-analytic and theoretical review', *Psychological Bulletin*, 128 (4), 2002: 439–579.

22. See *Childrenz Issues: Journal of the Children's Issues Centre*, Vol. 8, No. 2, 2004.

23. Durrant, J.'Whose Body is it Anyway? Physical Punishment, Children's Rights and Parental Responsibility', *Childrenz Issues: Journal of the Children's Issues Centre*, Vol. 8, No. 2, 2004: 23–26.

24. For example, see http://www.familyfirst.org.nz/index.cfm/Dr_Larzelere; accessed 2 September 2007.

25. For example, see http://tvnz.co.nz/view/page/411749/1024326; accessed 30 August 2007.

26. Fleming, G.'Helen Clark denies U-turn on smacking' *Herald on Sunday*, 15 March 2007. Retrieved 14 September 2007 from http://www.nzherald.co.nz/section/1/story.cfm?c_id=1&objectid=10428966

Chapter 2: **MILESTONES ALONG THE JOURNEY**

27. Salmond, A. *Two Worlds: First meetings between Māori and Europeans 1642–1772*, Viking, Auckland, 1991, p. 422.

Makereti 'The way it used to be', in: Ihimaera, W. (ed.) *Growing up Māori*, Tandem Press, Auckland, 1998, p. 24.

28. The Crimes Amendment Act 1941 abolished judicial flogging.

29 Personal communication with Marie Bell.

30. Department of Justice. *Crime in New Zealand*, Department of Justice, Wellington, 1968.

31. Retrieved 15 September 2007 from http://www.ohchr.org/english/law/ccpr.htm

32. Ritchie, J. and Ritchie, J. *Spare the Rod*, George Allen & Unwin, Sydney, 1981, p. 132.

33. Ritchie, J. and Ritchie, J. *Punishment Ideology and the Law*. Paper presented at The Rights of the Child and the Law Conference held in Christchurch, November 1979.

34. Ritchie, J. and Ritchie, J. *Spare the Rod*, Allen & Unwin, Sydney, 1981.

35. Suddens, D. 'Caveat teacher', *Broadsheet*, 92, 1981: 12.

36. Report of the Human Rights Commission on representations by the Auckland Committee on Racism and Discrimination: Children and Young Persons Homes Administered by the Department of Social Welfare, Human Rights Commission, Wellington, 1982.

37. Child care regulations were administered by the Department of Social Welfare at this time. They can now be found in sections 33(d) and 34 of the Education (Early Childhood Centres) Regulations 1998.

38. They can now be found in Regulation 20, Children, Young Persons and their Families (Residential Care) Regulations 1996.

39. For further information on the development of Office of the Children's Commissioner see: Barrington, J. *A Voice for Children. The Office of the*

Commissioner for Children 1989–2003, Dunmore Publishing, Wellington, 2004.

40. Caldwell, J.L. 'Parental Physical Punishment and the Law', *New Zealand Universities Law Review*, 13, 1989: 370–88.

41. *The United Nations Convention on the Rights of the Child*, United Nations, 1992. Retrieved 25 September 2007 from http://www.unicef.org/crc/

42. Max, L. *Children: Endangered Species*, Penguin Books, Auckland, 1990.

43. Max, L. 'The killing of Delcelia Witika and the banality of evil, Part 2', *Metro*, June 1992, pp. 108–14.

44. Hassall, I. B. 'Hitting Children', *CHILDREN: A newsletter from the Office of the Commissioner for Children*, No. 7, 1992: 8.

    Hassall, I.B. 'The Physical Punishment of Children', *CHILDREN: A newsletter from the Office of the Commissioner for Children*, No 8, 1993, pp. 2–4.

45. Maxwell, G. *Physical Punishment in the Home in New Zealand*, Office of the Commissioner for Children, Wellington, 1993.

46. Wood, B. *Hey! We don't hit anybody here*, Office of the Commissioner for Children, Wellington, 1995.

47. Ritchie, J. and Ritchie, J. *The Next Generation: Child Rearing in New Zealand*, Penguin, Auckland, 1997.

48. Ministry of Foreign Affairs and Trade. *Convention on the Rights of the Child: Presentation of the Initial Report of the Government of New Zealand*, Ministry of Foreign Affairs and Trade, Wellington, 1997.

49. [Authors unknown] *Our Children* series, *New Zealand Herald*, 14–17 June 1997.

50. Aldridge, V. 'Whipping Boy', *Dominion*, 15 November 1997, p. 20.

51. [Author unknown] 'Toddler died after bashing court hears', *Evening Post*, 8 May 2000, p. 8.

52. Ludbrook, R. and Wood, B. *Children's Rights to Safety and Physical Integrity: An examination of messages that influence attitudes about physical punishment*

of children. Paper presented at the Children's Issue Centre Conference, Otago University, Dunedin, June 1999.

53. Coddington, D.'Disciplined to Death', *North & South* magazine, February 2000.

54. CAB (00) M 32/7. (Obtained under the Official Information Act 1982.)

55. Hill, R.'Acquittal for son's beating outrages DOVE', *Hawkes Bay Today*, 24 February 2001.

56. SEQ (01) 15. (Obtained under the Official Information Act 1982.)

57. Office of the Commissioner for Children and EPOCH New Zealand. *Choose to hug, not to smack: Awhitia, Kaua e Papakitia*, Office of the Commissioner for Children, Wellington, 2003.

58. Carswell, S. *Survey on public attitudes towards the physical discipline of children*, Ministry of Justice, Wellington, 2001. Retrieved 14 November 2007 from http://www.justice.govt.nz/pubs/reports/2001/children/index.html

59. CAB (01) 645. (Obtained under the Official Information Act 1982.)

60. CAB (01) 37/5A. (Obtained under the Official Information Act 1982.)

61. Ministry of Social Development. *New Zealand's Agenda for Children*, Ministry of Social Development, Wellington, 2002. Retrieved 14 November 2007 from http://www.msd.govt.nz/publications/agenda-for-children-public-report/index.html

62. Institute of Public Policy at Auckland University of Technology, Children's Agenda and UNICEF New Zealand. *Making it Happen: implementing New Zealand's Agenda for Children*, UNICEF, Wellington, 2002.

63. CAB Min (02) 32/4B. (Obtained under the Official Information Act 1982.)

64. CAB Min (02) 32/4B. (Obtained under the Official Information Act 1982.)

65. Action for Children and Youth Aotearoa. *Children and Young People in Aotearoa New Zealand*, Action for Children and Youth Aotearoa, Auckland, 2003. Retrieved 14 November 2007 from http://www.acya.org.nz/site_resources/library/Documents/Reports_to_UN/ChildrenYouthAotearoa2003_FullReport.pdf

66. Retrieved 15 September 2007 from http://www.familyservices.govt.nz/info-for-families/skip/

67. *Maharey Notes*, Issues 88, 15 May 2003. Retrieved 31 August 2007 from http://www.beehive.govt.nz/Portfolio.aspx?PortfolioID=59&tid=3

68. Retrieved 23 October 2007 from http://www.unhchr.ch/tbs/doc.nsf/(Symbol)/CRC.C.OPAC.CO.2003.NZL.En?Opendocument

69. UNICEF. *A League Table of Child Maltreatment Deaths in Rich Nations: Innocenti Report Card No. 5*, Innocenti Research Centre, Florence, 2003. Retrieved 14 November 2007 from http://www.unicef-icdc.org/publications/pdf/repcard5e.pdf

70. Wood, B. and Davies, E. *Changing Attitudes about Physical Punishment of Children in Aotearoa: One component of primary prevention of child abuse.* Presentation made at the ISPCAN Conference in Brisbane, September 2004.

71. Institute of Public Policy at Auckland University of Technology and UNICEF New Zealand. *Protect and Treasure New Zealand's Children*, IPP at AUT and UNICEF, Wellington, 2004.

72. Retrieved 17 September 2007 from http://www.msd.govt.nz/media-information/press-releases/2004/pr-2004-05-06.html

73. Retrieved 31 August 2007 from http://www.unhchr.ch/tbs/doc.nsf/(Symbol)/CAT.C.CR.32.4.En?Opendocument

74. Smith, A.B., Gollop, M., Taylor, N.J. and Marshall, K. *The Discipline and Guidance of Children: A Summary of Research*, Office of the Children's Commissioner, Wellington, 2004. Retrieved 14 November 2007 from http://www.occ.org.nz/media/files/discipline_guidance

75. *Childrenz Issues: Journal of the Children's Issues Centre*, Vol. 8, No. 2, 2004.

76. Retrieved 31 August 2007 from http://www.hrc.co.nz/report/actionplan/0foreword.html

77. *EPOCH New Zealand Occasional Newsletter*, No. 23, July 2005. Retrieved 14 November 2007 from http://epochnz.org.nz/index.php?option=com_content&task=blogcategory&id=7&Itemid=15

See also the woman's own account of events at http://familyintegrity.blogspot.com/2007/04/riding-crop-case.html Retrieved 8 December 2007.

78. Dobbs, T. *INSIGHTS: Children & young people speak out about family discipline*, Save the Children New Zealand, Wellington, 2005.

79. Local government decisions were declarations of support and played no official part in the law-making process.

80. Millichamp, J., Martin J. and Langley J. 'On the receiving end: young adults describe their parents' use of physical punishment and other disciplinary measures during childhood', *New Zealand Medical Journal*, Vol. 119, No. 1228, 2006. Retrieved 31 August 2007 from http://www.nzma.org.nz/journal/119-1228/1818/

81. Beazley, H., Bessell, S., Ennew, J., and Waterson, R. *What Children say: Results of comparative research on the physical and emotional punishment of children in Southeast Asia and the Pacific*, Save the Children Sweden ROSEAP, Bangkok, 2005. Retrieved 20 November 2007 from http://seap.savethechildren.se/South_East_Asia/Misc/Puffs/What-Children-Say/

82. See http://www.nzfvc.org.nz/accan/papers-presentations/

83. Pritchard, R. *Children are Unbeatable: 7 very good reasons not to hit children*, Office of the Children's Commissioner and UNICEF New Zealand, Wellington, 2006.

84. Retrieved 31 August 2007 from http://www.unhchr.ch/tbs/doc.nsf/(Symbol)/CRC.C.GC.8.En?OpenDocument

85. Retrieved 31 August 2007 from http://www.epochnz.org.nz

86. Retrieved 31 August 2007 from http://www.violencestudy.org/r25

87. Retrieved 31 August 2007 from http://www.epochnz.org.nz

88. Debski, S., Buckley, S. and Russell, M. *Just who do we think children are? An analysis of submissions to the Justice and Electoral Select Committee 2006*, Health Services Research Centre, School of Government, Victoria University of Wellington, 2007, p. 13. Retrieved 3 September 2007 from http://www.victoria.ac.nz/hsrc/reports/new-reports.aspx

89. Retrieved 31 August 2007 from http://www.epochnz.org.nz

90. The process whereby a bill becomes law is explained in appendix 4.

91. *Māori Party Position on Repeal of Section 59,* press release of the Māori Party, 13 March 2007. Retrieved 31 August 2007 from http://www.scoop.co.nz/stories/PA0703/S00229.htm

92. *Bradford welcomes show of support for section 59 repeal,* press release of the Green Party, 28 March 2007. Retrieved 31 August 2007 from http://www.scoop.co.nz/stories/PA0703/S00590.htm

93. Retrieved 31 August 2007 from http://www.scoop.co.nz/PO0705/S00015.htm

94. See the Global Initiative to End all Corporal Punishment of Children website: http://www.endcorporalpunishment.org/pages/frame.html; accessed 6 November 2007.

Chapter 3: **CHILDREN'S RIGHTS**

95. *The United Nations Convention on the Rights of the Child,* United Nations, 1992. Retrieved 25 September 2007 from http://www.unicef.org/crc/

96. The Convention came into force after the first 20 countries had ratified it.

97. In signing the Convention, a state signals its intent to proceed to ratification provided the Convention is compatible with the laws and conditions of that state. In ratifying the Convention, the state gives it official sanction, i.e. it agrees to its terms. In New Zealand this does not give it the force of domestic law but it does give the Convention a formal status.

98. The 1969 Vienna Convention on the Law on Treaties can be retrieved from http://untreaty.un.org/ilc/texts/instruments/english/conventions/1_1_1969.pdf

99. Ludbrook, R.'Victims of Tokenism and Hypocrisy', *Human Rights Law and Practice,* Vol. 5, No. 2, 2 October 1999, para 1.2.

100. Committee on the Rights of the Child. *General Comment No. 8,* United Nations, 2006, p. 3. Retrieved 2 September 2007 from http://www.unhchr.ch/tbs/doc.nsf/898586b1dc7b4043c1256a450044f331/6545c032cb57bff5c12571fc002e834d/$FILE/G0740771.pdf

101. Ibid, p. 3.

102. Ibid, p. 2.

103. Ibid, p. 5.

104. CRC/C/15/Add.188, p. 9. Retrieved 6 November 2007 from http://www.unhchr.ch/tbs/doc.nsf/898586b1dc7b4043c1256a450044f331/2f2744b7e0d015d6c1256c76004b3ab7/$FILE/G0245381.pdf

105. Hassall, I. and Davies, E. *A note of caution on using the UN Convention on the Rights of the Child*, posted 2 May 2003. Retrieved 27 September 2007 from http://www.onlineopinion.com.au/view.asp?article=316

106. Belich, J. *Paradise Reforged: A History of the New Zealanders From the 1800s to the Year 2000*, Allen Lane, The Penguin Press, Auckland, 2001, p. 357.

107. Smith, C. *Royal Assent has been granted*. Retrieved 25 May 2007 from http://familyintegrity.blogspot.com/2007_05_01_archive.html

108. Wishart, I. *Eve's Bite*, Howling At The Moon Publishing, Auckland, 2007, p. 150.

109. Letter to the editor, *Press*, 10 October 2003.

110. Committee on the Rights of the Child. *General Comment No. 8*, United Nations, 2006 (see url above).

111. For recent examples of High Court decisions see: *P v K, NZLR*: 787, 2003; *L v A, FRNZ* 23: 583, 2003; *Ding v Minister of Immigration FRNZ* 25: 568, 2006. For earlier cases see: Tapp, P. *UNCROC in the Family Court*, presentation to the New Zealand Law Society Conference, 1998.

112. The Care of Children Bill was concerned with guardianship and care arrangements following the breakdown of marriages and de facto relationships.

113. *Care of Children Act 2004*, section 5(e).

114. *The United Nations Convention on the Rights of the Child*, United Nations, 1992, Article 44 (see url above).

115. New Zealand Ministry of Foreign Affairs and Trade. *Convention on the Rights of the Child. Presentation of the initial report of the Government of New Zealand.*

Information Bulletin No 2. New Zealand Ministry of Foreign Affairs and Trade, Wellington, 1997, p. 30.

116. Including CAB (00) M32/7 and CAB Min (01) 37/5A. (Obtained under the Official Information Act 1982.)

117. Ministry of Youth Affairs. *Children in New Zealand: United Nations Convention on the Rights of the Child. Second Periodic Report of New Zealand*, Ministry of Youth Affairs, Wellington, 2000.

118. *Concluding observations: New Zealand*. Office of the United Nations High Commissioner for Human Rights, 27 October 2003. Retrieved 31 August 2007 from http://www.unhchr.ch/tbs/doc.nsf/(Symbol)/CRC.C.15.Add.216.En?Opendocument

119. CAB (02) 32/4B. (Obtained under the Official Information Act 1982.)

120. Maharey, S. *Maharey Notes*, Issue 88, 6 March 2003. Retrieved 21 September 2007 from: http://www.beehive.govt.nz/ViewNewsletter.aspx?DocumentID=16846

121. *Universal Declaration of Human Rights*, United Nations, 1948. Retrieved 25 September 2007 from http://www.un.org/Overview/rights.html

122. *International Covenant on Civil and Political Rights*, United Nations, 1966. Retrieved 25 September 2007 from http://www.unhchr.ch/html/menu3/b/a_ccpr.htm

123. *Convention against Torture and Other Cruel, Inhuman or Degrading Treatment or Punishment*, United Nations, 1984. Retrieved 25 September 2007 from http://www.ohchr.org/english/law/cat.htm

124. *Conclusions and recommendations of the Committee against Torture: New Zealand*. United Nations, 2004, para 7(e). Retrieved 25 September 2007 from http://www.unhchr.ch/tbs/doc.nsf/(Symbol)CAT.C.CR.32.4.En?Opendocument

125. *Human Rights Act 1993*, section 21(1)(i).

126. *Human Rights in New Zealand Today Ngā Tika Tangata O Te Motu*, Human Rights Commission, 2004, pp. 57, 66.

127. The Human Rights Amendment Act 2001 came into force on 1 January 2002.

128. See http://www.hrc.co.nz/index.php?p=55484%20; accessed 25 September 2007.

129. See http://www.hrc.co.nz/report/actionplan/0foreword.html; accessed 25 September 2007.

130. See http://www.hrc.co.nz/report/actionplan/2children.html#saf; accessed 25 September 2007.

131. Retrieved 26 September 2007 from http://www.occ.org.nz/childcomm/about_us/the_children_s_commissioner_role

132. *Children's Commissioner Act 2003*, section 3(c). Retrieved 26 November 2007 from http://www.legislation.govt.nz/libraries/contents/om_isapi.dll?clientID=986393507&infobase=pal_statutes.nfo&jump=a2003-121&softpage=DOC

133. Ibid, section 12 (1)(c) and (d).

134. Retrieved 25 September 2007 from http://www.occ.org.nz/childcomm/resources_links/submissions

135. Tapp, P., Paterson, A. and Blaiklock, A. *The non-governmental report to the United Nations Committee on the Rights of the Child*. Action for Children in Aotearoa, Auckland, 1996, p. 62.

136. See http://www.acya.org.nz/; accessed 25 September 2007.

137. See http://www.acya.org.nz/?t=8; accessed 25 September 2007.

138. *Children and Youth in Aotearoa 2003*. Action for Children and Youth Aotearoa, Auckland, 2003. Retrieved 25 September 2007 from http://www.acya.org.nz/?t=27

139. *Whakaronga Mai: Listen Up* (video). Action for Children and Youth Aotearoa, Auckland, 2003.

140. *Report to the UN Committee Against Torture*, Action for Children and Youth Aotearoa, Auckland, 2004. Retrieved 10 October 2007 from http://www.acya.org.nz/site_resources/library/Documents/submissions/ACYAReporttoCAT_21April2004.rtf

141. *Report of the Justice and Electoral Select Committee on the Crimes (Abolition of Force as a Justification for Child Discipline) Amendment Bill.* Retrieved 25 September 2007 from http://www.parliament.nz/en-NZ/SC/Reports/c/b/b/cbb1a14c7ddf4e2bbd3154c9c4bc08f5.htm

142. *ACYA submission to the Justice and Electoral Select Committee.* Retrieved 25 September 2007 from http://www.acya.org.nz/?t=28

143. *Under 18 Delegates' Keynote Address,* Children's Forum East Asia Pacific Regional Consultation for the United Nations Study on Violence against Children. Retrieved 6 November 2007 from http://www.crin.org/violence/search/closeup.asp?infoID=5730

144. Pinheiro, P.S. *Report of the independent expert for the United Nations study on violence against children,* United Nations, 2006. Retrieved 7 November 2007 from http://violencestudy.org/IMG/pdf/English.pdf

Chapter 4: **THE LEGAL ISSUES**

145. NZPA.'Jury clears mother over "six of the best"', *New Zealand Herald,* 27 May 2007. Retrieved 28 November 2007 from http://www.nzherald.co.nz/topic/story.cfm?c_id=240&objectid=10127755

146. Kiro, C.'When discipline goes too far', *New Zealand Herald,* 22 June 2006. Retrieved 28 September 2007 from http://www.nzherald.co.nz/topic/story.cfm?c_id=124&objectid=10387699

George, G.'Woman tells of losing son in court farce', *New Zealand Herald,* 15 June 2006. Retrieved 28 September 2007 from http://www.nzherald.co.nz/section/1/story.cfm?c_id=1&objectid=10386574&pnum=0

Hughes, P.'Removal of child is always a last resort', *New Zealand Herald,* 22 June 2006. Retrieved 28 September 2007 from http://www.nzherald.co.nz/topic/story.cfm?c_id=124&objectid=10387700&pnum=0

See also the woman's own account of events at http://familyintegrity.blogspot.com/2007/04/riding-crop-case.html Retrieved 8 December 2007.

147. The term 'common law' is used to describe customary law as defined and developed by the courts.

148. Blackstone, William, *Commentaries on the Law of England*, 1786, 1 Bl Comm 440.

149. Ibid, Comm 441.

150. *In Re Agar Ellis* [1883] 24 Ch D 317, 326. Another judge in the case described a father's right to the custody and control of his children as a 'sacred right'.

151. Lord Cockburn CJ 2 F and F 202, 206.

152. *Everybody's Pocket Lawyer*, Saxon and Co, London, circa 1900.

153. *Age of Majority Act 1970.*

154. For example, *Y v Y* HC, Auckland, 27/2/98. Lucius Seneca, the Roman essayist and playwright writing in the first century AD, considered corporal punishment was only suitable for children who were incapable of reason.

155. *Gillick v West Norfolk and Wisbech Area Health Authority* [1986] AC 112; [1985] 3. All ER 402.

156. Stephen Sedley QC, in 'Child Welfare Limits Parents' Right to Punish or Restrain', *Childright Bulletin*, No. 18, 26 April 1986, argues that this decision means that parents cannot administer physical punishment to children who are capable of making their own decisions.

157. *R v Hopley* 2 F & F 202, 206; *R v Terry* [1955] VLR 114, 116.

158. Caldwell, L.J. 'Parental Physical Punishment and the Law', *New Zealand Universities Law Review*, 13: 370, 1989; *R v Haberstock* [1970] 1 CCC (2d) 433.

159. *R v Drake* [1902] NZLR 478.

160. Christchurch District Court 23/8/99.

161. 'Man who chained stepdaughter goes free', *New Zealand Herald*, 17 November 1999.

162. 'Parents not guilty of assault over bamboo stick beating', *New Zealand Herald*, 6 September 2001.

163. 'Father acquitted in pipe beating', *New Zealand Herald*, 3 November 2001.

164. 'Smacking laws stay unchanged for now', *Dominion*, 21 December 2001.

165. 'Belting OK for wild boys says jury', *New Zealand Herald*, 21 July 2002.

166. 'Smacking father discharged', *Dominion*, 23 February 2001.

167. Many cases are not reported in the sense that they are not published in any series of law reports. They are less likely to be put before the court by counsel.

168. *Hibbs v Police* HC Auckland AP205/95 26/10/95.

169. *R v Mc Farlane* CA29/01 17/5/01.

170. *Sadie v Police*, AP 50/95, 26/10/95, HC Williams J.

171. 'Man attacked son with broom handle', *New Zealand Press Association*, 9 July 2007.

172. *Crimes Act 1961*, section 2. Retrieved 27 November 2007 from http://www.legislation.govt.nz/libraries/contents/om_isapi.dll?clientID=982780185&infobase=pal_statutes.nfo&jump=a1961-043&softpage=DOC

173. The Domestic Protection Act 1982 enabled the Family Court to make a non-molestation or protection order against a parent who had been violent towards a child of the household.

174. *Domestic Violence Act 1995*, section 19(1). Retrieved 27 November 2007 from http://gpacts.knowledge-basket.co.nz/gpacts/public/text/1995/an/086.html

175. *A v A [protection order]* [1997] 17 FRNZ 13, also reported as *Ausage v Ausage* [1998] NZFLR 72.

176. *Sharma v Police* [2003] 2 NZLR 473.

177. See section 2 of the Guardianship of Infants Act 1926, section 23(1) of the Guardianship Act 1968, section 4 of the Care of Children Act 2004, and section 6 of the Children, Young Persons, and Their Families Act 1989.

178. *Care of Children Act 2004*. Retrieved 26 November 2007 from http://www.legislation.govt.nz/libraries/contents/om_isapi.dll?clientID=986394162&infobase=pal_statutes.nfo&jump=a2004-090&softpage=DOC

179. *T v T*, 9/7/99, Judge Robinson, Family Court Auckland FP004/919/90.

180. *Care of Children Act 2004*, section 14(1)(a). There are a number of other grounds described in section 14.

181. *L v A* [2003] 23 FRNZ 583, [2004] NZFLR 298.

182. *Y v Y* 27/2/98, Baragwanath J, HC Auckland 122/97.

183. *Sharma v Police* [2003] 2 NZLR 473.

184. See O'Reilly, L.'Child Abuse and the Law' in Abbott, X. (ed.), *Child Abuse Prevention in New Zealand,* Mental Health Foundation, 1983. Later editions of *Family Law Practice* and subsequent Brookers publications, Trapski's *Family Law* and *Brookers Family Law (Child Law I)* have been more openly critical of section 59.

185. Ludbrook, R., Tapp, P. and O'Reilly, L. *Family Law Practice,* Brooker and Friend, June 1982, para 12I. 01.

186. Caldwell, J. L.'Parental Physical Punishment and the Law', *NZ Universities Law Review,* Vol. 13, 1989: 370, 373.

187. See Breen, C.'The Corporal Punishment of Children: the Case for Abolition', *New Zealand Law Review,* 2002: 359; Taylor, N.'Physical Punishment of Children: International Legal Developments', *N.Z. Family Law Journal,* March 2005: 14.

188. Adhar. R. and Allan, J.'Taking Smacking Seriously: The Case for Retaining the Legality of Parental Smacking in New Zealand', *New Zealand Law Review,* 2001.

189. *Criminal Responsibility for Domestic Discipline: The Repeal or Amendment of s59 Crimes Act 1961.* The paper is signed by David R. James on behalf of the committee.

190. See Halsbury's *Laws of England* Vol. 5(3) Children and Young Persons 1 *Childhood and Legal Relationships* (para 4).

191. Youth Law Tino Rangatiratanga Taitamariki (formerly Youth Law Project) pressed for repeal of section 59 from 1988 onwards in its bulletin *Youth Law Review* and at conferences. It played a small but significant part in the move to abolish corporal punishment in schools in 1980: see YELP 1 *A Shame and a Disappointment,* which looks at the Lange Government's failure to honour its election promise to banish corporal punishment in schools.

192. 'Supernanny Busted:"Time Out" illegal under new Bill', *Investigate,* Vol. 6, Issue 65, 28 June 2006.

193. Katterns, T. 'Three smacks and he's guilty', *Dominion Post*, 22 November 2007. Retrieved 27 November 2007 from http://www.stuff.co.nz/stuff/4283366a10.html

Katterns, T. 'Smacking father had past assault conviction', *Dominion Post*, 25 November, 2007. Retrieved 27 November from http://www.stuff.co.nz/stuff/dominionpost/4285940a6000.html

194. New Zealand Police National News Release, 20 December 2007. Retrieved 5 January 2008 from http://www.police.govt.nz/news/release.html?id=3585

Chapter 5: **THE ROLE OF RELIGION**

195. A recently established Christian church with a strong Māori and Pacific following and conservative values opposed to social reforms such as repealing section 59.

196. The Civil Union Bill proposed the introduction of 'civil unions', which could be entered into by both heterosexual and homosexual couples. The bill passed into law in 2004.

197. *Religious Affiliation – 2006 Census*, Statistics New Zealand. Retrieved 15 October 2006 from http://www.stats.govt.nz/census/2006-census-data/quickstats-about-culture-identity/quickstats-about-culture-and-identity.htm?page=para012Master

198. Data downloaded 11 October 2007 from http://www.stats.govt.nz/census/2006-census-data/classification-counts/about-people/religious-affiliation.htm

See also http://www.stats.govt.nz/census/2006-census-data/quickstats-about-culture-identity/quickstats-about-culture-and-identity.htm?page=para012Master

199. The state in New Zealand is officially neutral in matters of religion and there is no state religion.

200. The three high profile pro-smacking Christian lobby groups were Family First New Zealand (see http://www.familyfirst.org.nz/), Family Integrity (see http://www.familyintegrity.org.nz/), and later the Destiny Church (see http://www.destinychurch.org.nz).

201. The Ringatu Church was founded in 1868 by the prophet Te Kooti Rikirangi, and the more influential Rātana Church was established by the visionary T. W. Rātana during the 1920s.

202. The video-stream for this interview was accessed on 5 October 2007 from http://tvnz.co.nz/view/page/425825/1037215

203. Mata'afa, M., Dever, G. and Tupou, T. *Child abuse and neglect in Pacific Island countries*, combined keynote address at the Twelfth International Congress of the International Society for the Prevention of Child Abuse and Neglect, September 1998.

204. Greven, P. *Spare the Child: The Religious Roots of Punishment and the Psychological Impact of Physical Abuse*, Vintage Books, New York, 1992, p. 6.

205. Ibid, p. 64.

206. These proverbs are often quoted in the language of the seventeenth-century King James translation.

207. Holy Bible, Authorised King James Version, Proverbs chapter 23 verses 13–14.

208. Greven, P. *Spare the Child: The Religious Roots of Punishment and the Psychological Impact of Physical Abuse*, Vintage Books, New York, 1992, p. 65.

209. Holy Bible, Authorised King James Version, Mark chapter 10 verse 14.

210. Greven, P. *Spare the Child: The Religious Roots of Punishment and the Psychological Impact of Physical Abuse*, Vintage Books, New York, 1992, p. 97.

211. *Corporal Punishment*, Joint Methodist-Presbyterian Public Questions Committee, July 1994. Retrieved 10 October 2007 from http://www.casi.org.nz/publications/cpunish.html

212. Media release from Church leaders in Auckland on 8 December 2002. Signed by Bishop Patrick Dunn (Roman Catholic Bishop of Auckland), the Reverend Douglas Lendrum (St David's Presbyterian Church), the Reverend David Pratt (Methodist Church, Auckland), the Reverend Ron O'Grady (Associated Churches of Christ), and Anglican Bishop Richard Randerson, Dean of Holy Trinity Cathedral.

213. Lindsell, S. 'Say no to smacking', *The Tablet*, May 2004.

214. In this context, 'Christian Scriptures' refers to the New Testament.

215. Cardy, G. *What does God think about hitting children?* Address to a UNICEF and IPP at AUT forum held in Auckland during November 2002.

216. Vailaau, N. *Does Biblical Theology Support Punishment of Children?*, Address to a UNICEF and IPP at AUT forum held in Wellington during November 2002.

217. Easton, P. and NZPA. 'Bishops offer muted support for smacking bill', *Dominion Post*, 27 April 2007.

218. The document is not available on the Internet but a copy is held by Beth Wood.

219. Lane, N. and Martin, K. 'Church against Church', *Dominion Post*, 2 May 2007.

220. In 2005 Graham Capill was charged with and convicted of offences involving the sexual abuse of children. His conduct was quickly condemned by the Christian Heritage Party. The Party was dissolved in 2006, its demise being blamed on Capill's disgrace. See the Wikipedia article retrieved 27 November 2007 from http://en.wikipedia.org/wiki/Graham_Capill

221. Quoted in the article: Varnham, M. 'The Christians who won't spare the Rod', *Evening Post*, 30 September 1993.

222. This became apparent when two of its members who had regularly contributed opinion pieces to *Press* newspaper lost their roles as commentators after accusations of plagiarism.

223. *Maxim Institute written submission on the Crimes (Abolition of Force as a Justification for Child Discipline) Amendment Bill.* Retrieved 10 October 2007 from http://www.maxim.org.nz/files/pdf/submission_crimesamendmentbill.pdf

224. 'School in corporal punishment stoplight', *TVNZ News*, 18 February 2007. Retrieved 9 October 2007 from http://tvnz.co.nz/view/page/411749/994345.

225. Trevett, C. 'Parents asked to OK school's use of strap', *New Zealand Herald*, 23 August 2006. Retrieved 15 October 2007 from http://www.nzherald.co.nz/section/1/story.cfm?c_id=1&objectid=10397624

226. Letter from the Ministry of Education (National Operations, Christchurch) to the Commissioner for Children, dated 3 March 1998.

227. Crewdson, P. 'School refuses to deny smacking', *Dominion Post*, 13 February 2007, p. A4.

228. Collins, S. 'Schools show how to smack', *New Zealand Herald*, 25 August 2005. Retrieved 9 October 2007 from http://www.nzherald.co.nz/section/1/story.cfm?c_id=1&objectid=10342325

229. Scoop is an online, independent repository of New Zealand news. It publishes all media releases in full without any editorial comment. See http://www.scoop.co.nz

230. *Organisations Opposing 'Anti-*Smacking' *Bill*, Family First press release, 28 March 2007. Retrieved 10 October 2007 from http://www.scoop.co.nz/stories/PO0703/S00358.htm

231 Smith, C. *The Christian Foundations of the Institution of Corporal Correction*, Family Integrity, 2005. Retrieved 11 October 2007 from http://www.familyintegrity.org.nz/

232. Houlahan, M. 'Church leaders turn up the heat on smacking bill', *New Zealand Herald*, 2 May 2007. Retrieved 10 October 2007 from http://www.nzherald.co.nz/section/1/story.cfm?c_id=1&objectid=10437294&pnum=0

233. Family Integrity, the most vocal lobby group of them all, only ever had one spokesperson, Craig Smith; Family First's spokesperson was invariably Bob McCoskrie; and Brain Tamaki was usually the only member of the Destiny Church who fronted up. Other commentators included the media personality Simon Barnett (a member of the Grace Vineyard Church, see http://www.grace.org.nz) and Christine Rankin, chief executive of Light One Life/For the Sake of our Children Trust which has links to Family First (see http://www.lightonelife.org.nz).

234. See: *Barnett says smacking bill 'home invasion'*, ChristianNews, no date given. Retrieved 10 October 2007 from http://christiannews.co.nz/?s=Barnett and 'Campaign against smacking bill hots up', *TVNZ One News*, 20 February 2007. Retrieved 29 August 2007 from http://www.tvnz.co.nz/view/page/423466/996860

235. Debski, S., Buckley, S. and Russell, M. *Just who do we think children are? An analysis of submissions to the Justice and Electoral Select Committee 2006*, Health Services Research Centre, School of Government, Victoria University of Wellington, 2007, p. 14. Retrieved 3 September 2007 from http://www.victoria.ac.nz/hsrc/reports/new-reports.aspx

236. See, for example, the article: Smith, A.B. 'What do Children Learn from being Smacked? Messages from Social Science Theory and Research', *Childrenz Issues Journal of the Children's Issues Centre*, Vol. 8, No. 2, 2004: 7–15.

237. A list of organisations opposed to the Bill was published later in a 2007 media release. (See: *Organisations Opposing 'Anti-Smacking' Bill*, Family First Press Release, 28 March 2007. Retrieved 15 October 2007 from http://www.scoop.co.nz/stories/PO0703/S00358.htm.) Only 47 organisations were named at this stage, with some of them being branches of the same organisation.

238. *Swedish Lawyer being brought to NZ by Coalition*, Family First Lobby press release, 12 June 2006. Retrieved 29 September 2007 from http://www.scoop.co.nz/stories/PO0606/S00105.htm

239. *Ruby Harrold-Claesson's oral submission to the section 59 of the Crimes Act Select Committee in Hamilton 27 July 2006*. Retrieved 11 October 2007 from http://familyintegrity.blogspot.com/2007/03/ruby-harrold-claessons-oral-submission.html

240. *Swedish Lawyer being brought to NZ by Coalition*, Family First Lobby press release, 12 June 2006. Retrieved 29 September 2007 from http://www.scoop.co.nz/stories/PO0606/S00105.htm

241. The collective response of Swedish academics can be downloaded from http://www.epochnz.org.nz/images/sweden_letter.pdf

242. For example, figures purporting to show high child mortality in Sweden in fact showed the mortality rate to be about half that of New Zealand. Numbers of children 'in care' in New Zealand and Sweden were not comparable because the Swedish figure included those in the youth justice system and those children whose families remained intact, although under supervision.

243. Larzelere, R.E. *Sweden's Smacking Ban: More Harm than Good*. Families First and the Christian Institute, 2004. Retrieved 10 October 2007 from http://www.christian.org.uk/pdfpublications/sweden_smacking.pdf

244. Durrant, J.E. *Law Reform and Corporal Punishment in Sweden: Response to Robert Larzelere, The Christian Institute and Families First.* Department of Family Social Sciences, University of Manitoba, 2005. Retrieved 10 October 2007 from http://umanitoba.ca/faculties/human_ecology/family/Staff/pdf_files/Durrant Response to Larzelere, the Christian Institute and Families First.pdf

245. Dobbs, T. *INSIGHTS: Children & young people speak out about family discipline,* Save the Children New Zealand, Wellington, 2005.

Chapter 6: **ADVOCATES FOR CHANGE**

246. Ritchie, J. and Ritchie, J. *Child rearing patterns in New Zealand,* A.H. & A.W. Reed, Dunedin, 1970.

247. Ritchie, J. and Ritchie, J. *Growing up in New Zealand,* George Allen & Unwin, Sydney, 1997.

248. Ibid, p. 132.

249. Ludbrook, R. and Wood, B. *Children's rights to safety and physical integrity: An examination of messages that influence attitudes about physical punishment of children.* Paper presented at the Children's Issues Centre Third Child and Family Policy conference, Dunedin, New Zealand, July 1999.

250. Personal communication from Rae Julian.

251. During the Committee of the Whole House stage, amendments to a bill can be proposed. Usually these changes are published before the debate in a Supplementary Order Paper (SOP).

252. Hassall, I.'New Zealand: A commissioner for children', in Flekkoy, M. (ed.) *Models for monitoring the protection of children's rights.* Florence: Innocenti Research Centre, 1990, p. 18.

253. Blaiklock, A., Kiro, C., Belgrave, M., Low, W., Davenport, E., and Hassall, I. *When the invisible hand rocks the cradle: New Zealand children in a time of change,* Innocenti Working Paper No. 93, UNICEF Innocenti Research Centre, Florence, 2002. Retrieved 3 October 2007 from http://www.unicef-icdc.org/publications/pdf/iwp93.pdf

254. Bryder, L. *A voice for mothers: The Plunket Society and infant welfare 1907–2000*, Auckland University Press, Auckland, 2003, p. 231.

255. UNICEF New Zealand and Institute of Public Policy at Auckland University of Technology. *Protect and Treasure New Zealand's Children*, UNICEF and IPP at AUT, Wellington, 2004.

256. Barrington, J. *A voice for children. The Office of the Children's Commissioner in New Zealand 1989–2003*, Dunmore Press, Wellington, 2004, p. 15.

257. *Children's Commissioner Act 2003*, section 3(c). Accessible from http://www.legislation.govt.nz/browse_vw.asp?content-set=pal_statutes

258. *Children's Commissioner should stay out of politics and stick to her day job*, press release from the National Party, 15 March 2007. Retrieved 10 October 2007 from http://www.judithcollins.co.nz/pressreleasedetail2007.asp?Ref=ChildrenCommissionershouldstayoutof &month=March&Year=2007

259. See http://www.epochnz.org.nz/

260. Debski, S., Buckley, S. and Russell, M. *Just who do we think children are? An analysis of submissions to the Justice and Electoral Select Committee 2006*, Health Services Research Centre, School of Government, Victoria University of Wellington, 2007, p. 14. Retrieved 3 September 2007 from http://www.victoria.ac.nz/hsrc/reports/new-reports.aspx

261. UNICEF also gave generously of Beth Wood's time in her role as Advocacy Manager.

262. Address delivered by the then Governor General, Dame Sylvia Cartwright, to the national conference of Save the Children, New Zealand, held in June 2003.

263. 'Children's advocates take heart at anti-smacking speech', *New Zealand Herald*, 17 June 2002. Retrieved 27 November 2007 from http://www.nzherald.co.nz/section/1/story.cfm?c_id=1&objectid=2047094

264. Dobbs, T. *INSIGHTS: Children & young people speak out about family discipline*, Save the Children, Wellington, 2005.

265. Ibid, p. 9.

266. Ritchie, J. and Ritchie, J. *Child rearing patterns in New Zealand*, A.H. & A.W. Reed, Wellington, 1970.

267. UNICEF New Zealand and Institute of Public Policy at Auckland University of Technology. *Protect and Treasure New Zealand's Children*, UNICEF and IPP at AUT, Wellington, 2004.

268. Edridge, M. 'No place for violence in the home', *Dominion Post*, 3 April 2007, p. B5.

269. See http://www.endcorporalpunishment.org

270. See http://www.childrenareunbeatable.org.uk/

271. Retrieved 4 October 2007 from http://www.hrc.co.nz/home/hrc/newsandissues/repealofsection59.php

272. Retrieved April 2006 from http://www.cyf.govt.nz/484.htm

273. *New Zealand Public Service Code of Conduct*, State Services Commission, 2005, p. 11. Retrieved 2 October 2007 from http://www.ssc.govt.nz/display/document.asp?docid=5208

274. See the Justice and Electoral Select Committee's report back to the House on Sue Bradford's Bill. Accessed 15 November 2007 from http://www.parliament.nz/NR/rdonlyres/65FA800D-9CFB-4016-A0EC-854DF1CFD4F3/48376/DBSCH_SCR_3587_4051.pdf

275. *Education Act 1989*, section 162(a)(v). Accessible from http://www.legislation.govt.nz/browse_vw.asp?content-set=pal_statutes

276. Taylor, N. 'Physical Punishment of children; international legal developments', *Family Law Journal* Vol. 5, Part I, March 2005: 14–22.

277. Davies, E. 'Smacking bill in need of more clarity', *New Zealand Herald*, 23 November 2006, p. A17.

278. Chamberlain, J. 'Our shame', *North & South* magazine, May 2006, p. 55.

279. Breen, C. 'The Corporal Punishment of Children in New Zealand: the Case for Abolition', *New Zealand Law Review*, (3), 2002: 359–91.

280. Sourced from http://news.bbc.co.uk/nolpda/ukfs_news/hi/newsid_6661000/6661823.stm?4d

281. 'Ngongotaha Working To Be NZ's First Smack Free Zone', *Family and community services NEWS*, Ministry of Social Development, April 2004.

282. Data retrieved 4 October 2007 from http://www.stats.govt.nz/census/2006-census-data/quickstats-about-culture-identity/quickstats-about-culture-and-identity.htm?page=para002Master

283. Pereira, T.'A Pacific Perspective on Physical Punishment', *Childrenz Issues*, Vol 8, No 2, 2004: pp. 27–29.

284. *Physical Punishment of Children Not Culturally Mandated*, Amokura – Family Violence Prevention Consortium Press Release – Repeal of s59, 8 June 2006.

285. Chapple, I.'Turia support for Bradford bill waivers: Māori and Pacific Islanders will be targeted', *Sunday Star Times*, 11 March, 2007, p. A5.

286. *Crime to Sentence: Trends in Criminal Justice, 1986–1996*, Chapter 3 Court Prosecutions, Ministry of Justice, 1998. Retrieved 8 October 2007 from http://www.courts.govt.nz/pubs/reports/1998/crime_sentence_86_96/chapter_3_1.html

287. *Anglican Māori support repeal of section 59*, press release Māori Anglican Church, 1 May 2007. Retrieved 2 September 2007 from http://www.scoop.co.nz/stories/PO0705/S00014.htm

288. A number of these submissions can be viewed on the EPOCH New Zealand website. See http://epochnz.org.nz/index.php?option=com_content&task=view&id=92&Itemid=22; accessed 18 November 2007.

     Save the Children's submission can found at http://www.savethechildren.net/new_zealand/newsroom/main.html

289. Smith, A.B., Gollop, M., Taylor, N.J. and Marshall, K. *The Discipline and Guidance of Children: Messages from Research*, Office of the Children's Commissioner, Wellington, 2005. Retrieved 14 November 2007 from http://www.nzfvc.org.nz/PublicationDetails.aspx?publication=12285

290. The briefing sheets can be viewed at http://epochnz.org.nz/index.php?option=com_content&task=view&id=92&Itemid=22

291. The media kit can be downloaded from http://www.everychildcounts.org.nz/docs/Section59MediaKitApril07.pdf

Chapter 7: **PUBLIC ATTITUDES**

292. Ritchie, J. and Ritchie, J. *Child rearing patterns in New Zealand*, A.H. & A.W. Reed, Wellington, 1970, p. 157.

293. Ibid, p. 157.

294. Ibid, p. 112.

295. Ritchie, J. *Boys will be boys; New Zealanders' approval of violence.* A paper presented at the Women's Studies Association Conference, Wellington, 1981.

296. Maxwell, G. *Physical punishment in the home in New Zealand*, Office of the Commissioner for Children, Wellington, 1993, p. 9.

297. Ibid, p. 9.

298. Cheng, D. 'MPs cheered as passions paraded', *New Zealand Herald*, 15 March 2007, p. A5. Retrieved 17 November 2007 from http://www.nzherald.co.nz/topic/story.cfm?c_id=146&objectid=10428888&pnum=0

299. The *Hansard* record was retrieved 20 September 2007 from http://www.parliament.nz/en-NZ/PB/Debates/Debates/3/d/e/48HansD_20070314_0001195-Crimes-Substituted-Section-59-Amendment.htm

300. Ritchie, J. and Ritchie, J. *Spare the Rod*, George Allen & Unwin, Sydney, 1981.

301. Ibid, p. 4.

302. Ibid, p. 10.

303. Mansfield, K. *The collected stories of Katherine Mansfield*, Ware Wordsworth Editions, Herts, England, 2006.

304. Hulme, K. *The Bone People*, Spiral, Wellington, 1983.

305. Duff, A. *Once Were Warriors*, Tandem Press, Auckland, 1990.

306. Crump, C. *In endless fear: A true story*, Penguin, Auckland, 2002.

307. Hubbard, H. 'Sir Ed Hillary: The man mountain', *Sunday Star-Times*, 6 April 2002, p. C4.

308. A birth cohort study involves selecting all of the people born during a particular period or year in a particular location.

309. Millichamp, J., Martin, J. and Langley, J.'On the receiving end: young adults describe their parents' use of physical punishment and other disciplinary measures during childhood', *New Zealand Medical Journal* 119, 2006: 1228. Retrieved 17 November 2007 from http://www.nzma.org.nz/journal/119-1228/1818/

310. Fergusson, D. and Lynskey, M.'Physical punishment/maltreatment during childhood and adjustment in young adulthood', *Child Abuse and Neglect* 21, 1997: 617–30. Figures have been rounded to the nearest whole percent.

311. Ritchie, J. and Ritchie, J. *Spare the Rod*, George Allen and Unwin, Sydney, 1981, p. 31.

312. [Author unknown].'The great celebrity smacking debate', *New Zealand Woman's Weekly*, 30 September 1996, pp. 8–9.

313. *Tots to Teens* is a free magazine for parents with children aged 0–12 years old. It is distributed through retailers, libraries, family venues as well as Plunket, schools and childcare facilities. It has a national circulation of 130,000 per issue, with regional editions in Auckland, Wellington and Christchurch.

314. *What do parents think?*, Littlies Lobby, 26 July, 2005. Retrieved 21 June 2007, from http://www.littlieslobby.org.nz/documents/Research_Results_Guiding_Children_To_Behave_Well.pdf

315. Collins, S.'Smackers in retreat: Survey', *New Zealand Herald*, 30 March 2005, p. A5. Retrieved 17 November 2007 from http://www.nzherald.co.nz/topic/story.cfm?c_id=146&objectid=10117744

316. Dobbs, T. *INSIGHTS: Children & young people speak out about family discipline*, Save the Children New Zealand, Wellington, 2005, p. 42.

317. Ibid, pp. 9–10.

318. Ibid, p. 44.

319. Ibid, pp. 43 and 46.

320. [Author unknown].'Does sparing the rod spoil the child?', *New Zealand Listener*, 14–20 January 1995, p. 13.

321. Carswell, S. *Survey on public attitudes towards the physical discipline of children,*

Ministry of Justice, Wellington, 2001. Retrieved 17 November 2007 from http://www.justice.govt.nz/pubs/reports/2001/children/index.html

322. Kiro, C. *Public opinion regarding ending of Section 59 of the Crimes Act*, Office of the Children's Commissioner, Wellington, 2006.

323. Cordemans, D. 'Most Kiwis Against Smacking', *The Epoch Times*, 21 February 2006. Retrieved 22 September 2007 from http://en.epochtimes.com/news/6-2-21/38513.html

324. Thomson, A. and Macbrane, R. 'Smacking law – voters say leave it alone', *New Zealand Herald*, 2 July 2005. Retrieved 22 September 2007 from http://www.nzherald.co.nz/section/1/story.cfm?c_id=1&objectid=10333802

325. [Author unknown]. *Anti-Smacking Bill*, Colmar Brunton, 25 March 2007. Pdf file downloaded 21 September 2007.

326. Kiro, C. *Public opinion regarding ending of Section 59 of the Crimes Act*, Office of the Children's Commissioner, Wellington, 2006.

327. Misa, T. 'Pacific people take up anti-smacking message', *New Zealand Herald*, 5 December 2007. Retrieved 6 December 2007 from http://www.nzherald.co.nz/topic/story.cfm?c_id=146&objectid=10480300&pnum=0

328. NZPA. 'Jury clears mother over "six of the best"', *New Zealand Herald*, 27 May 2007. Retrieved 28 November 2007 from http://www.nzherald.co.nz/topic/story.cfm?c_id=240&objectid=10127755

329. A fundamentalist Christian church. See the interview with the Exclusive Brethren member Neville Simmons. Video stream accessible from http://www.abc.net.au/4corners/special_eds/20071015/brethren/default.htm

330. For a more extensive discussion of the issues, see the book: Hager, N. *The Hollow Men: A study in the politics of deception*, Craig Potton Publishing, Nelson, 2006, pp. 18–39.

331. Buntain-Ricklefs, J., Kemper, K, Bell, M. and Babonis, T. 'Punishments: What predicts adult approval', *Child Abuse and Neglect* 18, 1994: 945–55.

332. Winnicott, D. *The maturational process and the facilitative environment*, International Universities Press, New York, 1965.

333. *Report of the Justice and Electoral Select Committee on the Crimes (Abolition of*

Force as a Justification for Child Discipline) Amendment Bill, p. 6. Retrieved 17 November 2007 from http://www.parliament.nz/NR/rdonlyres/65FA800D-9CFB-4016-A0EC-854DF1CFD4F3/48376/DBSCH_SCR_3587_4051.pdf

334. *Police Practice Guide for new Section 59*, New Zealand Police, 19 June 2007. Retrieved 23 September 2007 from http://www.police.govt.nz/news/release/3149.html

335. Young, A. 'Mixed views on who did most to help smacking bill', *New Zealand Herald*, 28 May 2007. Retrieved 22 September 2007 from http://www.nzherald.co.nz/section/1/story.cfm?c_id=1&objectid=10442145

336. Rogers, E. *Diffusion of innovations*, 5th edition, Free Press, New York, 2003.

Chapter 8: **THE ROLE OF THE MEDIA**

337. Tourelle, G, ' Hundreds protest anti-smacking bill', *New Zealand Herald*, 28 March 2007. Retrieved 24 October from http://www.nzherald.co.nz/topic/story.cfm?c_id=146&objectid=10431333

338. Coddington, D. 'Bradford's law will save our children', *New Zealand Herald*, 18 March 2007. Retrieved 17 November 2007 from http://www.nzherald.co.nz/topic/story.cfm?c_id=124&objectid=10429339

339. See, for example, Decision No. 2006–058 of the Broadcasting Standards Authority regarding the complaint brought by the Department of Child, Youth and Family Services against Television New Zealand. Retrieved 10 October 2007 from http://www.bsa.govt.nz/decisions/2006/2006-058.htm

340. A typical anti-repeal blog could be viewed at http://section59.blogspot.com/; accessed 10 October 2007.

341. See:

radio code of broadcasting practice, Broadcasting Standards Authority, 2006. Retrieved 5 October 2007 from http://www.bsa.govt.nz/codesstandards-radio.php

free to air television code of broadcasting practice, Broadcasting Standards Authority, 2006. Retrieved 5 October 2007 from http://www.bsa.govt.nz/codesstandards-freetv.php

New Zealand Press Council Principles, New Zealand Press Council. Retrieved 5 October 2007 from http://www.presscouncil.org.nz/principles_2.html

342. See: Vincent, R., Westaway, J. and Parker, C. 'Memories of smacks and "psychological warfare"', *New Zealand Woman's Weekly,* 7 September 1987, pp. 26–28; Neustatter, A. 'Is smacking children wrong?', *New Zealand Woman's Weekly,* 4 April 1988, pp. 56–57; and Woodfield, S. 'The great celebrity smacking debate', *New Zealand Woman's Weekly,* 30 September 1996, pp. 8–9.

343. Suddens, D. 'Caveat teacher', *Broadsheet* 92, 1981: 12.

344. Ritchie, J. and Ritchie, J. *Spare the Rod,* George Allen & Unwin, Sydney, 1981, p. 132.

345. Welch, D. 'Force of habit', *New Zealand Listener,* 13 November 1993, pp. 16–20.

346. UNICEF. *A league table of child maltreatment deaths in rich nations. Innocenti Report Card Issue No. 5,* Innocenti Research Centre, Florence, 2003. Retrieved 10 October 2007 from http://www.unicef-irc.org/cgi-bin/unicef/download_insert.sql?ProductID=353

347. Editor. 'Kids no longer safe in Godzone', *Sunday Star-Times,* 21 September 2003, p. C8.

348. For example: Coddington, D. 'Disciplined to Death', *North & South* magazine, February 2000.

349. Editor. 'We must never have another Teresa', *Dominion Post,* 10 October 2002, p. B4.

350. Editor. 'Cycle of abuse must stop', *New Zealand Herald,* 10 October 2002. Retrieved 8 October 2007 from http://www.nzherald.co.nz/topic/story.cfm?c_id=146&objectid=2998372

351. Editor. 'Spare the rod', *Press,* 15 October 2002, p. A8.

352. UNICEF. *A league table of child maltreatment deaths in rich nations. Innocenti Report Card Issue No. 5,* Innocenti Research Centre, Florence, 2003 (see above url).

353. *Concluding observations: New Zealand,* United Nations Committee on the

Rights of the Child. Retrieved 10 October 2007 from http://www.unhchr.ch/tbs/doc.nsf/(Symbol)/CRC.C.15.Add.216.En?Opendocument

354. Letter to the Editor, *Press*, 17 October 2003.

355. Letter to the Editor, *Press*, 17 October 2003.

356. Small, V. 'Smacking bill a focus for disaffection', *Dominion Post*, 29 March 2007.

357. For example: 'Anti-smacking bill passes first hurdle', *One News TVNZ*, 28 July 2005. Retrieved on 10 October 2007 from http://tvnz.co.nz/view/page/423465/600339 and 'Child smacking bill on election agenda', *New Zealand Herald*, 10 June 2005. Retrieved 10 October 2007 from http://www.nzherald.co.nz/section/1/story.cfm?c_id=1&objectid=10329981

358. de Bueger, J. 'Why you just can't beat a good caning', *Otago Daily Times*, 30 May 2005.

359. Ansley, B. 'Hands off', *New Zealand Listener*, 6 August 2005, p. 22.

360. Kay, M. 'Smacking bill's time out', *Dominion Post*, 15 March 2007.

361. McMillan, N. 'Reasonable force or unreasonable Bradford?', *Greymouth Star*, 4 April 2007, p. 4.

362. Editor. 'Bill will not take the heat out of smacking', *New Zealand Herald*, 13 June 2005. Retrieved 9 October 2007 from http://www.nzherald.co.nz/topic/story.cfm?c_id=146&objectid=10330329

363. *free to air television code of broadcasting practice*, Broadcasting Standards Authority, 2006, p. 5 (see above url).

364. *The TVNZ Charter*, TVNZ. Retrieved 10 October 2007 from http://tvnz.co.nz/view/page/816462/823782'

365. The video-stream for this interview was accessed on 5 October 2007 from http://tvnz.co.nz/view/page/425825/1037215

366. *free to air television code of broadcasting practice*, Broadcasting Standards Authority, 2006, p. 5 (see above url).

367. *New Zealand Press Council Principles*, New Zealand Press Council (see above url).

368. The three highest profile pro-smacking lobby groups were Family First New Zealand (see its website at http://www.familyfirst.org.nz/), Family Integrity (see its website at http://www.familyintegrity.org.nz/) and later the Destiny Church (see its website at http://www.destinychurch.org.nz).

369. See the data from the NZ Audit Bureau of Circulations. Sourced 8 October 2007 from http://www.abc.org.nz/audit/press.html

370. Editor. 'Good parents don't hit their children', *Dominion Post*, 19 July 2005.

371. Editor. 'Time for honesty over smacking', *Dominion Post*, 1 May 2007.

372. Editor. 'Ban on smacking is too hard hitting', *New Zealand Herald*, 10 May 2001. Retrieved 10 October 2007 from http://www.nzherald.co.nz/section/1/story.cfm?c_id=1&objectid=187949

373. Editor. 'Law rewrite to protect young', *New Zealand Herald*, 24 September 2003. Retrieved 10 October 2007 from http://www.nzherald.co.nz/topic/story.cfm?c_id=146&objectid=3525025

374. Editor. 'Bill will not take the heat out of smacking', *New Zealand Herald*, 13 June 2005. Retrieved 10 October 2007 from http://www.nzherald.co.nz/topic/story.cfm?c_id=146&objectid=10330329

375. Editor. 'Attitude not law needs to change', *New Zealand Herald*, 23 November 2006. Retrieved 10 October 2007 from http://www.nzherald.co.nz/topic/story.cfm?c_id=146&objectid=10411975&pnum=0

376. Editor. 'Democracy will survive the smacks', *New Zealand Herald*, 2 April 2007. Retrieved 10 October 2007 from http://www.nzherald.co.nz/section/1/story.cfm?c_id=1&objectid=10432027&pnum=0

377. Editor. 'Smacking bill unity all too rare', *New Zealand Herald*, 3 May 2007. Retrieved 10 October 2007 from http://www.nzherald.co.nz/topic/story.cfm?c_id=146&objectid=10437442&pnum=0

378. Regular commentators opposed to repeal included: Garth George and Jim Hopkins (*New Zealand Herald*), Richard Long (*Dominion Post*), Karl Du Fresne (*Press*), Michael Laws and Chris Trotter (*Sunday Star-Times*). Those who supported repeal included: Case Avery, Tapu Misa, Paul Thomas and John Roughan (*New Zealand Herald*), Finlay Macdonald and Raybon Kan (*Sunday Star-Times*), and Deborah Coddington (*Herald on Sunday*).

379. Misa, T. 'Smacking law change can lead to attitude change', *New Zealand Herald*, 2 November 2005. Retrieved 9 October 2007 from http://www.nzherald.co.nz/topic/story.cfm?c_id=146&objectid=10356489

380. Editor. 'Good parents don't hit their children', *Dominion Post*, 29 July 2005.

381. Editor. 'Ban the rod', *Press*, 14 March 2007.

382. George, G. 'Here's a revised declaration of the rights of the child', *New Zealand Herald*, 5 August 2004. Retrieved 10 October from http://www.nzherald.co.nz/section/1/story.cfm?c_id=1&objectid=3582230

383. Read, C. *From Innocents to Agents – children and children's rights in New Zealand*, Maxim Institute, 2006, quoted in George, G. 'Childhood under threat', *New Zealand Herald*, 7 December 2006. Retrieved 10 October 2007 from http://www.nzherald.co.nz/topic/story.cfm?c_id=500818&objectid=10414150&pnum=0

384. Editor. 'Time to stand firm', *Press*, 3 April 2007.

385. Positive parenting involves responding to children's strengths and desirable behaviours with praise and warmth rather than responding to negative behaviour with criticism and punishment. See the SKIP positive parenting resources at http://www.familyservices.govt.nz/info-for-families/skip/managing-behaviour.html

     See also the book: Durrant, J. E. *Positive Discipline: What is it and how do we do it?* Save the Children Southeast Asia and the Pacific, 2007. The pdf file of the book can be retrieved from http://seap.savethechildren.se/upload/scs/SEAP/publication/publication%20pdf/violence/Positive%20Discipline%20Report%2023Aug07.pdf

386. Avery, C. 'Legislation only way to stop parents hitting kids', *New Zealand Herald*, 9 December 2002. Retrieved 10 October 2007 from http://www.nzherald.co.nz/topic/story.cfm?c_id=146&objectid=3008360

387. Cromer, R. 'Fearful of Bradford's bill', *Timaru Herald*, 3 March 2007.

388. Editor. 'Clark's team should ditch their caution', *New Zealand Herald*, 18 February 2006. Retrieved 16 November 2007 from http://www.nzherald.co.nz/section/1/story.cfm?c_id=1&objectid=10368916

389. Katterns, T. 'Three smacks and he's "guilty"', *Dominion Post*, 22 November 2007. Retrieved 27 November 2007 from http://www.stuff.co.nz/stuff/4283366a10.html

Katterns, T. 'Smacking father had past assault conviction', *Dominion Post*, 25 November, 2007. Retrieved 27 November from http://www.stuff.co.nz/stuff/dominionpost/4285940a6000.html

390. Ibid.

391. Editor. 'Smacking law is working and critics need to accept the fact', *Herald on Sunday*, 25 November 2007. Retrieved 27 November 2007 from http://www.nzherald.co.nz/section/1/story.cfm?c_id=1&objectid=10478159

Editor. 'Hitting back, *The Press*, 27 November 2007. Retrieved 27 November 2007 from http://www.stuff.co.nz/thepress/4288708a24077.html

392. *Media Kit on the Crimes (Substituted Section 59) Amendment Bill*. Retrieved 20 September 2007 from http://www.everychildcounts.org.nz/docs/Section59MediaKitApril07.pdf

393. See http://www.scoop.co.nz/news/politics.html Accessed 8 October 2007.

394. Opinion pieces were contributed by John Bowis (SCNZ), Murray Edridge (Barnardos), Cindy Kiro (OCC), Ian Hassall and Emma Davies (IPP at AUT), and Beth Wood (UNICEF).

395. For example, the advertisement '300,000 signatures to make them listen', *New Zealand Herald*, 27 March 2007, p. A13.

396. A 'citizens initiated referendum' is a non-binding referendum held under the Citizens Initiated Referenda Act 1993. A petition signed by at least 10% of all registered electors is required to trigger the referendum.

397. See the advertisement 'Parents, don't accept the anti-smacking bill', *New Zealand Herald*, 16 May 2007, p. 21.

398. Information retrieved 27 November 2007 from http://www.familyfirst.org.nz/index.cfm/cases.html

Chapter 9: **THE POLITICAL SPHERE**

399. In New Zealand, individual MPs can place bills in a ballot that gets drawn from time to time. Such bills were called Member's Bills.
400. Personal communication with Dianne Yates.
401. EPOCH New Zealand. *Occasional Newsletter*, No. 7, November 1999.
402. Masters, C. 'Capill to fight for parents' right to smack', *New Zealand Herald*, 28 January 1997.
403. Letter from Roger Sowry to Mandy Gill, Convenor of EPOCH New Zealand, dated 15 November 1999.
404. EPOCH New Zealand. *Occasional Newsletter*, No. 4, December 1998.
405. [Author unknown]. 'Nats would allow children to be hit', *Dominion Post*, 11 September 2001.
406. CAB Min (01) 32/7. (Obtained under the Official Information Act 1982.)
407. SEQ (01) 15, p. 6. (Obtained under the Official Information Act 1982.)
408. Letter from Phil Goff to Beth Wood, dated 19 May 2000.
409. Letter from Phil Goff to Jane Ritchie, dated 4 April 2000.
410. SEQ (01) 15. (Obtained under the Official Information Act 1982.)
411. POL (02) 187. (Obtained under the Official Information Act 1982.)
412. CAB Min (02) 32/4B. (Obtained under the Official Information Act 1982.)
413. New Zealand First press release, 22 August 2000.
414. Rilkoff, M. *Alliance Opposes Smacking*, Alliance Party press release, 15 February 2001.
415. Letter from Sue Bradford to EPOCH, dated 4 October 2001.
416. Carswell, S. *Survey on public attitudes towards the physical discipline of children*, Ministry of Justice, Wellington, 2001. Retrieved 14 November 2007 from http://www.justice.govt.nz/pubs/reports/2001/children/index.html
417. Wycherley, G. 'Government puts off move to outlaw smacking', *New Zealand Herald*, 1 December 2001. Retrieved 14 November 2007 from http://www.nzherald.co.nz/section/1/story.cfm?c_id=1&objectid=383556

418. *Likely Effects of Repealing Section 59 of the Crimes Act.* An address by ACT MP Stephen Franks to a Barnardos forum in October 2001.

419. Berry, R. 'Minister defends Right to Smack', *Dominion Post*, 11 October 2002.

420. [Author unknown]. *Smacking: Section 59 and Children*, New Zealand Government press release, 4 December 2002.

421. [Author unknown]. 'Smacking ban still a live issue for Cabinet', *Dominion Post*, 12 December 2002.

422. Maharey, S. *Maharey Notes*, Issue 88, 6 March 2003. Retrieved 21 September 2007 from: http://www.beehive.govt.nz/ViewNewsletter.aspx?DocumentID=16846

423. Letter from Phil Goff to Beth Wood, dated 23 February 2005.

424. Letter from Phil Goff to George Hook, dated 11 June 2005.

425. [Author unknown]. *Greens draw-up their own anti-smacking bill*, Green Party media release, 6 October 2003.

426. The Bill's title was unfortunately nonsensical. It should have read *Crimes (Abolition of Child Discipline as a Justification for Force) Amendment Bill.*

427. Retrieved 18 September 2007 from http://www.parliament.nz/en-NZ/PB/Legislation/Bills/b/2/4/b24fba96f2224b1985bc254efac71c63.htm

428. The *Hansard* record of this debate was retrieved 18 September 2007 from http://www.parliament.nz/en-NZ/PB/Debates/Debates b/1/6/47Hans_20050727_00001406-Crimes-Abolition-of-Force-as-a-Justification.htm

429. Ibid.

430. Ibid.

431. Debski, S., Buckley, S. and Russell, M. *Just who do we think children are? An analysis of submissions to the Justice and Electoral Select Committee 2006*, Health Services Research Centre, School of Government, Victoria University of Wellington, 2007, p. 14. Retrieved 3 September 2007 from http://www.victoria.ac.nz/hsrc/reports/downloads/children_23_April.pdf

432. The *Hansard* record of this debate was retrieved 3 September 2007

from http://www.hansard.parliament.govt.nz/hansard/Final/FINAL_2007_02_21.htm

433. Māori electorates are a special type of electorate that voters of Māori descent can choose to vote in. Currently there are seven Māori electorates, which encompass large areas of the country, overlapping normal electorate boundaries.

434. [Author unknown]. *Māori Party Position on Repeal of Section 59*, Māori Party press release, 13 March 2007. Retrieved 20 September 2007 from http://www.scoop.co.nz/stories/PA0703/S00229.htm

435. The Hansard record of this debate was retrieved 19 September 2007 from http://www.hansard.parliament.govt.nz/hansard/Final/FINAL_2007_02_21.htm

436. [Author unknown]. *Bradford lauds Key's s59 efforts*, Green Party press release, 18 April 2007. Retrieved 16 November from http://www.scoop.co.nz/stories/PA0704/S00293.htm

437. List, K. *Grand Coalition Unites To Repeal Section 59*, 2 May 2007. Retrieved 3 September 2007 from http://www.scoop.co.nz/stories/HL0705/S00063.htm.

Audio recording of the press conference retrieved 21 September 2007 from http://www.scoop.co.nz/stories/HL0705/S00063.htm

438. For a more extensive discussion of the issues, see the book: Hager, N. *The Hollow Men: A study in the politics of deception*, Craig Potton Publishing, Nelson, 2006, pp. 18–39.

439. Small, V. 'Key's unwanted date with Destiny', *Dominion Post*, 19 April 2007.

440. Chapple, I. 'NZ First rows over bill', *Sunday Star-Times*, 25 March 2007.

441. Small, V. 'Labour takes it on the chin', *Dominion Post*, 29 May 2007.

442. Mcfie, R. and Welch D. 'The People Who Shape Our World', *New Zealand Listener*, 22 September 2007, p. 22.

Chapter 10: **THE WAY FORWARD**

443. Elements 3 and 5 were in fact already provided for under other statutes or common law.

444. *Police Practice Guide For New Section 59*, New Zealand Police press release, 19 June 2007. Retrieved 15 October 2007 from http://www.scoop.co.nz/stories/print.html?path=PA0706/S00371.htm

445. See the *TVNZ One News* item on the evening of 16 May 2007. Video-stream retrieved 15 October 2007 from http://tvnz.co.nz/view/video_popup_windows_skin/1191886?bandwidth=128k

     and the *TV3 News* item on the same evening. Video-stream retrieved 15 October 2007 from http://www.tv3.co.nz/VideoBrowseAll/PoliticsVideo/tabid/370/articleID/29254/Default.aspx#video?articleID=29254

446. See the article: 'Anti-smacking guide for police', *TVNZ One News*, 21 June 2007. Retrieved 15 October 2007 from http://tvnz.co.nz/view/page/1190535

     and the article: 'Guidelines issued to police on how to handle smacking law', *TV3 News*, 21 June 2007. Retrieved 15 October 2007 from http://www.tv3.co.nz/News/PoliticalNews/Story/tabid/419/articleID/29254/Default.aspx

447. *Crimes (Substituted Section 59) Amendment Act 2007.*

448. Ibid, section 5(4).

449. The Police Commissioner's view as quoted in the opinion piece: Hassall, I. *Perspective On The New Section 59*, 2 May 2007. Retrieved 15 October 2007 from http://www.scoop.co.nz/stories/print.html?path=HL0705/S00108.htm

450. The three-month review of police activity following the amendment of the law, which was released on 20 December 2007, did not contain any data that would answer this question. The review can be accessed from http://www.police.govt.nz/resources/2007/section-59-activity-review/

451. The judgement made in the case of a Masterton man who hit his son (see chapter 4) did not involve any interpretation of the meaning of the new law.

The defendant pleaded guilty so the court did not have to consider the legal effect of the substituted section 59.

452. *Crimes (Substituted Section 59) Amendment Act 2007*, section 4.

453. It is unlikely that a definitive ruling on the scope of the *Parental control* provisions will be made for some time. It would require a case in which the defence was raised successfully or unsuccessfully and the Crown or the defendant took the case on appeal to the High Court.

454. *Police Practice Guide For New Section 59*, New Zealand Police press release, 19 June 2007 (see url above).

455. *Crimes (Substituted Section 59) Amendment Act 2007*, section 4 Purpose.

456. The Police are responsible for administering the law but the Ministry of Justice has responsibility for the legislation.

457. See the information sheets retrieved 15 October 2007 from:

http://www.epochnz.org.nz/images/new_law_notice_1.pdf

http://www.occ.org.nz/childcomm/resources_links/reports_publications/good_parents_relax_a_quick_guide_to_the_changes_to_section_59_of_the_crimes_act?eZSESSIDchildcomm=0c8b4ed777b007328fb8e5112dc78e28

Barnardos New Zealand also produced a fact sheet *Child discipline and the law*, which can be obtained in hard copy from any Barnardos New Zealand office.

458. The EPOCH pamphlet *New Zealand's new child discipline law* lists some of the many sources of information about positive parenting. The pamphlet is downloadable from http://www.epochnz.org.nz/images/new_law_notice_1.pdf

459. Plunket offers parenting classes around the country which include positive parenting approaches.

460. SKIP positive parenting resources can be viewed on the website http://www.familyservices.govt.nz/info-for-families/skip/index.html

461. *Police Practice Guide For New Section 59*, New Zealand Police press release, 19 June 2007, pp. 15–16 (see url above).

462. Ibid, pp. 7–8.

463. Letter from Peter Hughes, chief executive of the Ministry of Social Development, to George Hook, dated 19 December 2007.

464. Ibid.

465. *Crimes (Substituted Section 59) Amendment Act 2007*, sections 7(1) and 4.

466. Letter from Peter Hughes, chief executive of the Ministry of Social Development, to George Hook, dated 19 December 2007. The monitoring plan had yet to be presented to the Chief Executive for approval.

467. Durrant, J.E. 'Evaluating the success of Sweden's corporal punishment ban', *Child Abuse and Neglect*, 23(5), 1999: 435–48.

468. *Longitudinal Study of New Zealand Children and Families: Development Phase*, Ministry of Social Development. Retrieved 28 November 2007 from http://www.msd.govt.nz/work-areas/cross-sectoral-work/longitudinal-study.html

469. *Section 59 of the Crimes Act: Where to from here?*, May 2007. A briefing sheet published by Barnardos NZ, EPOCH NZ, National Council of Independent Women's Refuges, Plunket, Save the Children NZ and UNICEF. The briefing sheet can be accessed from http://epochnz.org.nz/index.php?option=com_content&task=view&id=92&Itemid=22

470. *The United Nations Convention on the Rights of the Child*, United Nations, 1998, Articles 12 and 42. Retrieved 18 October 2007 from http://www.unhchr.ch/html/menu3/b/k2crc.htm

471. Mcfie, R. and Welsh, D. 'The people who shape our world', *New Zealand Listener*, 22 September 2007, p. 22.

Appendix 1

TEXT OF SUE BRADFORD'S BILL

Crimes (Abolition of Force as a Justification for Child Discipline) Amendment Bill

Member's Bill

The Parliament of New Zealand enacts as follows:

1 Title

(1) This Act is the Crimes (Abolition of Force as a Justification for Child Discipline) Amendment Act 2005.

(2) In this Act, the Crimes Act 1961 is called 'the principal Act'.

2 Commencement

This Act comes into force on the day after the date on which it receives the Royal assent.

3 Purpose

The purpose of this Act is to amend the principal Act to abolish the use of reasonable force by parents as a justification for disciplining children.

4 Domestic discipline

Section 59 of the principal Act is repealed.

5 Consequential amendments to Education Act 1989

(1) Section 139A(1) of the Education Act 1989 is amended by omitting the words ", unless that person is a guardian of the student or child".

(2) Section 139A(2) of the Education Act 1989 is amended by omitting the words ", unless that person is a guardian of the student or child".

Appendix 2

TEXT OF THE AMENDED BILL

The Crimes (Substituted Section 59) Amendment Bill

as recommended by the majority of the Select Committee November 2006

The Parliament of New Zealand enacts as follows:

1 Title

This Act is the Crimes (Substituted Section 59) Amendment Act 2007.

2 Commencement

This Act comes into force on the day after the date on which it receives the Royal assent.

3 Principal Act amended

This Act amends the Crimes Act 1961.

4 Purpose

The purpose of this Act is to amend the principal Act to make better provision for children to live in a safe and secure environment free from violence by abolishing the use of parental force for the purpose of correction.

5 New section 59 substituted

Section 59 is repealed and the following section substituted:

59 Parental control

(1) Every parent of a child and every person in the place of a parent of the child is justified in using force if the force used is reasonable in the circumstances and is for the purpose of:

(a) preventing or minimising harm to the child or another person; or

(b) preventing the child from engaging or continuing to engage in conduct that amounts to a criminal offence; or

(c) preventing the child from engaging or continuing to engage inoffensive or disruptive behaviour; or

(d) performing the normal daily tasks that are incidental to good care and parenting.

(2) Nothing in subsection (1) or in any rule of common law justifies the use of force for the purpose of correction.

(3) Subsection (2) prevails over subsection (1).

6 (Consequential) Amendments to Education Act 1989

(1) Section 139A(1) of the Education Act 1989 is amended by omitting ", unless that person is a guardian of the student or child".

(2) Section 139A(2) of the Education Act 1989 is amended by omitting ", unless that person is a guardian of the student or child".

Appendix 3

TEXT OF THE ACT

Crimes (Substituted Section 59) Amendment Act 2007

Commenced: 21 June 2007

The Parliament of New Zealand enacts as follows:

1 Title

This Act is the Crimes (Substituted Section 59) Amendment Act 2007.

2 Commencement

This Act comes into force one month after the date on which it receives the Royal assent.

3 Principal Act amended

This Act amends the Crimes Act 1961.

4 Purpose

The purpose of this Act is to amend the principal Act to make better provision for children to live in a safe and secure environment free from violence by abolishing the use of parental force for the purpose of correction.

5 New section 59 substituted

Section 59 is repealed and the following section substituted:

59 Parental control

(1) Every parent of a child and every person in the place of a parent of the child is justified in using force if the force used is reasonable in the circumstances and is for the purpose of:

(a) preventing or minimising harm to the child or another person; or

(b) preventing the child from engaging or continuing to engage in conduct that amounts to a criminal offence; or

(c) preventing the child from engaging or continuing to engage in offensive or disruptive behaviour; or

(d) performing the normal daily tasks that are incidental to good care and parenting.

(2) Nothing in subsection (1) or in any rule of common law justifies the use of force for the purpose of correction.

(3) Subsection (2) prevails over subsection (1).

(4) To avoid doubt, it is affirmed that the Police have the discretion not to prosecute complaints against a parent of a child or person in the place of a parent of a child in relation to an offence involving the use of force against a child, where the offence is considered to be so inconsequential that there is no public interest in proceeding with a prosecution.

6 Amendments to Education Act 1989

(1) This section amends the Education Act 1989.

(2) Section 139A(1) and (2) of the Education Act 1989 are amended by omitting ", unless that person is a guardian of the student or child".

7 Chief executive to monitor effects of this Act

(1) The chief executive must, in accordance with this section, monitor, and advise the Minister on the effects of this Act, including the extent to which this Act is achieving its purpose as set out in section 4 of this Act, and of any additional impacts.

(2) As soon as practicable after the expiry of the period of 2 years after the date of the commencement of this Act, the chief executive must:

(a) review the available data and any trends indicated by that data about the matters referred to in subsection (1); and

(b) report the chief executive's findings to the Minister.

(3) As soon as practicable after receiving the report under subsection

(2), the Minister must present a copy of that report to the House of Representatives.

(4) In this section, chief executive and Minister have the same meanings as in section 2(1) of the Children, Young Persons, and Their Families Act 1989.

Appendix 4

HOW LAWS ARE MADE IN NEW ZEALAND

New laws can be proposed by government ministers and by other Members of Parliament (MPs). The proposed legislation is called a bill.

If the bill is sponsored by a Minister of the Crown it is called a Government Bill. Other MPs can put forward 'draft bills', but these must go into a ballot from which the lucky ones are drawn from time to time. These bills are known as Member's Bills. (Green MP Sue Bradford's Member's Bill to repeal section 59 was one of the 'lucky bills' as there are usually about 40 bills in each ballot.) Having been drawn from the ballot, a Member's Bill goes through essentially the same process as a Government Bill.

Each bill must pass through seven stages that ensure the proposed law is subject to public debate and careful parliamentary scrutiny before being passed. (Where Sue Bradford's bill is referred to below it is simply called 'the Bill'.)

1. **Introduction**
   This is an administrative procedure that announces a bill's arrival in Parliament. The text of the bill is now available to all MPs and the public.

2. **First reading**
   This stage provides the first opportunity for MPs to debate the merits of a bill. For Member's Bills, the debate is limited to one hour. At the end of the debate the House decides whether a bill should be 'read a first time'. (This is a little confusing as only the title is read out loud.) If a bill receives a majority of the votes cast it proceeds to the select committee stage. If the vote is lost that is the end of the bill. (The Bill passed its first reading by 63 votes in favour and 54 against.)

3. **Select Committee**
   This is a standing committee of a small group of politicians from various parties who scrutinise bills. Usually the committee invites

the public to make either written or oral submissions or both. The committee debates the issues that arise and sometimes it makes changes to a bill called amendments. The select committee has to report back to the House, usually within six months. (The committee considering the Bill was eventually allowed 16 months because of the large number of submissions involved.) The report may recommend amendments and if so usually includes a commentary. If the members of a select committee do not agree on the form of a bill, the majority vote prevails. Dissenting views are also presented in a separate section of the report. (The Bill was amended at this stage and a dissenting opinion was included in the report as well.)

4 **Second reading**
During this stage, MPs argue over the main principles of a bill and the changes recommended by the select committee during a two-hour debate. But the wording of a bill cannot be changed from the form put forward by the select committee. Again, there must be a majority in favour of a bill being 'read', otherwise it fails. (The Bill passed its second reading by 70 votes in favour and 51 against.)

5. **Committee of the Whole House**
At this stage the House forms itself into a committee comprising all MPs and a bill's provisions are debated in detail. There is no time limit on this debate and any MP may address the bill. (The National Party mounted a filibuster at this stage to delay the progress of the Bill.) Any member can propose amendments to a bill, which are then voted on individually. (Several amendments were made to the Bill at this stage including the 'last minute' compromise amendment jointly agreed to by Labour, National and the Bill's sponsor.) Once the final content of a bill has been agreed to by majority vote, it is then reprinted to show the changes made to the bill.

6. **Third reading**
This is the final stage in the House and it usually takes the form of a summing up debate and general comment on a bill in its final form. A bill cannot be modified at this stage and the debate takes less than two hours. The vote taken at the end of the debate is the final one and

there must be a majority in favour of a bill receiving its third reading otherwise that is the end of the bill. (The Bill passed its third reading by 113 votes in favour and 8 against.)

7. **Royal assent**
   A bill does not finally become law until it is signed by the Queen's representative, the Governor General. (Sue Bradford's Bill passed into law on 20 May 2007.)

Appendix 5

HOW NEW ZEALAND IS GOVERNED

New Zealand is a parliamentary democracy. Every three years the people elect those who will represent them in the House of Representatives, which is usually referred to as Parliament. Parliament is the supreme law-making body in the land and technically it also includes the Head of State.

New Zealand's Head of State is a hereditary monarch, whose functions are mostly performed by his or her representative, the Governor General. Those functions include appointing and dismissing Governments, opening and closing Parliament, and giving royal assent to bills passed by the House of Representatives so that they become part of the law of the land.

The people's representatives are called Members of Parliament (MPs). Usually there are about 120 MPs in the House and they all sit in a single chamber. There is no Upper House or Senate in New Zealand.

The Formation of Governments

By convention, after each election, the leader of the political party with the largest number of MPs in the House takes the initiative in seeking parliamentary support to form a Government. Usually this requires the negotiation of coalition agreements with minor political parties. If that leader can secure the support of a majority of MPs, then he or she approaches the Governor General, who then gives leave for the leader to form the Government. By convention, the leader of the party with majority support in the House becomes the Head of Government, the Prime Minister.

The Prime Minister or the party's caucus, depending on the party involved, then selects senior MPs to serve as Ministers of the Crown. Only sitting MPs can serve as ministers. All of the ministers, including the Prime Minister, are then sworn in by the Governor General. (After that event the Governor General usually acts only on the advice of the Prime Minister.)

The Prime Minister decides which ministers will become part of Cabinet, the executive decision-making arm of the Government. Usually all senior ministers are invited to become part of Cabinet.

Ministers usually have the responsibility for overseeing a number of government departments, which do the work of government in administering the laws of the land as enacted by Parliament. (The judiciary also plays a role in governance by interpreting those laws.)

As used in this book, the word 'Government' usually refers to Cabinet, although sometimes it refers to the parliamentary coalition that is in power, and sometimes it includes government departments.

Mixed-Member-Proportional Representation

Members of Parliament are elected using a mixed-member-proportional (MMP) representation voting system. Each member of the public aged 18 years or over has two votes – one for their local representative (electorate vote) and the other for the political party of their choice (party vote).

The electorate vote results in 60 New Zealanders becoming *electorate MPs*, each representing the people in a particular geographical region. The results of the party vote are used to ensure that the overall composition of Parliament reflects the proportion of votes given nationwide to each party. Some party members, as ranked on party lists, join the electorate MPs in the House as *list MPs* in order to ensure that their party is proportionately represented. This swells the ranks of Parliament to about 120 members.

Coalitions for Governance and Law-making

In practice, the MMP system means that major parties are unlikely to ever get an absolute majority in Parliament. The major party that gets to form the Government must rely on the support of minor parties to govern. Getting specific legislation through the House can be a difficult matter. Often the Government will have to assemble a working coalition to get a Government Bill passed. The same is true for Member's Bills put forward by individual MPs, such as the one put forward by Green MP Sue Bradford.

Political Parties Represented in Parliament during the Bill's Passage

Sue Bradford's Bill received its first reading in July 2005 and the final form of the Bill was approved by Parliament in May 2007.

Party	July 2002 Election	October 2005 Election
ACT	9	2
Green Party	9	6
Labour Party	52	50
Māori Party	–	4
National Party	27	48
New Zealand First	13	7
Progressive Coalition/Party	2	1
United Future	8	3

Appendix 6

ORGANISATIONS THAT SUPPORTED REPEAL

Organisations committed to positive non-violent parenting and the repeal of section 59 of the Crimes Act 1961, according to a list held by EPOCH New Zealand in July 2006.

Action for Children and Youth Aotearoa (Auckland)

Ahu Whakatika Challenge Violence Trust (Rotorua)

Alternatives to Violence Project

Amnesty International New Zealand

Anger Change Trust Auckland

Aotearoa New Zealand Association of Social Workers

Arai Te Uru Whare Hauora (Dunedin)

Auckland Women's Centre

Awhina Whānau Services Inc. (Hastings)

Barnardos New Zealand

Birthright New Zealand Inc.

Bream Bay Community Support Trust (Ruakaka)

Canterbury Home Birth Association

Catholic Social Services (Wellington)

CCS New Zealand

Central Hawkes Bay Support and Counselling Services

Central Plateau REAP (Taupo)

Child Abuse Prevention Services (National Office Wellington)

Child Development Foundation (Auckland)

Child Helpline Trust (Christchurch)

Child Poverty Action Group

Children's Agenda (Auckland)

Children's Issues Centre (Dunedin)

Childwise Methodist Mission (Christchurch)

Dannevirke Family Services Inc.

Domestic Violence Centre (Preventing Violence in the Home)

DOVE Hawkes Bay

Eastbay REAP (Whakatane)

Education for Change (Christchurch)

Every Child Counts

Family Focus (Greymouth)

Family Help Centre (Rotorua)

Family Support Services Whanganui Trust

Foundation for Peace Studies (Auckland)

Hamilton Abuse Intervention Project

Hamilton Refuge and Support Services

Hauraki Safety Network

Healing and Rape Crisis Centre (Te Awamutu)

Hinengakau Maatua Whangai (Taumarunui)

Home and Family Society Inc. (Auckland)

Home and Family Society Inc. (Christchurch)

Horowhenua Family Violence Intervention

Human Rights Foundation of Aotearoa New Zealand

Humanists for Non-violence

Inner City Group for Men (Auckland)

Inner City Women's Group (Grey Lynn)

James Family Presbyterian Support Northern (Auckland)

Kaitaia Homebased Whānau Support

Kapiti Men for Non Violence Inc.

La Leche League NZ

Le Lafitaga Trust (Auckland)

Linton Camp Community Services

Living Without Violence (Porirua)

Living Without Violence (Waiheke Network)

Mana Social Services Trust (Rotorua)

Manawatu Alternatives to Violence

Māori Women's Welfare League

Methodist Mission Northern (Glen Eden)

Motueka Women's Support Link

Naku Enei Tamariki (Lower Hutt)

Napier Women's Refuge

National Collective of Independent Women's Refuges

National Council for Young Catholics

National Council of Women of New Zealand

National Network of Stopping Violence Services

Natural Parenting New Zealand Ltd (Christchurch)

Nelson Rape and Sexual Abuse Network

New Zealand Association for Adolescent Health and Development

New Zealand Association of Counsellors

New Zealand Family Planning Association

New Zealand Family Research Trust (Auckland)

New Zealand Federation of Business and Professional Women

New Zealand Playcentre Inc.

New Zealand Psychological Society

North Harbour Living Without Violence Inc. (Takapuna)

North Shore Women's Centre (Glenfield)

North Taranaki Kindergarten Association (New Plymouth)

Office of the Children's Commissioner

OMEP Aotearoa New Zealand

Pacific Foundation (Auckland)

Pacifica

Paediatric Society of New Zealand

Parent and Family Counselling Service (Whangarei)

Parent Help Wellington Inc.

ParentingWorx

Parentline Charitable Trust (Hamilton)

Parentline Hawkes Bay Inc.

Parentline Manawatu

Parents' Centre NZ Inc.

Peace Movement Aotearoa

Peppertree House – South Auckland Family Refuge

PORSE In-Home Childcare Network (NZ) Ltd

Presbyterian Support New Zealand

Public Health Association of New Zealand Inc.

Quaker Peace and Service

Quakers

Rahui Pokeka Maatua Whaangai Justice (Huntly)

Relationship Services NZ Inc.

Rodney Stopping Violence Services

Royal New Zealand Plunket Society

Safer Families Foundation (Takapuna)

Save the Children New Zealand

South Canterbury Violence Intervention Project

South Canterbury Women's Refuge

Start Inc. (Christchurch)

Stopping Violence Services Nelson

Stopping Violence Services Wairarapa

Supportline Women's Refuge (Auckland)

Taranaki Social Services (New Plymouth)

Te Aupouri Iwi Social Services (Kaitaia)

Te Awamutu Women's Centre

Te Awamutu Women's Refuge – Nga Maunga Hei Kakahu Inc.

Te Awhina Support (Murupara)

Te Hauauru Mahi A Iwi (Kaikohe)

Te Korowai Aroha O Ngati Whatua (Wellsford)

Te Manawa Services (Fielding)

Te Puna O Te Aroha Māori Women's Refuge (Whangarei)

Te Roopu Whakaruruhau (Palmerston North)

Te Ruru Resources

Te Tari Puna o Aotearoa/NZ Childcare Association

Te Whānau O Te Mangarongo (Lower Hutt)

Te Whare Oranga Wairua Women's Refuge (Taupo)

Te Whariki Manawahine O Hauraki (Thames)

Thames Women's Resource Centre

The Body Shop

The Brainwave Trust

The Dove Group for Children (New Plymouth)

The Women's International League for Peace and Freedom

Tongan Tamaki Community Centre (Auckland)

Tongariro Whānau Support Trust (Turangi)

Tu Tama Wahine o Taranaki Inc. (New Plymouth)

Tupoho Maatua Whangai Trust (Whanganui)

UNICEF New Zealand

Violence Free Waitakere

Wairarapa Community Counselling Centre

Wairarapa Women's Refuge

Waitakere Abuse and Trauma Counselling Service Inc.

Wellington Community Law Centre

Wellington Ending Violence and Abuse

Wesley Community Action

Whānau Awhina Women's Refuge (Whanganui)

Whanganui Living Without Violence Trust

Women of the Kaipara Resource Centre (Dargaville)

Women's Centre (Christchurch)

Youth Law/Tino Rangatiratanga Taitamariki

Youthline Auckland Charitable Trust

Appendix 7

SUMMARY OF ADVOCACY ACTIVITIES

Before the Bill's Arrival

- Raising public awareness of section 59 and positive non-violent discipline through presentations at conferences and meetings.
- Writing articles for newspapers, journals and websites.
- Establishing a website devoted to ending physical punishment.
- Issuing media releases and making public appearances.
- Developing materials (pamphlets, flyers and booklets) about the repeal of section 59 and positive non-violent parenting.
- Distributing materials at conferences and meetings, in waiting rooms, through member agencies and letter-box drops.
- Engaging the support of a wide range of organisations.
- Creating an informal network of supportive organisations and maintaining an information flow to members through newsletters and bulletins.
- Engaging the support of staff, clients and members of larger agencies sympathetic to the cause.
- Regularly lobbying politicians though visits, letters and later emails to MPs.
- Organising forums and meetings and inviting local and overseas speakers.
- Publicising the findings of research into the effects of physical discipline.

After the Bill's Arrival

- Making informed submissions to the Select Committee considering the Bill.
- Setting up regular coordination meetings in large cities.
- Developing and implementing an advocacy strategy that included:
  - a communication strategy focused largely on engaging proactively and reactively with the media
  - setting up systems to monitor the media
  - lobbying of politicians regularly through visits, letters and emails
  - tracking the stances of political parties and individual MPs
  - writing information sheets on issues relating to section 59 and distributing them to MPs and other supporters
  - encouraging supportive agencies to become involved in the public debate through writing letters to the media, and emailing or writing letters to MPs
  - developing an electronic system to make it easy for supporters to email MPs
  - commenting on claims made by those opposed to repeal, either in the media or directly to MPs.
- Maintaining a close working relationship with the leading law reformer and other MPs supportive of repeal.
- Engaging and encouraging public support for law change from individuals and organisations including celebrities and Christian supporters.

ACRONYMS AND ORGANISATIONS

ACCAN – *Australasian Conference on Child Abuse and Neglect*
A biennial conference held in either Australia or New Zealand.

ACYA – *Action for Children and Youth Aotearoa*
A New Zealand non-governmental organisation that coordinates a report to the UN Committee on the Rights of the Child and promotes the Convention on the Rights of the Child.

Barnardos – *Barnardos New Zealand*
A major child and family service provider that also has a child advocacy role.

CAT – *Convention against Torture and Other Cruel, Inhuman or Degrading Treatment or Punishment*
A convention adopted by the United Nations General Assembly in 1984.

CAVE – *Campaign Against Violence in Education*
A lobby group, which existed in New Zealand during the 1980s, that campaigned against use of corporal punishment in schools.

CRC – *United Nations Committee on the Rights of the Child*
A body of independent experts that monitors the implementation of the Convention on the Rights of the Child by states which have ratified the Convention on the Rights of the Child.

CROC – see **UNCROC** below

ECC – *Every Child Counts*
A coalition of Plunket, Barnardos, IPP at AUT, Save the Children New Zealand and UNICEF New Zealand, which aimed to increase children's profile and priority on the political agenda.

EPOCH NZ – *End Physical Punishment of Children New Zealand*
A non-governmental organisation that lobbied for the repeal of the law that sanctioned the physical (corporal) punishment of children and promoted positive, non-violent discipline.

Families Commission
An independent government-funded organisation promoting the interest of families and organising research into family issues.

ICCPR – *International Covenant on Civil and Political Rights*
A covenant adopted by the United Nations General Assembly in 1966.

IPP at AUT – *The Institute of Public Policy at Auckland University of Technology*
An institute that provides 'independent research and advice on economic and social development in New Zealand and comparative countries'.

ISPCAN – *International Society for the Prevention of Child Abuse and Neglect*
An international organisation which brings together professionals 'to work towards the prevention and treatment of child abuse, neglect and exploitation globally.'

OCC – *Office of the Children's Commissioner*
An independent body funded by the New Zealand Government to protect and promote children's interests in a variety of ways.

OECD – *Organisation for Economic Co-operation and Development*
An organisation that provides a setting in which member governments 'compare policy experiences, seek answers to common problems, identify good practice and co-ordinate domestic and international policies.'

Plunket – *Royal New Zealand Plunket Society*
A large non-governmental organisation providing preventative child health services and parenting advice to families with children under five years of age

SCNZ – *Save the Children New Zealand*
The New Zealand arm of the international organisation that fundraises for international development purposes and which also has a domestic programme.

SKIP – *Strategies with Kids: Information for Parents*
A government-funded initiative promoting positive parenting.

UDHR – *Universal Declaration of Human Rights*
An advisory declaration adopted by the United Nations General Assembly in 1948.

UN – *United Nations*

An international organisation whose stated aims are 'to facilitate cooperation in international law, international security, economic development, social progress and human rights issues'.

UNCROC – *United Nations Convention on the Rights of the Child*

The abbreviation commonly used in New Zealand for the instrument in international law that specifies the human rights of children, although in other places **CROC** is more commonly used.

UNICEF – *UNICEF New Zealand*

A country office of the international organisation United Nations Children's Fund, which fundraises for international development purposes and provides a domestic advocacy service.

GLOSSARY

act – a *statute*/a *bill* which has become part of the law

'advocates' – those organisations and individuals who sought the repeal of *section 59*

Aotearoa – *Māori* word for New Zealand, sometimes used in conjunction with the words 'New Zealand', as in 'Aotearoa New Zealand', and sometimes used by itself as the name of the country

'assault' – most New Zealanders would consider the term to mean a situation in which one person applies considerable force to another, but in the law an assault includes any application of force no matter how 'inconsequential', including mild *smacking*

'(the) ballot' – the system in which legislation proposed by individual *MPs* (*Member's Bills*) are drawn in a ballot and placed on the parliamentary agenda

bill – a proposed piece of legislation that has been introduced into *Parliament* for its consideration

'(the) Bill' – refers to the various versions (see appendixes 1–3) of the proposed legislation to repeal *section 59* which were debated in New Zealand's *Parliament*

blog – a website that provides an online opportunity for members of the public to make personal comments on issues

Cabinet – the group of senior *ministers* which serve as the executive decision-making arm of the *Government*

caucus – a closed meeting of those *MPs* belonging to a particular *parliamentary party*; caucus decisions are usually binding on the way members of the caucus vote in *Parliament*

civil law – statutes that govern the relations between private individuals

Committee of the Whole House – a stage in the law-making progress in which all *MPs* are allowed to comment on a *bill* and propose amendments

common law – law established through court decisions rather than by *Parliament* (cf. *statute*)

conscience vote – a situation in which a parliamentary party allows its *MPs* to vote according to their conscience rather than the party's policy or position

corporal punishment – the punishment of children by striking them with an object such as a hand or an instrument (it has a similar meaning to the term *physical punishment*)

criminal law – *statutes* that are concerned with defining crimes against members of the public or the state and the penalties associated with them

Crown – a term which usually refers to the *sovereign*

electorate MP – an *MP* who represents the members of the public living in a particular geographical area of the country (cf. *list MP*)

electorate vote – one of two votes in a general election, in which adult New Zealanders chose an individual to represent their electorate (cf. *party vote*)

filibuster – filling the time allocated for the discussion of bills during the *Committee of the Whole House* stage with pointless and/or repetitive speeches in order to delay progress

'(the) Government' – those *MPs* who are appointed by the Queen's representative, the Governor General, as *ministers* of the Crown (see appendix 5)

'(the) House' – the House of Representatives (there is only one House in New Zealand)/sometimes used to refer to the parliamentary setting

hui – *Māori* word for a meeting

iwi – *Māori* word for a tribe

kaumātua – *Māori* word for a respected male elder

list MP – an MP who is appointed from a party list in order to ensure that the proportion of MPs from each party reflects the overall *party vote* of the nation (cf. *electorate MP*)

Māori – the indigenous people of *Aotearoa* New Zealand

marae – *Māori* name for a meeting house and the surrounding grounds and buildings

'(the) media' – term used to collectively describe all forms of mass communication, including television, radio, newspapers and magazines; also used to refer to the people who produce the communications involved

Member of Parliament– an individual selected to represent the public in *Parliament*, either by an *electorate* (*electorate MP*) or from a *political party*'s list (*list MP*)

Member's Bill – proposed legislation put forward by an individual *MP*

ministers (of the Crown) – MPs selected either by the Prime Minister or by a caucus vote (depending on the party in power) to serve as ministers of the Crown, with responsibilities for different government departments

mixed-member-proportional (MMP) representation – New Zealand's system of electing *MPs*, some of whom are appointed as a result of the *electorate vote*, others of whom are appointed from a party list in order to ensure that the proportion of *MPs* in the *House* reflects the *party vote* of the nation

MP – *Member of Parliament*

non-governmental organisation (NGO) – a not-for-profit, independent organisation working within the community

opinion poll – a survey of public opinion, whether statistically valid or not, that purports to reflect the views of the public

'(the) opposition' – term used to refer collectively to those groups and individuals opposed to the repeal of *section 59*

'(the) Opposition' – the main *political party* that opposes the *Government* in *Parliament*; during the passage of the Bill this was the National Party

Pākehā – *Māori* word used to describe New Zealanders of non-Māori descent, usually those of European origin

Parliament – the supreme law-making body in New Zealand (technically it includes the *sovereign* as well)/sometimes referred to as the House of Representatives

parliamentary party – the group of *MPs* who belong to a particular *political party*, including both *electorate* and *list MPs*

party vote – one of two votes in a general election, in which New Zealanders vote to indicate the *political party* of their choice (cf. *electorate vote*)

(parliamentary) party vote – occurs when *MPs* belonging to a particular *parliamentary party* vote en bloc for or against a motion before the *House* (cf. *conscience vote*)

physical punishment – the punishment of children by applying physical force to them with an object such as a hand or an instrument (it has a very similar meaning to the term *corporal punishment*)

political party – a registered political party (cf. *parliamentary party*)

positive parenting – involves responding to children's strengths and desirable behaviours with praise and warmth rather than responding to negative behaviour with criticism and punishment

'reading' – a term that refers to various stages in the law-making process (first, second and third) when *Parliament* is considering a *bill* (see appendix 4); at the end of each session a vote is taken on whether the bill is taken to be 'read' or not by the *House*

'section 59' – the old section of the Crimes Act 1961, containing the *statutory defence* available to adults who *assault* their children for the purpose of correcting them

select committee – a small group of *MPs* from various *parliamentary parties*, with the responsibility for investigating and reporting on a specific matter, for example, proposed legislation (a *bill*)

smacking – hitting a child's body with an open hand or an instrument with the intention of causing pain in order to punish or correct the child; generally smacking would be less forceful than beating

sovereign – the Head of State in a constitutional monarchy like New Zealand

spanking – this term is less often used in New Zealand but it would generally be recognised as having a similar meaning as *smacking*

statute – a law enacted by *Parliament* (cf. *common law*)

statutory defence – a defence enshrined in law for an action that would otherwise be deemed illegal, for example *section* 59 of the Crimes Act 1961 provided parents who *assault* their children with such a legal defence in some circumstances

'submission' – oral or written reports made by individuals, organisations and government departments to the Justice and Electoral *Select Committee* considering the *section* 59 repeal *bill*

tāngata whenua – *Māori* word for the original inhabitants of New Zealand/the indigenous people of New Zealand, the *Māori*

Te Tai Tokerau – the northern part of Aotearoa New Zealand

whānau – *Māori* name for an extended family or family group

'whipped' – term used in the parliamentary setting to indicate that *MPs* will vote according to their party's policy or position (cf. *conscience vote*)

INDEX